DRUG EFFECTS

Advances in Critical Medical Anthropology
Series Editors: Merrill Singer and Pamela Erickson

This book series advances our understanding of the complex and rapidly changing landscape of health, disease, and treatment around the world with original
and innovative books in the spirit of critical medical anthropology that exemplify
and extend its theoretical and empirical dimensions. Books in the series address
topics across the broad range of subjects addressed by medical anthropologists
and other scholars and practitioners working at the intersections of social science
and medicine.

DRUG EFFECTS

Khat in Biocultural and Socioeconomic Perspective

Lisa L. Gezon

Walnut Creek, California

Left Coast Press, Inc. is committed to preserving ancient forests and natural resources. We elected to print this title on 30% post consumer recycled paper, processed chlorine free. As a result, for this printing, we have saved:

3 Trees (40' tall and 6-8" diameter)
1 Million BTUs of Total Energy
234 Pounds of Greenhouse Gases
1,056 Gallons of Wastewater
67 Pounds of Solid Waste

Left Coast Press, Inc. made this paper choice because our printer, Thomson-Shore, Inc., is a member of Green Press Initiative, a nonprofit program dedicated to supporting authors, publishers, and suppliers in their efforts to reduce their use of fiber obtained from endangered forests.

For more information, visit www.greenpressinitiative.org

Environmental impact estimates were made using the Environmental Defense Paper Calculator. For more information visit: www.papercalculator.org.

LEFT COAST PRESS, INC.
1630 North Main Street, #400
Walnut Creek, CA 94596
http://www.LCoastPress.com

Copyright © 2012 by Left Coast Press, Inc.

ISBN 978-1-59874-490-3 hardcover
ISBN 978-1-59874-491-0 paperback
ISBN 978-1-61132-788-5 institutional electronic

Library of Congress Cataloging-in-Publication Data:

Gezon, Lisa L.
Drug effects : khat in biocultural and socioeconomic perspective / Lisa L. Gezon.
    p. cm. — (Advances in critical medical anthropology; v. 3)
  ISBN 978-1-59874-490-3 (hbk. : perm paper) — ISBN 978-1-59874-491-0 (paperback : perm paper) — ISBN 978-1-61132-788-5 (eBook)
  1. Khat—Social aspects. 2. Khat—Economic aspects. 3. Khat—Political aspects. I. Title.
HV5822.Q3G49 2011
583'.85—dc23
                    2011030972

Printed in the United States of America

∞ ™ The paper used in this publication meets the minimum requirements of American National Standard for Information Sciences—Permanence of Paper for Printed Library Materials, ANSI/NISO Z39.48–1992.

Cover design by Piper Wallis

Dedication

To my children, Evan and Adam, who supported my long hours of work and whose presence with me in Madagascar opened so many doors to friendship and understanding.

CONTENTS

LIST OF ILLUSTRATIONS

ACKNOWLEDGMENTS

This project has been in progress since 2000—more than ten years before writing these acknowledgments. It was then that I began to write grant proposals to study how urban consumption patterns affect patterns of exploitation of forest products within the region surrounding the city. Coming from a political ecology perspective, I wanted to build on my interest in the human dynamics of conservation and land use change. My earlier work (Gezon 2006) centered on the micropolitics of protected area management around the Ankarana Special Reserve, which lies to the south of the Amber Mountain National Park, the focus of this current research on khat. For this project, I wished to concentrate not only on the proximate drivers of deforestation but on the entire commodity chain, in order to consider how consumer demand shapes land use decisions. This focus would connect local land use practices directly with regional, national, and global influences.

Knowing that farmers around Amber Mountain have a long history of producing cash crops (fruits and vegetables in particular), and recognizing its proximity to the urban consumers and transportation networks of the city of Diego Suarez, this seemed like a logical place to do fieldwork. At the time I wrote my grant proposals, I was not yet aware of how important khat was to the economic and ecological transformation of the region—and how central it would become to my study. Early fieldwork revealed the importance of khat to farmers, traders, and consumers. Later fieldwork showed the complex relationship between vegetable and khat production that I describe in Chapter 5.

After several attempts and much refining of my ideas, my research on commodity chains and land use in northern Madagascar was funded in 2003 by the National Geographic Society (Grant Number 7413.03), the National Science Foundation (Award Number BCS-0318640), and a U.S. Department of Education Fulbright-Hays Faculty Research Abroad Fellowship. I went to Madagascar for one month in 2003, six months in 2004, and one month each in 2005, 2007, and 2010. The trip in 2010 was funded by the University of West Georgia College of Arts and Sciences Faculty Research Grant Program and by a collaborative grant from the Canadian Social Sciences and Humanities Research Council International Opportunities Fund Grant (PIs Andrew Walsh and Ian Calquhoun). I am thankful to all the reviewers and program officers for their confidence in my project in its various phases.

My interest in the medical aspects of khat emerged as I realized that khat's drug qualities shaped people's experience with it as a commodity: Fears about the dangers khat poses to health, combined with experiences of pleasure, sociability, and people's high willingness to pay for it renders khat heavy with implications. From a political ecology perspective, its status as a drug influenced people's decisions to transform rice fields and even forests into khat fields. It seemed like a critical medical anthropology (CMA) perspective would be the best one for getting at khat's multiple aspects. Inquiring holistically into khat's effects as a drug would include, but go beyond, a political ecology analysis. As I became more immersed in the CMA approach, my analysis became increasingly framed around forming an understanding of khat's multifaceted drug effects. The result is this book, which addresses a question that weighs heavily on the minds of many in northern Madagascar: Is khat good or bad? Although the question is simple, the answer is, not surprisingly, complicated. My hope is that this exploration of drug effects will inspire studies of other drugs as situated in biocultural and socioeconomic contexts.

I am thankful to many people who, over the many years since I began this project, have contributed in one way or another to it. My apologies to those I may leave out. All shortcomings are fully my own responsibility. For the writing up of this work, my first thanks go to my editors, Jennifer Collier, Pam Erickson, and Merrill Singer, who believed in this project and gave me the encouragement I needed to finish this manuscript. Their insightful comments helped me find my voice. I also thank my colleagues at the University of West Georgia (UWG) for supporting me along the way. First of all, I thank my chair, Marjorie Snipes, whose bright smile and caring words have gotten me through both challenging and good times. I thank Karl Steinen for generating the map of northern Madagascar. Warm friendship and moral support have come from various other colleagues at UWG, including Aran MacKinnon, Jeannette Diaz-Laplante, Chris Aanstoos, Cita Cook, Jane McCandless, Thomas Foster, and many others too numerous to name. Supportive academic colleagues beyond UWG include Conrad Kottak, Bruce Mannheim, my entire cohort from the University of Michigan, Susan Paulson, Andrew Walsh (Jao Ankarana), Ben Freed, Janice Harper, Rebecca Green, Betina Torbjornsen, Ann Kingsolver, Laurent Berger, Sophie Blanchy, Louise Lamphere, Carol Stack, Jennifer Cole, Andrew Mathews, and the list could go on.

Within Madagascar, I especially value of the stimulating conversations, intellectual guidance, and friendship I had with colleagues Alex Totomarovariou, Pierre Mbima, Marteline Be Razafindravola, and Jean-Louis Boutouhely at the Université d'Antsiranana, and with Jean-Aimé Rakotoarisoa at the Musée d'Art et d'Archéologie in Antananarivo, Madagascar. Professor Alex Totomarovariou (director of the Ango-American Studies Program at the Université d'Antsiranana) and his wife Laurette deserve special mention because of their support on a daily basis as my neighbors and friends in Diego Suarez. Their friendship was invaluable in 2004 as I found and set up a home for myself, my two children, and several research assistants, including Jess and Robert Cook and Blandine R. Alex also was the main point person for finding the excellent students I worked with at the Université d'Antsiranana, who enthusiastically helped administer surveys and conduct interviews in 2007 and 2010. As for friends in Diego Suarez, there are too many to mention by name, but I am grateful for the depth of connection I have had with many people, and I am thankful for their generosity in supporting me personally and professionally. I do wish specifically acknowledge the support of Ghislain Gaspard and Jacqueline Benivo-Gaspard for having welcomed me and my fellow researchers into their home and shared their wealth of knowledge with us.

For logistical support in the United States, I thank the Department of Anthropology office manager, Brenda Simonds. For vital research assistance, I thank Keri Adams for developing the index and working masterfully with Endnote to complete the references. Heather McGuire and Bobby Moore have provided important bibliographic support in earlier stages of writing. Eve Copeland diligently worked at data coding and entry, which became the basis for statistical analyses.

For making this project possible, I thank not only the agencies that funded my research, but also and especially the people I have known in Madagascar who have generously given me their time, their warmth, and their stories. It has been an honor and a privilege to share lives with each other, amid the achievements, personal challenges, and daily living that we shared. Through these deep human connections, I have made friends at the same time that I found cultural consultants.

Those who truly made this project possible are my two children, Evan and Adam Block, who, at ages six and seven, accompanied me to Madagascar for nearly six months of fieldwork in 2004. Their delight and joy in experiencing a new world opened up doors to interpersonal connections and understanding with people of all ages, both in the city and in the countryside. Having my kids with me made me more interesting as a researcher and lent me a certain legitimacy as a parent and a fellow human.

1

KHAT COMES TO MADAGASCAR

It is noon on a hot, dusty day in Diego Suarez, the capital of the northern province of Antsiranana in Madagascar. Most people are in their homes preparing the noonday meal. A few enterprising others are busy on the otherwise quiet street, preparing for the shipment of freshly picked khat to arrive by local transport from the surrounding agricultural areas. When it arrives, people stir from their midday rest to purchase a packet of the tender leaves, preparing to spend the afternoon chewing either by themselves, on the job, or with friends (see Figure 1.1). Such is the daily ritual for many in Diego. Khat fuels the local informal economy and is indeed "green gold" for many farmers and traders.

Khat is a bushy plant whose leaves when chewed produce a mild amphetamine-like effect. Its popularity is growing throughout the Indian Ocean, including Madagascar. The major producers of khat are Yemen, Ethiopia, and Kenya, but wherever it is grown, it tends to be cultivated by small holders (with most farming less than 2 hectares) and distributed through small-scale traders (Carrier 2005a; Gebissa 2004; Kennedy 1987). This is also the case in Madagascar. The labor input is minimal, so it is a good investment for just about any household that has available land.

Khat came to Madagascar during the French colonial era, introduced by Yemeni dock workers who brought khat with them to Diego Suarez, or Antsiranana, in the far north of Madagascar and planted it on a small scale in kitchen gardens. Until recently, the primary consumers of khat in Madagascar were immigrants of Yemeni descent, known locally as *arabou*. They used it in the

Figure 1.1   This man is buying khat in the city of Diego Suarez

traditional Yemeni pattern, chewing it socially in the afternoons as a stimulus for good conversation and introspection (Kennedy 1987). The first to grow khat commercially in Madagascar, according to my interviewees, were Creoles—farmers of French descent—who came over from the French-controlled Ile de la Réunion (about 540 miles east of Madagascar) around the turn of the century. They established small plantations on Amber Mountain (or Mt. d'Amber, as it is called in French), about 20–30 miles inland from the coastal city of Diego Suarez. When the French were forced to leave the country in the mid-1970s amid a socialist revolution, the Creoles either sold or abandoned their khat farms. The oldest of the highly productive establishments on Amber Mountain today is owned by a family that bought their land from a Creole family and identify themselves as a mix of Yemeni, Malagasy, and Creole descent.

Since around the 1980s, more and more non-Yemeni-descended Malagasy have begun chewing khat both socially and alone. Most local people concur that taxi drivers were among the first to chew it in order to stay awake while they worked at night. Khat has also become popular as a recreational substance, most visibly among urban youth and men. Although users speak expansively about the experiences of the high they feel while chewing khat, its effects have commonly been likened to drinking several cups of strong coffee. The pulse of the street economy of Diego Suarez is fueled by khat, with sellers and chewers and people stopping to shop and chat along well-traveled streets. When trucks with khat arrive, people flock around the most popular street merchants to buy their share. Khat has become the lifeblood of the informal economy of the north, providing significant income to small-scale farmers and producers.

Wherever khat is grown throughout the world, it is critical to local economies. Where it is chewed, it is central to local identity (Carrier and Gezon 2009; Mains 2010). The apparent simplicity of this scenario—people chewing khat and farmers and traders making money from it—masks the complexity of the issues it raises, because khat is a scheduled drug. It is a psychotropic substance that acts on the mind, affecting emotions, perception, and behavior. More simply, khat is a drug and affects the central nervous system as a stimulant. The terms "drug" and "psychoactive substance" are used interchangeably with reference to a broad range of substances that have an effect on mental states and behavior, without reference to whether or not they are illegal (Page and Singer 2010:5). Some psychoactive substances are legal throughout much of the world and are perceived to have effects that are either not significantly dangerous to individuals or social life (such as caffeine), to be unhealthy physically but not mentally (tobacco), or to be manageable by adults of a certain age (alcohol). Other substances—the ones we often call drugs—are formally assessed as having potential for abuse. Some of these are controlled as pharmaceuticals, and all controlled drugs are illegal as recreational or self-medicating substances.

The primary active compounds found in khat have been identified as drugs by the World Health Organization (WHO) and have been scheduled into two different categories. When it is fresh, khat contains cathinone, which is in the category of substances that are the most highly potent and subject to abuse. Schedule I drugs are defined as ones that have no acceptable medical use and cannot be used safely even under medical supervision. This schedule also includes heroin, cocaine, marijuana, and methamphetamine. After twenty-four–forty-eight hours, cathinone breaks down into cathine, which is a Schedule IV drug, defined as having low abuse potential, a currently accepted medical use, and some risk of low-level dependence. Because it contains these active compounds, it is illegal to possess the khat plant in the United States and much of Europe.[1] In many countries where it is grown and consumed, khat has an ambiguous or highly debated legal status, leading Cassanelli (1986) to identify it as having a quasi-legal status.

Because of its legal status, khat faces constraints that other commodity crops do not. Even though it is legal in Madagascar, it is illegal in places where it could potentially be marketed and in countries on which Madagascar depends for foreign aid. It is not exported and therefore not a source of hard currency for the government, making it not only a low priority but even perhaps a hindrance to economic growth according to the terms of neoliberal capitalism that is dependent on global capital flows. Despite its prominence in local economies around the world, khat receives little attention at national and global levels, aside from occasional debates about its legal status. In Madagascar, it is virtually ignored at the national level. Even in countries where it provides an important source of tax revenue to governments, such as Ethiopia and Kenya, it rarely if ever receives constructive attention by agronomists who might help develop more efficient and sustainable ways of growing this valuable plant (Gebissa 2004). A final layer of complexity is related to khat's general association with Islam and its particular association with Somali terrorists and pirates, who are often described as "khat-crazed" in the popular media (http://www.washingtontimes.com/news/2009/apr/29/khat-crazed-kids/print/; accessed September 30, 2011). These negative connotations threaten people's ability to produce, trade, and consume khat freely and make its status different from other globally sanctioned cash crops.

The increasing popularity of khat globally raises several questions about its effects as a drug and about the role it plays in people's lives: Why has khat become increasingly popular? What are khat's effects on physical and mental health? How does it affect local livelihood strategies—is it a viable means of survival? What consequences do official positions on khat have for local people? What follows is an ethnographic study of a psychotropic plant in the everyday lives of producers, traders, and consumers in northern Madagascar, where local experiences are contextualized within critical assessments of the cultural politics of health, state and global power, economic development, gender relations, and environmental sustainability.

Any discussion of khat as a health issue encounters high stakes political debates about the drug's effects on human beings. One side takes WHO and national legal classifications of drugs at face value and assumes that all illegal psychotropic substances are harmful—by virtue of the fact that they are illegal. Those who take this position often have genuine concerns for health and social welfare, but there is a circular nature to this argument: The substances *must* be bad *because* they are illegal. There are several problems with this assessment. First, it often rests on eth-nocentric moral evaluations and a resistance to engage critically with the legiti-macy of the status of illegality. It too easily parrots the language of the schedules in lumping a mild amphetamine such as khat with a highly physically addictive narcotic like heroin. In addition to disregarding differences in chemical make-up and physiological effects, automatic condemnation also ignores the social and cultural contexts that affect how drugs are consumed and the varied effects they have on people due to such factors as chemical potency and cultural expectations.

The other side of the khat debate takes into account the social and cultural contexts of drug use, arguing that drugs, in and of themselves, are not necessarily harmful, regardless of their legal status (Weil and Rosen 1983). In so doing, this side has responded to what has seemed to be the shortsightedness of the mainstream conservative discourse, which consistently vilifies drugs and imbues them with great negative social consequences—including social and moral condemnation and legal repercussions. This alternative approach introduces a culturally sensitive appreciation of context. A problem with this perspective, however, is that an overly apologetic analysis can prevent a balanced examination of the possibility of deleterious physical and social effects of consumption. Furthermore, it ignores how drug use may differently affect diverse segments of the population—notably its gendered effects.

I side with the second perspective in the drug debate and argue that khat, in itself, is neither good nor bad. What is valuable in evaluating khat's effects are criteria for evaluating its health effects—broadly defined—on a population in particular contexts. Debates on drugs are often highly emotionally charged and closely correlated with broader political and economic contexts—the political War on Drugs, for example. This influences many to take a negative perspective on drug use. It is therefore important to determine how drugs are framed politically and economically, in addition to identifying direct health concerns surrounding consumption. A single drug, like khat, may have both costs and benefits.

Framing Khat: Interrelated Perspectives

Every drug has the potential for abuse, just as each one has the potential for productive and responsible use. In this book, I blend critical medical and political ecological approaches to understanding khat in Madagascar.

Approaches within Medical Anthropology

There are several dominant approaches taken within medical anthropology, described by Singer and Baer (2007) as medical ecology, meaning-centered medical anthropology, and critical medical anthropology.

Medical ecology understands health in an adaptive context, considering health risks and cultural adaptations to them, as well as the health repercussions of various survival strategies (McElroy and Townsend 2009). Agriculture, for example, while increasing land productivity and providing large amounts of surplus, has had deleterious effects on human health. Crops are vulnerable to drought and disease; people eating cereal crops as a dietary staple often suffer nutritional deficiencies; incidence of tooth decay increases; and exposure to animal-borne diseases increases due to relatively high population densities.

An important critique of the medical ecology approach is that it ignores the cultural context of all but adaptation and it takes conditions of ill-health as etic categories, ignoring cultural contexts (Singer and Baer 2007:32). Referring to a critique by Byron Good (1994), Singer and Baer argue that what is lost "is a full appreciation of the human cultural/symbolic construction of the world we inhabit" (Singer and Baer 2007:32).

Meaning-centered medical anthropology fills this gap by focusing on cultural systems of health and illness, understanding health care systems as situated within locally embedded worldviews and practices. This perspective interrogates cultural construction and experience of health and the relationship between mind and body, considering such factors as culture bound syndromes and the cultural effectiveness of placebo effect. It might analyze the cultural construction of pain or the role of shamanism in healing (Strathern and Stewart 2010), for example. While this is a critical component of any medical anthropology analysis, a critique of this approach is that it remains focused on the local level, ignoring wider political and economic frameworks influencing health conditions and perceptions of them.

Critical medical anthropology (CMA) is the name of the approach that builds on insights from the previous two perspectives by contextualizing the local within broader factors of political economy and farther reaching cultural influences. According to Singer and Baer, "CMA emphasizes structures of power and inequality in health care systems and the contributions of health ideas and practices in reinforcing inequalities in the wider society" (2007:33). Paul Farmer, while not intentionally defining CMA, calls on an approach that interrogates "how large-scale social forces come to have their effects on the bodies of the poor and marginalized" (2000:xiii). This work on khat in Madagascar follows a CMA approach in its insistence on examining local social and individual effects alongside broader cultural politics and economics of production, trade, and consumption.

Political Ecology and CMA

Political ecology emerged within anthropology with an explicit interest in understanding how extra-local dynamics affect local environmental processes. Eric Wolf is credited with making the first written mention of "political ecology" (1972), when he argued that local ecological and social practices must be understood in the context of nonlocal interests.[2] Studies in political ecology have since made the important point that local resource use practices are best understood when broader political and economic conditions are taken into consideration. More specifically, political ecology considers power relations and social hierarchies, examining who has and does not have access to resources. CMA's emphasis has resonated with that of political ecology, in that CMA "involves paying close attention to what has been called the 'vertical links' that connect the social group of interest to the larger regional, national, and global human society" (Singer and Baer 2007:33). Both political ecology and CMA seek to understand, in Merrill Singer's words, the "wider causes and determinants of decision making and behavior" (Singer and Baer 2007:33).

Early case studies illustrate political ecology's focus on linking local events to broader political and economic dynamics. Lucy Jarosz (1993), for example, using a historical political ecology approach, put contemporary slash-and-burn horticultural practices in the eastern rainforests of Madagascar into broader perspective. While current conservation proponents tend to blame local people for forest destruction, Jarosz showed how French colonial practices drove people to their unsustainable land use practices. During the colonial era, the French took people's fertile agricultural land from them, forcing them to find other means of subsistence. Many moved to the edges of the rainforest and then survived by cutting down the forest to farm on. In addition, she pointed out how colonial logging itself directly eliminated vast tracts of forest. Some political ecology has produced ethnographically rich studies of micropolitics in the context of resource management. My earlier work examined the politics of park management (Gezon 2006) and jurisdiction over access to marine resources (Gezon 1999a), arguing that despite their subordinate political positions, local people can play an important role in shaping the way resources are allocated and used. Religious and local political leaders negotiate and often effectively resist restrictions from above.

Some political ecological scholarship has explicitly combined with a medical anthropology analysis. Janice Harper (2002) examines the health correlates of conservation in the eastern rainforest of Madagascar. She studied local uses of traditional medicines and examined the consequences of restricting local people from these resources when they have limited access to Western-trained medical professionals and cannot afford pharmaceuticals. She also criticized the conservation effort for ignoring local health issues such as malnutrition and those related to poor sanitation. In another example of a fusion between critical medical and ecological approaches, Singer and Baer examined the relationship between health and productive subsistence systems in their study of global warming. They explain that global warming affects health, for example, when it results in droughts that leave people hungry or malnourished and vulnerable to disease, the spread of tropical diseases to larger areas, and heat waves (Baer and Singer 2009; Singer and Baer 2007:189–193).

Because khat is a cultivated plant, it is easy to make the connection to political ecology; to comprehend the dynamics of local production systems, a study of khat needs to be grounded in an understanding of nonlocalized demand for the product. As a psychotropic substance, khat also invites a CMA analysis since its consumption cannot be understood without looking to broader issues of health effects, poverty, global drug policies, and local social change. Political ecology and CMA converge to provide a nuanced analysis of khat in Madagascar.

Drugs in a CMA Context

In evaluating psychotropic substances, CMA uses two important strategies. First, it examines drug consumption within a social context of inequality, considering its effects on various segments of the population—especially the poor (Singer 2008a). Second, it goes beyond analyzing consumption to consider the political and economic material and discursive contexts of drug production and availability. The CMA approach builds on traditional medical anthropology approaches by examining the cultural contexts of use and by considering how drug-related decision-making may serve some adaptive purpose. These meaning-centered accounts have typically emphasized a culturally relativist analysis of drugs from the perspective of the user, who often does not see drug use as deviant. Bennett and Cook explain that this has led to a disjuncture between anthropological analyses and the goals of clinicians and policy makers, who focus on how to eradicate or at least lessen harmful effects of drug use (Bennett and Cook 1996:237).

CMA analyses take into account the cultural contexts of drug use within a broader political and economic framework, considering the three stages in a commodity chain: production and trade as well as consumption. In focusing on systems of power, both horizontally within communities and vertically, CMA considers how social relationships of class, age, ethnicity, and gender (among others) structure unequal access to health care and exposure to health risks from drugs. In his book, *Drugging the Poor*, Singer argues that both legal and illegal drugs "contribute to maintaining an unjust structure of social and economic relations" (2008a:230). This occurs in several ways. First, in pacifying poor and working classes, drugs help prevent collective action. On the other hand, Singer and his colleagues note the tendency of people to self-medicate "the hidden injuries of oppression" (Baer et al. 2003:169), using drugs as "a means of coping with the stresses and demands of being at the bottom of an oppressive class structure" (Singer 2008a:23).

Another connection between drugs and poverty is the physical effects of heavy drug use, including *in utero* exposure, which has a negative impact on capacity and upward mobility. Singer (2008a:31) criticizes the use of tobacco, for example, arguing that it is a significant barrier to the well-being of consuming populations by causing and aggravating chronic illnesses in users and their families and by diverting funds from household budgets (regarding tobacco, see also Kingsolver 2011). Corporate business practices, including targeted advertising, make legal drugs attractive to poor segments of the population (Singer 2008a) and covert government practices increase the availability of debilitating illegal drugs.

There has been a historic connection between drug availability and capitalist interests because of the high revenue gains from drug sales. The case of opium represents a particularly egregious historic example of a highly addictive, debilitating drug being pushed to fill national coffers. The British directed a large portion of the Indian economy to the production of opium, which it sold forcibly to China after winning the Opium Wars of the early to mid-nineteenth century. The lucrative sale of opium effectively balanced Britain's trade deficit with China (Klein 2008; Singer 2008b:24). Later, the French largely financed their colonial endeavors in Southeast Asia with opium revenues by marketing it directly or taxing its sale in legal venues throughout areas controlled by the French. Drugs were not only a source of revenue for imperialist governments but also a means for controlling colonized populations. Although Vietnam did not officially become independent from the French until the mid-1950s, Singer (2008b:26) quotes Ho Chi Minh from a protest letter written in 1920 that the Vietnamese people had been conquered through selfish interests, brazenly exploited and oppressed, and "poisoned with opium, alcohol, etc."

Contemporary drug use also needs to be considered in light of who benefits politically and economically from drug availability and use. To be fully understood, the War on Drugs, for example, must be situated within a national context of anxiety over rebellious youth of the late 1960s and early 1970s and a fear of urban minorities, especially African American male youth (Baum 1996; Massing 1998:97). Internationally, it has been an adjunct to foreign policy interests. Chien et al. (2000) present poignant cases of how the Central Intelligence Agency (CIA) notoriously fostered relations with drug rings to support foreign interests in Latin America and South and Southeast Asia. The CIA has repeatedly funded leaders of smuggling operations whose political positions support U.S. interests. In his book on the politics of poppies through time, Chouvy writes, "the anti-Communist agenda of the CIA played a decisive role in stimulating the global illicit drug trade" (2009:95). As a result, the availability of cocaine and heroin to Americans has been assured. These scholars argue that the War on Drugs has served elite interests and has acted in contradiction to its own stated objectives of controlling drug production, trade, and consumption.

Drug consumption represents a complex intersection of power that includes direct manipulation of consumers and voluntary appropriation of drugs by consumers based on their pleasurable and symbolically meaningful experiences.

Scholarly studies of drug foods provide a good example of this. Sidney Mintz, for example, studied the role of sugar and other drug foods in enabling capitalism and in creating a working class. In his study of the role of sugar in modern history, Mintz wrote: "the hypothesis offered here is that sugar and other drug foods, by provisioning, sating—and, indeed, drugging—farm and factory workers, sharply reduced the overall cost of creating and reproducing the metropolitan proletariat" (1985:180). Sugar and tea not only taste good, but they give energy and suppress appetites. Mintz argued that the workers were not just passive victims of this capitalist strategy, however. They willingly worked harder to be able to consume these luxury products. Mintz wrote that "sugar, tea, and like products represented the growing freedom of ordinary folks, their opportunity to participate in the elevation of their own standards of living" (1985:183). In a similar way, people choose to consume khat partly because of the pleasurable and socially meaningful experience it provides.

The goal of CMA, then, is to consider the larger contexts of drug consumption and availability, analyzing broad political and economic dynamics of production and trade. Examining production and sale of drugs provides insight into the circumstances through which the substances have become available in the first place. It also provides insight into the cultural ideologies and social expectations that surround all aspects of a substance. CMA also builds on meaning-centered medical anthropology, which reveals the cultural and social contexts of drug use, focusing on consumer behavior and worldview. Along these lines, it evaluates the interrelatedness of biochemical effects, the drug's situation within social, political, and economic dynamics, and cultural expectations of drug effects.

Perceptions of health (and what is "good for you" and "bad for you") exist in a field of competing ideologies, where the ones held by those with power are more influential than others and will more likely be translated into action. In the case of khat, to be able to determine whether khat chewing ought to be acceptable or not, we must consult multiple sources of information, recognizing that people's stated experiences with khat—as users or those with opinions on it—are shaped by cultural perceptions of what khat is. Since perceptions of khat's effects will vary both within communities and cross-culturally, assessing its effects requires nuanced, sensitive analyses. CMA urges us to look well beyond overly simplistic dualistic evaluations that judge drug use to be straightforwardly either good or bad, acceptable or not.

Cultural Contexts of Drug Use

To understand the biocultural aspects of drug use, several factors must be considered, including: (1) drug action, or the chemical reactions of substances; (2) the social and cultural environment in which substances are consumed, including the physical setting; and (3) individual attitudes and perceptions about the substances. As to physiological effects of drugs, Erich Goode (2007) notes that these substances cannot be evaluated as to their physical and mental effects in a vacuum, isolated from all social and cultural contexts of use. Pharmacological studies of chemical reactions alone will not predict even the physical effects, since these depend on dose and "route of administration." Drugs may be consumed via needle, pill, tea, smoking, or chewing, and these routes will affect the strength of their effect. The intensity of coca, for example, increases dramatically when chewed as a leaf, snorted as cocaine, or smoked as crack. Similarly, a synthetic, concentrated pill version of cathine, which has been used as a rave drug in urban youth party contexts, is considerably more potent than the chewing of khat leaves. Many analysts agree that the ingestion of cathine from khat chewing is self-limiting because of the route of administration, which prevents large doses from being consumed at once. The same is true for coca leaves. One of the problems with the formal scheduling of drugs is that there is inadequate consideration of differences in effects due to the route of administration.

Physical drug effects also depend on how drugs are *mixed* with other drugs, food, and drink. In Madagascar, for example, one of the problems cited by medical doctors was that they saw increased gastrointestinal problems with khat when people did not eat a healthy meal either before or after chewing it. Psychiatric professionals said that khat by itself rarely caused problems; it was mixing with alcohol or marijuana that correlated with psychotic episodes.

Beyond direct physiological and psychological effects from the chemical substances, social contexts and cultural expectations also shape the user's experience of a substance. Perhaps the best way to think about this is to recognize the power of the placebo effect. With a placebo, a neutral substance can have a physical effect if a person believes it will have one. In clinical drug trials, placebos are administered as a control, to test the efficacy of the drug in question. Unexpectedly, in Western biomedical drug tests, inactive properties (such as sugar pills or saline solutions, for example), have produced results similar to the active ingredient in a significant number of cases for some ailments, and have been especially effective in pain relief.

Miller and Kaptchuk (2008), who work respectively for the National Institutes of Health and Harvard Medical School, argue that it is not the placebo itself—the sugar pill, for example—that is effective. They maintain that the total *context* of the healing encounter is a more important key to explaining a "placebo's" observable effects. They report, for example, that in a clinical test, pain medication proved to be significantly more effective when administered by a clinician and to the patient's knowledge than when administered by a machine without the patient being aware (Miller and Kaptchuk 2008:224). They write: "Factors that may play a role in contextual healing include the environment of the clinical setting, cognitive and affective communication of clinicians, and the ritual of administering treatment. . . . Attention to contextual healing signifies that there is more to medicine than diagnosing disease and administering proven effective treatments" (p. 224).

So it is with responses to psychoactive substances—legal or illegal: Cognitive expectations, culturally situated but individually experienced mind sets, and rituals of administration all influence the observable effects—both psychological *and* physiological. In 1964, Timothy Leary, who became famous for his studies and promotion of psychedelic drugs, and his colleagues wrote that "the nature of the [drug] experience depends almost entirely on set and setting" (Leary et al. 1964:11), where *set* refers to the individual's personality structure and mood, and *setting* to the physical conditions (weather, characteristics of the room, etc.), the relationship of the people to each other, and cultural worldviews.

In a later study, psychiatrist Norman E. Zinberg (1984:5) focused on setting, which he determined to be the least well understood. He proposed that setting includes social controls, consisting of patterned behaviors (social rituals) and values and rules of conduct (social sanctions). Social controls do not inevitably lead to controlled drug use, but Zinberg emphasizes that: "The social setting, with its formal and informal controls, its capacity to develop new informal social sanctions and rituals, and its transmission of information in numerous informal ways, is a crucial factor in the controlled use of any intoxicant" (p. 15). It does this by defining appropriate doses, identifying safe and appropriate social and physical settings, and compartmentalizing drug use to support the users' other commitments and relationships. Zinberg's general point is that drug effects are as much—if not more—related to social and cultural settings as they are to pharmacological drug action, per se.

Alcohol provides a poignant example of the cultural differences in the physical, psychological, and social experiences of those drinking it. In a cross-cultural comparison, MacAndrew and Edgerton (2003 [1969]) concluded that behavior while under the influence of alcohol is highly culturally variable and that explaining this behavior cannot be reduced to biochemical descriptions. In a contemporary iteration of scholarship first published in 1958, Heath writes about the unexpectedly high tolerance for alcohol among the Camba of Bolivia. Even though, in the 1950s, when he conducted his study, they were falling-down drunk about five days per month, they did not experience "any of the various so-called alcohol-related problems that are so often attributed to heavy drinkers" (Heath 2004:119–120). Patterns of drinking have changed since the 1950s, however, corresponding with shifts in economic opportunities and social organization.

Native American drinking has been observed to be quite different. Samson (2004), for example, argues that heavy drinking among the Innu of Labrador, Canada, has existed as a result of contact with European fur traders. Nevertheless, its debilitating effects, including "mass inebriation, social disorganization, marital disharmony, child neglect and untimely deaths" (Samson 2004:150–151) only emerged to a great extent in the late twentieth century, when these people, who were nomadic hunters, were forcibly settled—their land and livelihood stripped from them. With few to no alternatives, they were forced to rely on the Canadian government for assistance.

Much literature on alcohol has focused on problematic alcohol consumption, taking for granted certain assumptions about the effects of dose on behavior. Page and Singer point out that more recent studies, however, are beginning to identify "the importance of drinking places in the making of social lives, social relations, and personal identities that extend far beyond their immediate settings" (Page and Singer 2010:13; see also Gamburd 2008; Pine 2008).

As the example of alcohol reveals, in one cultural context, the use of a particular drug may tend to be individually harmful and socially disruptive and in another, it may not be. In a volume edited by Coomber and South (2004a), scholars explore various cultural contexts of drug use, illustrating through case studies that *socially integrated drug use results in fewer cases of abuse*. Some drugs typically thought of as individually and socially dangerous have controlled patterns of use in some settings, for example opium in India (Ganguly 2004), coca in Latin America (Spedding 2004), and *ganja* in Jamaica (Chevannes 2004). MacRae presented his study of the ritual use of *ayahuasca* in Brazil by the followers of the Santo Daime religious movement, which was founded in 1930. He identifies several social factors that effectively control its abuse, including its incorporation into a religious ritual context; prescriptions for diet and behavior before, during, and after consumption; a designated leader who is responsible for maintaining order; and protocols for controlling the dosage consumed (MacRae 2004:32).

The introduction of drugs to new populations of users is not always as socially integrated as in the case of *ayahuasca* for the Santo Diame movement. Some drugs have been introduced by outsiders, with devastating local effects. In what has been called the "spill-over" effect, for example, drugs flow into local markets in places where traffickers set up transit routes from producing countries to consuming countries. Many of these are in Africa (Nigeria and South Africa) and the Caribbean (Klein 2008). Klein explains that drug syndicates "cover their running expenses by developing a local market" (p. 134).

Local interest in drugs has also arisen in the wake of tourism. Tourist demand for cocaine has resulted in local demand for crack in Jamaica, for example. Heroin was introduced to the Kenya coast by tourists in the 1970s, and, as in most cases of new drug introductions, new Kenyan users were not aware of its effects or addictive properties. Klein (2008:133) points out that heroin use coincides with increased rates of crime and transmission of blood-borne diseases. In a more sympathetic vein, Beckerleg (2004) writes that heroin became increasingly socially integrated with the rise in the 1980s of a subculture concerned with its use and procurement. It includes specialized language, values, user etiquette, and patterned settings of use. Heroin use is condemned by health workers and community elders, but many families tolerate users and many continue to provide financial and other support. Beckerleg (2004) does not condone heroin use in Kenya but points out the importance of understanding its significance to users and the willingness of local nonusers to tolerate it.

As the case of heroin in Kenya suggests, just because social norms are in place does not mean that drug use is necessarily unproblematic for individuals and social groups. The introduction of drugs in recent times has coincided with the entrenchment of social inequality both at home and abroad through the exploitation of non-Western people and resources as well as through the systematic impoverishment of underclasses living in Western nations. These disruptions have created dependencies on new modes of production—and, in many cases, on new substances. Singer (2008b) points out several ways in which new patterns of drug use negatively affect prospects for individual and national economic gain in poor countries, thereby contributing to their impoverishment. Specifically, drug trade and use threaten the health and autonomy of producing populations, who are exposed to dangerous conditions (e.g., exposure to dangerous chemicals used in making heroin); drug use can also lower productivity when users are incapacitated due to intoxication; the high financial stakes of drug trade encourages governmental corruption; drug use has negative effects on families who rely on the using adult for financial and other kinds of support; and drug trade and use result in a rise in violence and crime, resulting in lower security for the overall population. Thus, socially disruptive drug use has strong moorings in processes of globalization.

Khat, while deeply culturally embedded in Yemen and parts of Ethiopia, has been only recently adopted by other populations throughout the western Indian Ocean, including Madagascar. The ramifications of this are explored in later chapters (especially Chapters 3 and 6).

Identifying Drug Use and Abuse

Just as it is difficult to define the social outcome of the use of different drugs, it is also hard to distinguish drug "use" from drug "abuse." Linda Bennett and Paul Cook (1996:242) argue that the distance "between acceptable usage . . . and dysfunctional-pathological usage is extremely complicated." This is particularly the case when cultural values either strongly condemn or affirm certain forms of drug use. Using Jamaica as an example, Bennett and Cook (1996) note that despite middle-class Jamaican insistence that *ganja* makes people lazy, an important study (Rubin and Comitas 1975) showed that in overall work productivity there was no correlation between those who consumed cannabis and those who do not. Chevannes (2004) notes that many Jamaican workers see *ganja* as a stimulant and smoke it on the job for that purpose. Stereotypes of *ganja* as either a stimulant or a depressant cloud the ability to understand its actual culturally mediated effects. Evaluating this requires examining multiple variables, including individual health, economic productivity, and social relationships.

One of the thorniest issues to tease out is the difference in analysis at individual versus societal levels. While at the individual level it may be relatively easy to connect drug abuse with dysfunctional social relationships and poor health, at the aggregate level it is difficult or impossible to blame drug abuse for what seem to be unacceptable social problems. The CMA perspective, by bringing macropolitical economic dynamics into the frame of analysis, confronts this dilemma of recognizing the consequences of individual actions while considering how choices are framed and constrained by forces beyond individuals' choices—such as the historical reality of loss of land and culture, in the case of Native Americans, or the economic reality of a changing global economy, where it is difficult to find jobs paying living wages because manufacturing jobs have gone to countries with cheap labor. Drug abuse is a symptom of these much greater problems and is not an ultimate cause of social breakdown.

The tendency for easy condemnation of drug use has led many anthropologists to avoid the language of use and abuse, in favor of meaning-centered approaches that describe rather than evaluate a drug's effects. In looking to intervention, however, critical medical applied anthropologists combine attention to political and economic factors—for example, calls for poverty reduction in general—with strategies to reduce harm to individuals and their communities. A discussion of applied efforts regarding khat use will be taken up in greater depth in the last chapter of this book.

What about Khat?: Interweaving Theoretical Frameworks

Khat (or any drug, for that matter), in itself, is neither good nor bad. Rather, criteria can be established for evaluating its effects on a population in particular contexts. An analysis of khat will not remain isolated to the effects of consumption alone but will also consider the political, economic, cultural, and social frameworks within which consumption exists. In the chapters to come, I will consider five major issues: (1) the individual physical and mental effects of khat; (2) the social and cultural effects on labor productivity, the quality of gendered interpersonal relationships, and ethnic identity; (3) the economic effects on household buying power where people spend money on khat and on buying power where people make money from khat; (4) the implications of khat production for food security and availability; and (5) the broader political and economic contexts of khat production and trade.

I weave several theoretical strands into the CMA and political ecology approaches for my analysis of the role of khat in Madagascar today. My interest in khat production and trade as well as consumption ties in with studies of commodity chains. A focus on relationships between local and extra-local phenomena engages studies in globalization. At the local level, studies of social differentiation—according to such factors as gender, class, or ethnicity—reveal how khat became a viable commodity in the first place. In this case, I particularly examine how gendered social networks organize local activities of production, trade, and consumption. Khat provides a valuable case study for illustrating how any drug can be studied from a CMA perspective by combining individual, social, cultural, political, and economic perspectives with the gaze focused at intersections between local and broader frames of interaction.

Commodity Chains

The khat phenomenon is complex and located at multiple scales. Studying it poses methodological challenges. A multi-sited analysis within the north of Madagascar allowed for observation into the multiple phases of the life of khat as a commodity—from production to distribution to consumption. One can trace the lineage of commodity chain-type analyses in anthropology to the cultural ecology studies of Julian Steward and through the students he influenced, including Sidney Mintz and Eric Wolf. Steward's (1955) analysis of Puerto Rico examined the ecology of industrial populations. Mintz's (1974, 1985) analyses of the history of the sugar plantation economy in Puerto Rico went beyond a description of agricultural processes to examine how demand for sugar abroad provided the impetus for changing local conditions. In *Europe and the People without History* (1982), Wolf argues that to understand contemporary economies, it is important to study the history of global connections and the movement of commodities. Commodity consumption—in this case, drugs—does not occur in a vacuum but is made possible through processes of production and trade.

Commodity chain analysis provides a framework for understanding how various localities are linked through economic processes. Early analyses by Hopkins and Wallerstein (1986) and Gereffi and Korzeniewicz (1994) focused on the labor and productive aspects of commodity formation and movement. One goal of these studies was to analyze production and markets as interconnected rather than isolated phenomena. This represents an offshoot of world system and dependency theories (Kenney and Florida 1994).

An important goal of these analyses was to argue that the poverty of one part of the world cannot be understood without analyzing the wealth of another—and vice versa. A study of the coca commodity chain, for example, analyzed comparative profit margins along the chain and, not surprisingly, found that the majority of the value was added once the processed cocaine arrived in the United States (Wilson and Zambrano 1994). This approach revealed why the coca-producing countries remain relatively impoverished. Although the Latin American elite controls coca production, the majority of the profits go to the wholesalers and retailers (not the low-level street sellers) in the already financially powerful consumer countries, who are already part of the global financial core.

Another approach built on these earlier studies is called *filière*, which means "thread" in French. *Filière* emphasizes "the series of relations through which an item passes, from extraction through conversion, exchange, transport, distribution and final use" (Ribot 1998:307). It differs from commodity chain approaches in that it does not privilege production and distribution, but rather focuses on consumption and on the cultural contexts of all three processes (Ribot 2005). Ribot and others developed this framework to emphasize empirical investigation of market relationships, moving away from formal neoclassical models that ignore the embeddedness of markets in broader political and social systems (Bernstein 1996; Ribot 1998, 2005). The *filière* approach is more closely aligned with an anthropological emphasis on ethnography and holism than is the commodity chain approach.

In *The Social Lives of Things*, Appadurai (1986) has similarly called attention to studies of commodities from cultural as well as political, economic, and social perspectives. He proposed that relations and contests of power connect the processes of production, distribution, and consumption. This perspective has influenced many current commodity chain and multi-sited perspectives in anthropology. A study of khat that appeared in that volume described changes in production and consumption in northeast Africa that provides a valuable "window on the cultural changes and social tension that exist in northeast Africa today" (Cassanelli 1986:255). In my analysis, the commodity chain approach provides a vantage point for evaluating khat's effects as a drug in Madagascar.

Livelihood Strategies: Gender, Globalization, and Social Difference

Khat provides opportunities for economically marginal populations, particularly for women. To understand why this is the case, I analyze gendered social networks in northern Madagascar, considering how they permeate the domains of production, trade, and consumption and paying close attention to local social differentiation (Page and Singer 2010).

CMA has been criticized for focusing too heavily on portraying individuals as victims of overarching systems of inequality (Harper 2002). Theoretical discussions often remain at the macro-level of analysis, missing a systematic fine-grained analysis of inequality, agency, and negotiation of systemic constraints at the everyday, person-to-person level (see Singer 2006 for an exception). In addressing this weakness, my analysis draws on feminist anthropology because of its strength in interpreting everyday interactions of difference and power. In this way, feminist anthropology provides a bridge between macro- and micro-level analyses and a theoretical context for presenting ethnographic data.

Feminist scholarship focuses on differences between individuals living within the same cultural context. Gender is an important point of departure, but gendered relationships are not isolated from other differences based on class, age, and ethnicity, for example. Power infuses all relationships, as certain social positions have greater access to power, prestige, and wealth. Feminist scholarship teases out the delicate task of navigating complex identities. The restrictions of received social structures juxtapose the agency of individual actors, who have the capacity to innovate and reinterpret creatively (Moore 1994, 1999) and who perform their gender roles through everyday actions. In this way, it is possible to trace local dynamics of adaptation to new circumstances—such as, in this case, the emerging khat phenomenon. By studying local performances of gendered identity and economic strategy, we learn about the triggers that encouraged the expansion of khat in the first place, as well as the processes through which it has become culturally and economically integrated within Malagasy life. Attention to local interactions also reveals the local sphere to be heterogeneous, or socially differentiated, in the opportunities it provides for of privilege, authority, and access to resources. It reveals how benefits and costs associated with drugs (in this case, khat) are unevenly distributed.

Analysis of women, who are embedded in relationships with men and shaped by multiple factors of differentiation (such as ethnicity, education, and class), offers a privileged window into the place where global processes meet local contexts. To understand health and the effects of khat as a drug commodity, it is critical to examine gendered relationships and household strategies. A recent edited volume by Gunewardena and Kingsolver (2007b), entitled *The Gender of Globalization: Women Navigating Cultural and Economic Marginalities*, makes three important points. First, women's experiences intersect with existing forms of social inequality. Second, and relatedly, women's (and, I might add, men's) agency is socially and culturally constrained by factors such as the availability of economic opportunities and gender ideologies. Third, women (and men) negotiate the effects of globalization—often experiencing increased disempowerment but sometimes taking advantage of new opportunities.

Women in northern Madagascar have found new opportunities in the areas of production and distribution, but women cannot be taken as a homogeneous category. This analysis demonstrates that the category of "women" must be understood in terms of many factors of differentiation, including marital and household status, ethnic identity, and position within the khat commodity chain.

Love, Affect, and Gendered Identity

My research on khat made it clear that a perspective based in economic rationality could provide some broad-stroke generalizations about how and why the khat economy thrives: Khat brings in more money than other commodities, therefore people grow and sell it. Khat makes people feel good, therefore they consume it. But to understand daily actions and decision-making required a broader, more holistic focus. It also revealed an irreducible aspect of decision-making that studies of rational behavior do not capture well—that of identity, affect, and attachment. Although I did not go to the field with the intention of studying sexuality, affect, domestic relationships, and "love," I found that these were ubiquitous idioms through which women and men alike understood, negotiated, and challenged the opportunities and constraints that they faced. Many consumers consider khat an aphrodisiac, fueling its desirability. For traders and producers, gendered strategies for survival occur within the context of affection and desire for connection. Sexuality, desire, and the meanings associated with them provide indicators of opportunity and constraint and metaphors for success and failure in the economic sphere in northern Madagascar. They also constitute ends in themselves and cannot be tied deterministically to economic processes.

This analysis elaborates medical anthropology's emphasis on "the importance of women's local moral worlds" and "the importance of understanding women's subjectivities" (Inhorn 2006:347) and leads to understanding women's position within health care systems. It situates gender directly within CMA, as it connects gendered intimate experiences to global processes. It points out desire as a kind of sensory experience that structures social relations (Nichter 2008). It also ties studies in the anthropology of affect to a CMA of drugs by investigating desire and attachment as local frameworks, or worldviews, for understanding consumption, trade, and production of a drug. This work joins a recent anthropological interest in the politics of affect and intimacy (Hirsch and Wardlow 2006; Ilouz 1997).

Gendered divisions of labor do not occur outside the politics of affection and "affairs of the heart" through which people track their choices. Rather, I argue, observable divisions of labor revolve around cultural constructions and lived experiences of desire and interpersonal connection as well as material needs for food and shelter for oneself and one's dependents. Studying these dynamics not only makes for a more interesting story, but makes any analysis of khat's effects more relevant to potential local needs for public health interventions by identifying patterns and logics of behavior. Thus, it situates gender analysis at the center of CMA and drug studies. A focus on gender as a particular form of inequality provides an important point of entry for investigating intersections between the local and the global, and feminist anthropology provides the theoretical toolkit for understanding that inequality. Gender is a particularly important axis of difference in the experience of drug effects within as well as between communities.

Khat on the Margins: Silence, State Perspectives, and Globalization

Broader questions emerge from localized gendered relationships: Why, given khat's economic success at the local level, is it ignored at the state level? Why does it remain marginal to formal economic development schemes? For insights into these questions, I consider recent anthropological scholarship on the state and secrecy, corruption, and on critical development theory. In keeping with both CMA and political ecology approaches, I propose that global discourses about drugs and economic development, as well as practices of governance and development interventions, provide a compelling framework for considering local experiences of khat on the ground.

Khat is the lifeblood of the economy of the far north of Madagascar. The informal khat economy has permitted producers on the margins of the global economy to survive in conditions where they have little chance for upward mobility—or even basic survival. Madagascar is one of the world's poorest countries. With undermaintained infrastructure and little access to the financial or social capital necessary to develop profitable business ventures, people throughout Madagascar, and in the north in particular in this case, lack the ability to participate as full members in the global capitalist economy. Khat has offered a local adaptation to the challenges associated with entrenched poverty.

Recognizing khat as a local adaptation to poverty underscores insights from scholars of globalization who have rejected an assumption that globalization results in an increasing homogenization of the world (Friedman 2000). Global capitalism results in a highly stratified world (Cole 2001; Smith 1984), despite the compression of time and space due to technological advances (Castells 1996; Harvey 1989). Throughout her work, Tsing points out that what we refer to as global is not a top-down project but is coproduced across scales (1993, 2000, 2005). Her concept of "friction" captures this sense: "As a metaphorical image, friction reminds us that heterogeneous and unequal encounters can lead to new arrangements of culture and power" (2005:5). Appadurai (1996) analyzes the cultural dimensions of globalization addressing the popular alarm that globalization will lead to homogenization. He introduces concepts such as ethnoscapes, mediascapes, and financescapes for understanding the fluidity and irregularity of global flows. As a case study, khat in Madagascar provides an example of a uniquely local rejoinder to economic change associated with globalization.

As a phenomenon of both production and consumption, khat weaves back and forth between the local, regional, national, and global. Understanding it as a drug that powerfully affects people's lives requires navigating its effects at these multiple levels. The physical effects of drugs are tightly interwoven with the political, economic, and cultural settings in which consumption takes place. Khat's effects, moreover, include not only its consequences on the body but also its indirect effects on livelihoods and perceptions of well-being.

The Local Context: Ethnic Identity Politics

Many current tensions within Madagascar have roots in ethnic identity politics of the precolonial and colonial eras. The Antankarana, as an ethnic-identity group, have been recognized as an important presence in the north for several centuries. Antankarana royalty arrived in the early 1600s, asserting political hegemony over autonomous fishing and small-scale agricultural populations in a dynastic expansion of the Sakalava kingdom to the south (Baré 1980; Vérin 1990). The Antankarana geographical seat lies to the southwest of Diego Suarez and to the west of the Ankarana massif, in the village of Ambatoaranana (Gezon 2006; Walsh 1998). In the nineteenth century, the Antankarana were forcibly subdued by the imperialist precolonial Merina state, which arose in the central highlands of Madagascar, with Antananarivo as its capital (Heseltine 1971; Larson 2000). Until 1896, when the French officially took over the country as a colony, the Antankarana struggled against their submission to the Merina through both direct resistance and by seeking help from outsiders (Gezon 2006). Contemporary national and local political and religious expressions remain marked by memories of their defeat (Lambek and Walsh 1997; Walsh 1998).

When the French took possession of Madagascar in 1896, the war against the Merina was finally over. Although the French had sided with the Antankarana throughout the nineteenth century, the Antankarana did not receive special treatment in the colonial era. The French made Antananarivo—the Merina capital—the national capital. Because of the influence of the British, the Merina had been Westernized to a greater extent than any of the coastal regions through formal education and missionary religious enculturation. They were therefore in a better position to take any positions that required specialized training or general familiarity with French ways. Many people in Diego Suarez feel that the privileging of the central highlands over the coastal regions has remained over the years. In local political discourse, people express resentment, and in local political action many resist the hegemony of the central highlands by supporting movements and candidates who promote coastal interests.

Despite the ethnic diversity of the northern region today, Antankarana history illustrates the types of tensions that continue to be found between central highlands–identifying people (especially Merina) and those identifying with the coasts. The history of these ethnic politics is also important for understanding khat, since khat tends to be associated with northern coastal populations and can in some contexts symbolize difference from the high plateau. Khat often takes on charged associations that go far beyond disinterested assessments of its health, social, or economic effects. Khat's perceived effect of making people lazy (avoidant of productive work), for example, aligns well with cultural stereotypes of coastal populations as generally prone to laziness. From the perspective of many khat chewers, national resistance to khat is interpreted as an example of identity politics aimed less at khat than at themselves as a group.

Methods and Evolution of the Study

This study came together over many years of research. My familiarity with Madagascar began in 1990 after my first year of graduate school, and I have returned frequently. I lived in a small village outside of the Ankarana Reserve in northern Madagascar for sixteen months in 1993–94, when I became fluent in the northern dialect of Malagasy. During that time, I conducted doctoral research on the micro-politics of conservation and land management (Gezon 1995, 2006). In a more recent study, I sought to move away from an approach common in conservation studies that is grounded in the activities immediately surrounding a protected area. I took the actual ecological pressures on forests as my point of departure, recognizing that this would lead me to explore commodity chains. I focused on a different protected area—Amber Mountain (Mt. d'Ambre in French) in northern Madagascar, which located about 30 kilometers from the regional capital city of Diego Suarez—where many people grow nonstaple food and cash crops in the zone surrounding the protected area. Amber Mountain has been a protected area since the colonial era, and the majority of it is currently managed as a national park (Gezon 1997a, 2000a, 2003; Gezon and Freed 1999). Cash cropping of fruit and

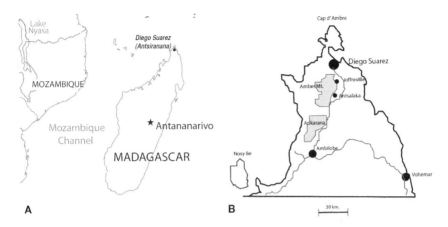

Figure 1.2   Map of Madagascar and a close-up of northern Madagascar

vegetables to serve the French population of the city dates to the early colonial era in this area. Because of this relationship between production and external markets, studying production alone would not reveal the complexities of contemporary forest degradation, local livelihoods, or conservation efforts. I thus developed a research design based on an interdisciplinary commodity chain approach.

After doing preliminary research in 2003, I found that the most significant dynamic was the expansion of khat production in the vicinity and on the edges of the Amber Mountain National Park (see Figure 1.2). I continued to inquire into the significance of vegetable production, as khat and vegetable commodity chains were interlinked in ways I could not have anticipated. After securing funding from the National Geographic Society, the National Science Foundation, and Fulbright-Hays,[3] I conducted six months of ethnographic fieldwork in 2004. I returned for follow-up research for a month each in 2005, 2007, and 2010. I also spent a month in France doing archival research in Paris and Aix-en-Provence in 2005. In the field, I observed extensively and collected reports and other grey literature. I conducted interviews with many types of interested parties, including khat consumers, traders, producers, government officials, and local scholars. I distributed daily food logs to trace urban vegetable consumption in 2004–05; I administered a structured interview schedule with producers, distributors, and consumers in 2007; and I continued informal interviewing in the summer of 2010. Students from the Université d'Antsiranana provided invaluable assistance with interviewing and administration of the surveys.

Because of my interest in commodity chains, I realized I would have to develop a multi-sited research design—albeit a rather localized one that would not span national boundaries (Gezon 2010). A theoretical interest in geographically dispersed processes and connections requires innovative methodological approaches. Those studying the anthropology of globalization have struggled with this challenge. In his influential review, George Marcus (1995) notes that understanding the local remains critical to globalization studies, and macro-theory does not obviate the need for ethnography. Page and Singer also call for a methodological approach to drug studies that is appropriate for an interconnected globe that affirms an ethnographically grounded approach while remaining "viable and vital in a changing world" (2010:89). Marcus identifies a strategy that requires "quite literally following connections, associations and putative relationships" (1995:97). It involves fieldwork in multiple geographic sites, with sensitivity to tracing the connections between them (see Figure 1.3).

My own approach was also influenced by the linkages methodology of Conrad Kottak and Elizabeth Colson (1994), who took inspiration from the world system approaches of Mintz (1985), Wolf (1982), and Wallerstein (1974). They also drew from scholarship coming out of the Rhodes-Livingstone Institute in northern Rhodesia (now Zambia) and the Manchester School under Max Gluckman. Scholars such as Gluckman (1958), Van Velsen (1979), and later Burawoy (1991) embraced the extended case method for identifying connections in time, space, and topic. Epstein wrote that "cases have their sources in the ceaseless flow of

Figure 1.3   Author with a khat trader from Diego Suarez

social life and, in turn, contribute to that flow" (1978 [1967]:230). Following case studies often means tracing geographical paths, as actors move around. Kottak and Colson's linkages methodology comprises many facets, including "a network approach (to trace the far-flung sets of relationships associated with geographical mobility and external interventions)" (Kottak and Colson 1994:397), ethnography combined with survey techniques, longitudinal research, and the collection of records through archives or government reports. This kind of research often takes time and a team approach, including experts from the country being studied. This kind of study also requires "studying up" (Nader 1972) to understand the perspectives of states and global financial institutions.

Studying production involved a two-stage process. The first focused on land cover change, as I gathered insight into the effects of khat production on forest cover, in keeping with my original research on conservation and deforestation. For this first part, I assembled a team of researchers in 2004 to examine the dynamics of land cover change through satellite images and ground-truthing. The second part was ethnographically based and involved in-depth interviews as well as spending unstructured time with khat farmers during my study of production on the ground around the Amber Mountain has lasted from 2003 to 2010.

I traced distribution networks by asking farmers to whom they sell and retail sellers where they purchase their khat. Studying consumption involved two main methods: (1) network sampling, where chewers were identified and their milieu studied; and (2) a structured interview schedule administered at the end of the study in 2007 to collect broader and more generalizable data about khat chewing in the general population of Diego Suarez.

Production, distribution (or trade), and consumption make up the khat commodity chain. While many studies of commodity chains are international in scope (Friedberg 2001; Hansen 2000), in Madagascar, khat's principle sites in the chain are primarily in the same region of the country. The majority of the nation's khat is produced within 50 miles of the northern city of Diego Suarez and the main consuming population is within that city, though it is increasingly being sent to urban populations in other parts of the country.

My multi-method study thus used a flexible research strategy that was aimed at discovering processes and connections in the commodity chain, grounded in ethnography, and made use of multiple data sources relevant to the topic.

Overview of Chapters

I begin with the end of the commodity chain in Chapters 2 and 3, focusing on understanding khat from the perspective of consumers. Chapter 2 presents consumption practices, identifying the kinds of social, cultural, and productive relationships established as a result of chewing khat. Chapter 3 focuses on khat's direct effects on physical and mental health, reviewing both scientific evidence as well as local perceptions of its effects and tracing political interpretations of its use over time. Chapter 4 concentrates on the indirect effects of khat by considering the beginning of the commodity chain. It describes the production and marketing of khat within the regional economy, highlighting its importance for local livelihoods. Chapter 5 addresses issues of food security from a political ecology perspective by considering the impact of khat production on the planting of food crops. Chapters 6 and 7 turn to broader issues of gender and globalization. Chapter 6 identifies the gendered dynamics of khat consumption, production, and trade, focusing on social differentiation at the local levels. Chapter 7 considers macro-level issues surrounding khat, identifying it as a site of struggle over ethnicity, religion, and economic philosophy embedded in the larger national and global contexts.

Chapter 8, the conclusion, brings the insights of the previous chapters together and evaluates the value of khat in its many local contexts as drug and cash crop using a critical perspective to analyze issues surrounding khat as a set of costs and benefits. Understanding khat (or any drug) requires complex evaluation of multiple effects of sometimes contradictory aspects of use that can only be accurately perceived in political, economic, social, and cultural contexts.

Notes

1. Armstrong (2008) has noted that defense professionals in the United States have argued in court that khat itself is not illegal, because it does not always contain the Schedule I drug, cathinone. He writes that "in two cases, courts have ruled for the appellants because khat is not specified in any law" (p. 637).
2. Important references in the study of political ecology include Blaikie and Brookfield (1987), Schmink and Wood (1987), Bassett (1988), Hecht and Cockburn (1990), Peet and Watts (1993, 2004), the entire special issue of the Annals of the Association of American Geographers (1993), Martinez-Alier (2002), Robbins (2004), Moore (2005), Paulson and Gezon (2005), Biersack and Greenberg (2006), Escobar (2008), and Peet et al. (2011).
3. National Science Foundation 2003, Award Number BCS-0318640; National Geographic Society 2003, Grant Number 7413.03; U.S. Department of Education Fulbright-Hays Faculty Research Abroad Fellowship 2003.

2

CONTEXTS OF CONSUMPTION

Cultivation of khat (Catha edulis) originated in the region surrounding the Red Sea and the western Indian Ocean. Khat is still consumed for its stimulating properties in the Arabian Peninsula, East and southern Africa, and Madagascar, but it is also popular with diaspora communities around the world. Usually consumed by chewing, users store a plug of chewed young stems and leaves in the cheek.

In the many places where khat is consumed, there are some commonalities due both to its pharmacological properties and to its shared cultural past. It has spread from Yemen and Ethiopia—major original centers of production—throughout the Horn of Africa, the eastern Indian Ocean, and much of the world (Carrier and Gezon 2009).[1] Many divergences also exist, which can be related to the various cultural and social contexts of consumption. A brief review of khat's chemical properties provides a framework for understanding these practices.

Khat has amphetamine-like characteristics and acts as a stimulant, causing the user to feel alert. As with all stimulants, a feeling of lethargy or sadness can follow the stimulating effects. The active property cathinone rapidly degrades into the less potent cathine postharvest, and after about twenty-four hours, khat loses potency. Wherever it is chewed in its leafy form, therefore, consumers usually want it to be as fresh as possible (see Carrier 2005a). The fact that it is perishable shapes its contexts of use.

Scholars have recognized that the consumption of psychotropic substances does not in itself predict negative or positive social, mental, or physical health outcomes. Coomber and South (2004b), for example, criticize the predominant Western notion that "drugs are inherently evil, their use inevitably undermines individual health and inexorably leads to the disintegration and destruction of community and society" (pp. 13–14). They argue instead that in many contexts, drugs are a sociocultural asset, associated with mutual support and the practice of morally grounded religious beliefs. Many drugs considered harmful stem from Western colonial influences and changes associated with globalization. But change and globalization do not uniformly bring about socially and individually destructive use of substances. Relatively recent substance use traditions, such as *ayahuasca* in the Santo Daime ritual context in Brazil (MacRae 2004), peyote in the United States (Schaefer 2004), and hallucinogens in the Bwiti religion practiced in Gabon encourage community building, the authors of these studies suggest. This implies that one role of drugs in adapting to globalization is the creation of contemporary, relevant forms of identity. Recent increase in the use of khat in Madagascar has similarly played a role in the formation of new multiethnic communities of identity in both rural and urban areas. In analyzing the effects of psychotropic substances, one cannot understand the health effects without knowing about the context in which they are produced, traded, and consumed.

Cultural expectations strongly shape the drug experience. Bennett and Cook (1996), for example, note "the power of culture to shape the drug encounter" (p. 239) and point out that "drug users have divergent experiences apparently related to wider cultural differences" (p. 239). In their edited volume, Coomber and South (2004b) identify that key elements in positive social use are social constraints that present what is acceptable and unacceptable use—how much to consume, how intoxicated to get, and when, where, and how to behave when intoxicated. These are informal controls. Because of the important role of cultural expectations, the same drug may be acceptable and even positive in one context but detrimental in another. As described in Chapter 1, opium (Ganguly 2004) and alcohol (Heath 2004; Samson 2004) are such examples.

This chapter is broken into two major sections. The first presents a history of khat use globally and identifies cross-cultural contexts of its consumption. The next section considers khat use in Madagascar in particular. Presenting a general description of khat chewing practices, it analyzes one aspect of health with regard to khat in Madagascar, namely, the social effects on both labor productivity and the quality of interpersonal relationships. The introduction outlined several aspects of health that need to be considered when analyzing the role of psychotropic substances, including: (1) the direct effects of consumption on social relationships, mental stability, and physical well-being; (2) the indirect effects, including the potentially negative consequences of spending for consumption on household budgets; (3) and the positive effects of khat as a viable means of income for farmers and traders. This chapter focuses on the first of the direct effects—social relationships, while the next chapter delves more deeply into the psychological and physical effects of khat use.

In addition to a review of newspaper and scholarly writings on khat, a large part of this chapter is based on interviews and observations conducted from 2003 to 2010 and a survey conducted in and around the city of Diego Suarez, Madagascar, in 2007. The research focused on khat users, nonusers within the social networks of users, and various officials throughout the city (e.g., politicians, bureaucrats, medical doctors, and clergy) who have a role in shaping public opinion and developing public policy surrounding khat use.

Practices of Consumption

The ultimate origins of the khat plant are unknown, and sources about this present different versions. John Kennedy (1987:60–62) summarizes the literature, identifying khat's origins variously as from Turkestan and Afghanistan (first mentioned in the eleventh century), from Ethiopia, and from Yemen. Kennedy, examining Schopen's (Schopen 1978, cited in Kennedy) evidence, notes that it is reasonable to assume that it was introduced to Ethiopia in the eleventh century, where it was first used recreationally. Although most writers accept that khat came to Yemen from Ethiopia, Kennedy (1987) proposes that there is some evidence that it went in the opposite direction. In any case, he notes that khat was probably used recreationally on a limited basis by the twelfth century in both places, but became widespread by the fourteenth century.

Khat has been chewed for centuries in Yemen and certain parts of Ethiopia and Kenya, and it continues to be an integral part of social and ritual life in those places (Carrier 2005a; Gebissa 2004; Kennedy 1987). Today, khat is consumed primarily in Yemen and East Africa, including Ethiopia, Kenya, Djibouti, and Somalia. It is increasingly consumed in the West and Australia, particularly as Somali refugees take root in new locales, including Great Britain, the United States, and Australia (Bures 2001; Dupont et al. 2005; Fahim 2006; Klein 2008). It has also been consumed in synthetic pill form as a rave drug by predominantly white youth in North America, Europe, and Israel (Al-Motarreb et al. 2010).

Chewing khat has been an important social ritual in Yemen for hundreds of years, mostly among men, but also among some women. Academic accounts identify khat as embedded within a centuries-long tradition of Yemeni poetry—much of which (but not all) is laudatory of khat's effects (Caton 1993; Wagner 2005; Weir 1985:66). These authors report that as early as the sixteenth century,

Sufi mystics debated the virtues of khat versus coffee, arguing over which provided a better sense of union with God. Mark Wagner (2005) provides examples of poems where the authors have endowed each of these stimulants with medical and supernatural properties and associated them with strongly positive affective and aesthetic characteristics. He quotes from a poem dated 1699: "Whenever I wanted my sight to rise to the sky, to existence, [khat] served as my stairs, [Allowing me] to cross the stars is one of its merits" (2005:24; second brackets in the original).

Wagner argues that in the seventeenth and eighteenth centuries, this poetic debate was mainly playful, but later poetic exchanges became serious, especially in the twentieth century, as the question of khat versus coffee has resonated with discourses of modernity, economic development, national and Arab Muslim identity, and participation in the global economy. The existence of poetic debates on the value of khat demonstrates it as an integrated part of Yemeni cultural practice, even if internally debated.

Yemen: Longstanding Traditions

In the contemporary era, khat is illegal throughout the majority of the Arabian peninsula except in Yemen. There, khat is a distinctly Yemeni marker of cultural identity and is not only legal but an integral part of Yemeni social and political life. Kennedy (1987:78) estimated that at the time of his research in the mid-1980s, at least 50–60% of women and 80–85% of men in what was then North Yemen chewed khat more than once a week. Many argue that khat chewing is the most important symbolic expression of a general preoccupation with autonomy among Yemenis. Daniel Varisco noted that "chewing khat is an act that is distinctively Yemeni and shared with no other Arab culture" (1986:3). In the 1980s and early 1990s, Yemen went through considerable political and economic changes: Oil was discovered in 1984 (Carapico and Myntti 1991:25). The Republic of Yemen was formed in 1990 by the unification of the socialist People's Democratic Republic of Yemen ("South" Yemen) with the conservative Yemen Arab Republic ("North" Yemen) (Milich and Al-Sabbry 1995). Varisco argued in 1997 that khat's role in marking Yemeni identity became salient as Yemen entered the world economy and as people began to identify themselves as citizens of a nation instead of merely members of tribes or classes.

At the time of her study, Shelagh Weir (1985:109) noted two kinds of khat-chewing parties in Yemen: one for special occasions like weddings, circumcisions, and other special events, and another that she calls "everyday" parties, where people bring their own khat and other consumables. Until the mid-twentieth century, khat was perceived as a luxury good affordable habitu-ally (several times per week) mainly by urban elites (in the early eighteenth, it was an urban luxury [Wagner 2005:129]). However, remittances from Yemeni family members working in oil-rich Arab countries beginning in the 1970s made habitual khat chewing more broadly available to the general public. This influx of money led to dramatic changes in the economy, including a shift from subsistence-based farming and livestock to more commoditized agriculture and wage-earning (Weir 1985:22). The influx of cash also increased the occur-rence of "'everyday' khat parties," as less wealthy segments of society became able to afford it. It is interesting to note that khat chewing has become more and not less important as Yemen has become incorporated into the regional and global economy.

Khat chewing in Yemen can be highly stylized. Wagner (2005) analyzes eighteenth-century poems that humorously describe the cultural norms of a khat-chewing party in terms that strikingly resemble some aspects of contem-porary Yemeni practices. One poem dated 1766 prescribes the proper number of participants (seven–nine), appropriate time of day, form of entertainment ("if it is an evening soiree we will have music") (Wagner 2005:130), the proper way to sit (without stretching one's legs), and the manner of speaking ("Since speech requires careful crafting do not talk over one another" [p. 130]). Schuyler (1997) draws parallels between early nineteenth-century and contemporary khat chewing both through his own ethnographic research and in his analysis of a poem from around the turn of the nineteenth century. He notes a common emphasis on conviviality as well as the importance of the participants contribut-ing to the event by way of story, reflection, or song.

Even if the specifics of the khat-chewing parties are not identical over the centuries, these poems suggest that the manner in which people consume khat—in social khat-chewing sessions—has been highly ritualized for centuries, and that affective ways of describing the experience have remained similar. Kennedy (1987:79–101), in identifying khat as a "social institution," wrote that people in contemporary Yemen give a great deal of consideration to preparing for and tak-ing part in these sessions, including such care in choosing the appropriate grade of khat and preferably eating a large hot meal before chewing. In the past as well as today, people prefer to chew in groups either in general purpose living rooms or, for the wealthier, in rooms set apart for khat chewing called *muffraj*, which are ideally located several stories up, with a good view (Weir 1985). Sometimes, there are separate rooms for women to chew khat. Kennedy writes: "It is obvious to any visitor that the whole purpose of the *muffraj* is the creation of an environment facilitating pleasure, relaxation and human companionship" (1987:84). He noted that many markers of social differentiation, such as class, gender, and rural versus urban, influence these khat-chewing settings and patterns. Nevertheless, there exists a standard model based on the practices of an urban elite class.

Many have written about the unfolding of khat-chewing sessions in both historical and contemporary contexts (Kennedy 1987; Schuyler 1997; Varisco 1997; Wedeen 2008; Weir 1985). In Yemen, the khat party is an important social institution and a formal affair with an identifiable structure. Such parties are not merely recreational: Not only does the seating arrangement reflect the social ranking of the attendees, but the parties are opportunities to do business and expand one's social networks, even to meet local politicians. Wedeen writes: "Qat chew conversations have consistently flourished since unification [of the Republic of Yemen] as a key enclave of publicity through which frank discussions among politicians and ordinary citizens take place" (2008:126).

On an affective level, several researchers have observed that Yemenis idealize the progression of moods through a khat-chewing session. During the first part of the four–five-hour-long khat-chewing session, people engage in alert conversation and gain a sense of community. The second part, the *kayf*, is characterized by a "euphoric optimistic state in which everything seems possible" (Kennedy 1987:112). Schuyler (1997:64) notes that it is a more intimate mood, both acoustically and emotionally. It is a time of more intimate conversation during which people may negotiate business transactions or seek personal guidance. During the last part, people experience introversion and sometimes a temporary depression or sadness. People often become silent, and song may replace conversation (Schuyler 1997:65).

Tobacco is a usual complement to khat chewing (Varisco 1997), and in many places, alcohol is used after the khat-chewing session. While Kennedy mentions alcohol use as a way to counteract the effects of khat, Schuyler (1997:68) analyzes it as a complement to khat. Some only drink a little to stimulate appetite and bring on sleep, but heavy drinking can bring out another mood at the end of a khat-chewing session. People may engage in boisterous conversation and dancing, but also belligerence, sarcasm, and arguments. Not enough is written about alcohol in khat-chewing sessions, however, to evaluate how frequent this practice is or the extent to which it crosses gender and class lines.

Khat in the Horn of Africa

Khat production and consumption also has a long tradition in Ethiopia. It is mainly produced in the Hererge highlands in eastern Ethiopia, which borders northern Somali (Gebissa 2004:36–37). Gebissa (2004:76) quotes Richard Burton on khat in Ethiopia among the Harer in 1853: Khat is considered to be "Food for the Pious, and literati remark that it has the singular properties of enlivening the imagination, clearing the ideas, cheering the heart, diminishing sleep, and taking the place of food." Khat use increased in Ethiopia as the Oromo pastoralists became sedentary farmers and began converting to Islam (Gebissa 2004:52). Gebissa writes: "By 1910 khat-chewing had become a widespread practice among the Islamized Oromo, among whom the leaf quickly attained social, cultural and religious importance. . . . Non-Muslims, however, considered khat-chewing to be a sign of conversion to the Islamic faith" (2004:52).

In Ethiopia, people consume khat to celebrate marriages and births and in other religious ceremonies (Brooke 1960). Varisco (1997) writes that while people in Yemen do not formally incorporate khat into their religious ceremonies, Ethiopian Muslims use khat in ceremonies to drive out evil spirits. In a recent edited volume on khat in Ethiopia (Gebissa 2010b), Ahmed (2010) identifies traditional ceremonial use of khat in northern Ethiopia, particularly among rural Oromo- and Amhara-identified people. Khat features prominently in a ritual performed in times of crisis. Most commonly, individuals call a ceremony to address specific personal or familial problems, such as illness or childlessness. A community may also hold a ceremony to address crises such as war, drought, or epidemics. The ceremonies last at least through one entire night, and sometimes for several days. The host ritually picks khat and distributes it. While in the state of euphoria, participants praise saints and shower blessings on the host. A ritual leader closes with blessings and prayer for the fulfillment of the host's wishes.

After the advent of military rule in Ethiopia in 1974, writes Gebissa (2010d), khat chewing began to appeal to urban youth. A combination of a reduction in public entertainment and sports and the movement of students into the rural (khat-chewing) areas to help with land redistribution created a climate for khat chewing to take off. Students took khat back to the cities and it became popular as a way to stay awake for studying as well as a form of entertainment. After the fall of the military regime, khat chewing became increasingly public and has become ubiquitous in the urban areas of Ethiopia. The urban context, according to Gebissa (2010d), differs in significant ways from the traditional rural one: In the urban setting, khat is often mixed with alcohol; it is only chewed (as opposed to being boiled as a tea used for medicinal purposes); and it is chewed in the afternoon, as opposed to morning or at night during worship. In rural areas, chewing is associated with community ritual, religious observance, or working. In the urban setting, khat is less ritualized.

Khat consumption in Somali-populated regions close to Ethiopia also has a long tradition that predates its recent popularity in southern Somalia. As in Ethiopia, it is consumed ritually in this part of Somalia. Though some Somali Muslim orders forbid khat, others advocate using it to aid in prayer and meditation (Migdalovitz 1993). The British were concerned enough about khat consumption in the northern part of the Somaliland Protectorate that they instituted one of the first legislative attempts against it in 1921 (see BritishSomaliland 1923:

291–292). Southern Somalis viewed khat consumption, according to Cassanelli, as a "somewhat eccentric and amusing habit" (1986:240) of northerners. Its popularity increased, however, in the late 1960s and early 1970s in Mogadishu and elsewhere when the idea that khat chewing offered protection against cholera and dysentery circulated. In the early 1980s, research showed that while khat chewing was common in both Hargeisa and Mogadishu, the proportion of consumers was still higher in Hargeisa, the more northern of the two cities: 55% in Hargeisa as opposed to 18% in Mogadishu.

Khat is also very popular in Djibouti, formerly French Somaliland. Because of khat's short "shelf life," consumption in southern Somalia and Djibouti was limited until the 1940s by its distance from major zones of production. When the Italians took over Ethiopia in 1835, they built over 2,000 miles of paved roads, enabling khat to reach many parts of Somalia and even Djibouti within forty-eight hours (Gebissa 2004:77). Increased consumption throughout the Horn of Africa is partly due to improved transportation infrastructure, which allows khat to be carried quickly from the site of production to consumption areas. Gebissa argues that it is also due to greater disposable income with the increase of civil servant jobs and the introduction of the habit to urban areas by farmers moving in. Consumption of khat in Djibouti, writes Gebissa (2004:83), began with Yemenis who had emigrated there and spread to the local population who imported it from both Yemen and the Ethiopian highlands. As khat became more available in Somalia, Gebissa (2004:81–82) argues that it also became a symbol of Somali identity. It also became a framework for expressing anti-colonial sentiment and for organizing against foreign control. Leaders of khat-trafficking operations became warlords, using their infrastructural and social networks to form a political base. Defending their right to chew khat has been intricately linked with Somali right to self-governance.

It is likely that this history of association between khat and rebellion in Somalia continued through the events of 1992, when the United States failed in its attempt to establish its authority and stabilize the government (Migdalovitz 1993:7). Aidan Hartley, a journalist in Mogadishu in the early 1990s, writes that "one of the common clichés produced by journalists and the US military at the time was that Somalia's war was fuelled by khat and that '[kh]at-crazed gunmen' were destroying the nation" (2004:236). More recently, it has been associated with Somali pirates, who have been reportedly paid in khat for overtaking ships in the western Indian Ocean and have been portrayed as great chewers of khat (Kingstone 2009). Not all in Somalia have been in favor of khat, however: There was strong governmental opposition under the secular socialist regime of Mohamed Said Barre, who presided until he was ousted in 1991. Barre banned khat in 1983. The prohibition failed in part because khat consumption was strongly associated with antigovernment sentiment. There has not been a stable government in Somalia since 1991, but opposition to khat has continued from Islamist political factions, certain Muslim religious communities, and those with public health concerns.

Although the Yemeni and Ethiopian diaspora consume khat in the West, many newspaper reports focus on khat consumption only among the Somalis living in Europe, North America, and Australia. Partly because of the sensationalized media coverage of the collapse of the Somali state, khat is associated throughout the world with Somalis. Much to the chagrin of Somalis who oppose it, khat consumption is increasingly seen as a "Somali thing."

Khat in Kenya

Another major zone of consumption as well as production is Kenya, especially in the mountain range to the northeast of Mount Kenya, the Nyambene Hills, where it is cultivated by the Bantu-speaking Meru (Carrier 2005a, 2007; Goldsmith 1999; Hjort 1974). Written accounts of the late nineteenth century show that in the Nyambenes, khat was already being cultivated and consumed prior to colonization. Meru oral testimony, supported by the extreme age of some khat bushes, suggests cultivation began much earlier. Besides the great economic importance of khat to the Meru, the trees also provide symbolic association with ancestors and form an important part of cultural identity. Khat is also used in many ceremonies, including marriage negotiations and circumcisions (Carrier 2005a:208–209, 2005b:540). Colonial authorities noted this traditional use of khat. They tolerated it, despite the disdain with which many viewed the substance (Anderson and Carrier 2009).

The cultural importance to the Meru of khat, which they call *miraa*, is well established. Ceremonial uses are particularly important, including both the preliminaries to circumcision and the preliminaries to marriage. Carrier (2007) reports that boys take khat to elders to let them know they are ready for their rite of passage, and a prospective son-in-law takes khat to the prospective bride's parents to request permission to marry her. The khat must be of the highest quality from the oldest trees in both cases and tied in a special bundle. The bundles are offered to senior men by their juniors, which symbolizes the power of the elders, in theory if not in practice. Both the Meru and the Yemeni emphasize khat's role in facilitating peaceful social interaction in contrast to the sometimes volatile sociability induced by alcohol.

While khat is a culturally integrated indigenous crop among the Meru, it has become increasingly popular in both rural areas and urban centers beyond the Meru, especially among youth. Inspired by the entrepreneurial Meru and Somalis, the khat trade developed over the last century and is now an economically important cash crop. It is taken by air from Nairobi to Mogadishu and elsewhere in Somalia each day (Carrier 2005a). It is then flown legally to the

United Kingdom and Holland, then illegally from there to other parts of Europe, Canada, and the United States.

In Kenya, consumption patterns of khat vary, unlike the more-or-less set times for chewing khat in Yemen and Djibouti. This is especially true for Kenyan youth; rather than formal structured settings, most Kenyan youth chew khat in informal settings, often while watching football or in a café. Similar to youthful chewing wherever it is documented, including in Madagascar, much bravado usually surrounds consumption. For those who work, chewing fits around work hours and is often limited to the weekend. For others, chewing is determined by ability to buy some khat or to obtain some from friends and can fill any free time they have. Weekend sessions can last into the night and are sometimes accompanied by alcoholic drinks. Employment seems to be a major factor in when and how often people chew. Carrier (Carrier and Gezon 2009) surmises that the notion that Somalis in the diaspora chew more than they did in Somalia is probably explained by high rates of unemployment in the diaspora rather than the breakdown of traditional cultural restraints. This hypothesis is also suggested by other scholars (Griffiths et al. 1997).

In addition to the main khat-consuming countries discussed above, khat is chewed elsewhere. In Africa, Beckerleg's research reveals its substantial history in Uganda (Beckerleg 2009), and people also chew it throughout much of eastern and southern Africa. Despite its illegality in Tanzania, consumption continues there (Carrier 2007:242). Khat has also spread throughout the Western world, where the leafy form is consumed by immigrants from Somalia, Yemen, or Kenya.

Khat in Madagascar

lepëpl mirëvo bontka quoi question'*ny l'habtid/* plaisir/ match *dé* foot/ *mormorengy am'* gymnase couvert *lépèpl* tous tous *socobis/ khâtman simple ou menlazen tranquillos voyagement yémen/katmandou* . . .

The people dream of chewing khat. It is a question of habit, of pleasure. During soccer games, while watching traditional boxing (*morengy*) at the covered gymnasium. Everyone has round cheeks, from simple amateurs to the great consumers of khat. All enjoy khat immensely [Yemen and Katmandou in the case of the quote above refer to the state of euphoric pleasure associated with khat chewing. A literal translation would be: All travel to Yemen and Katmandou]. (interview with a Malagasy youth, Mbima 2006:585)

People in Madagascar chew khat recreationally as well as to stay awake for work. Guards and taxi drivers chew khat alone on the job. Professionals and

Figure 2.1   Youth in Diego Suarez often chew khat and play cards in the afternoons

laborers chew recreationally on weekends, often with friends. Although khat is a stimulant, the recreational cultural contexts in which people chew—watching television, playing cards, or sitting around and chatting with friends—allows minds to wander and focus in ways that are not permitted at work. People report enjoying the way khat allows them to be *concentré*, or concentrated on philosophical musings or reflections on their lives. People often comment on how khat puts them into a mindset of dreaming of and planning for the future. Many see this as positive, though others—particularly nonchewers who are critical of the activity—see it as merely an escape that never pans out into anything practical. Men and women alike claim that one of the side effects—and benefits—of khat is that it serves as an aphrodisiac, and that men, especially, will be likely to seek out a sexual partner after chewing khat. Some point to this as part of the financial cost of khat chewing, since, unless a woman is a very steady girlfriend or a wife, she will expect to be entertained if not paid outright.

Khat cultivation in Madagascar dates back to the early twentieth century and is associated with "*arabou*," the word commonly used for people of Yemeni descent. The Yemenis arrived in Madagascar toward the beginning of the twentieth century as dock workers in the port in the regional capital city of Diego Suarez—an important military and commercial base. This migration of Yemenis to Madagascar probably coincides with the development of the port in the city of Aden in Yemen after World War I (Weir 1985:19). While these Yemenis brought khat with them and planted it in kitchen gardens, the Creoles were reportedly the first to grow it commercially. These white farmers of French descent came over from Ile de la Réunion around the turn of the century and established fields on Amber Mountain, near the colonial town of Joffreville, located about 30 kilometers from the city. Those of Yemeni descent, although maintaining a degree of social isolation and a strong cultural identity, have nevertheless mixed with others living locally.

When the French left the country en masse in the mid-1970s amid a socialist revolution and the coming to power of Didier Ratsiraka, others took over the Creole farms. The oldest and most productive establishment on Amber Mountain is owned by a family of mixed Yemeni, Malagasy, and Creole descent. As will be described in Chapter 3, farmers in the area once made their living growing vegetables. After the French departed, however, the market for vegetables declined considerably, and in the last twenty years, many took to growing khat instead. Supporting this growth in production has been an increase in consumption: In the past twenty or so years, khat chewing has gained significant popularity among the broader Malagasy population—particularly among those identifying as coastal peoples, or *côtiers*, and especially those in Diego Suarez, the city closest to the zones of production.

Khat and Youth Culture

As khat chewing gradually caught on, two main categories of men began chewing: laborers and professionals with stable incomes, who chew mainly on weekends, and *barbo*, urban youth reputed to be shiftless and in search of distraction. *Barbo*, which might be translated as hoodlum, usually work in the informal economy, often with the stated goal of making enough money to purchase more khat. Many work odd jobs in the mornings and reserve the afternoons for chewing with their friends (see Figure 2.1). Few have stable employment, though some are students. They often chew khat in groups, either in someone's living room or on the street, playing cards, sitting or talking, or watching television. Few are practicing Muslims, and they often drink beer, rather than the cold water or milk of Yemeni chewers who are generally practicing Muslims. They do this to "kill the [stimulant] effect" (*mamono ny dosy*) during and after chewing.

The Malagasy linguist, Pierre Mbima, studied male urban youth counterculture in Diego Suarez (2006) and the related slang called *koroko*. Those participating in the youth culture are often uniformly identified from the outside as *barbo*, and they themselves have appropriated the term, often referring to themselves in the third person as *barbo* (or *barbeaux* following French convention). Despite this stereotype, they actually come from a wide variety of socioeconomic circumstances. Mbima observed well-to-do mixed French-Malagasy individuals who possess French nationality and attend the elite Lycée Français chewing khat alongside young Comorians and Malagasys who go to public schools and are from families with stable incomes and consistent parental presence. Also in the mix are those from the poorest sector, who are often poorly educated and may not have consistent parental presence. Some are full-time students, while others have steady or at least seasonal jobs. Many work in the informal sector, taking jobs when and where they are available. The core of the *koroko* groups, however, and the speakers of the most complex *koroko* slang, are the semi-illiterate poor from marginalized and continuously stigmatized groups (Mbima 2006:38).

Despite these socioeconomic differences, what unifies youth is the common language of *koroko* and an association with drugs—in particular khat and marijuana. From the outside, people consider them uniformly to be drug users. Among *koroko* speakers, and among *barbo* in general, chewing and even selling khat is an important identity marker. Although *barbo* and *koroko* are not the only khat chewers in Diego Suarez, khat chewing in Diego is often associated with youth culture. Mbima identified eighteen different *koroko* groups located by *quartier* within the city, with members between the ages of twelve and twenty-seven. Each group has a name—often a music group or place, which are often in English. There are groups, for example, named Maiden, Dark Angel, Las Vegas, Dallas, Kosovo, and Woodstock. In each locale, they gather daily in a central public location to chat, play cards and music, and often chew khat. A minority of the groups work together in organized criminal activity.

Barbo and the *koroko* are often regarded with suspicion and vilified, especially by those who have received more Western education, who are not originally from the north, and who are more Western oriented in general. Many of these middle-to-upper-class Malagasy do not know how *barbo* afford khat and suspect them of stealing. Ethnographic interviews reveal that although this may, in fact, occur, it is not common. Mbima (2006) found that stealing was indeed part of the identity and practice of some of the *koroko* groups, and he explained that the *koroko* leaders from across town are aware of the major players in the local criminal element, even if they themselves do not participate. Some *koroko* may steal, but it is not the majority who do so.

Throughout the working and poorer neighborhoods of the city, I and my research associates did more than 100 surveys and interviews focusing on khat consumption in the city of Antsiranana. The surveys were administered by thirteen students at the University of Antsiranana, as part of an informal training in methods. Students provided feedback on the initial set of questions, pilot tested the survey, and helped revise it based on initial responses. They then fanned out throughout the city and interviewed people based on snowball sampling. Together, our team administered 147 surveys. Most of the respondents were people with less than a high school education and had lived in northern Madagascar—most of them in the city itself—for most of their lives. They live in neighborhoods where khat chewing is common, and many chew khat themselves. The survey results provide a general picture of how khat chewing is perceived and experienced in that milieu. These results do not represent as well the segment of the population that is most commonly critical of khat chewing: highly educated people and/or those with nonlocal identities.

In these surveys, concern about khat as an impetus for crime—stealing in particular—and other socially disruptive behavior was minimal. Out of 147 respondents, 85% said khat does not lead to social problems; 10% said yes, but, ironically, several responded that the social problem was that khat is not accepted—not that khat is a problem itself. Four percent said that it depends. Because of the strong association between khat and youth, it is unlikely that people from these neighborhoods see this segment of youth as a general threat. As for the segments of the population who were less tolerant of khat—higher income, more Westernized people—few had direct evidence of stealing as a threat.

One social problem that khat is identified with in many cultural contexts globally is so-called laziness, or an unwillingness to work productively. Even if they are not generally regarded as a public menace, these young men are seen—particularly by the middle class and professionals—as lazy and barriers to economic development. They gain this reputation not only because they chew khat in public while other people are working, but also because they are content to work informally or not to work at all rather than taking a steady job. In the survey of 147 respondents, we found that, contrary to common stereotypes, common citizens of Diego Suarez do not tend to find that khat makes people lazy. Only 7% responded that it makes people lazy; 77% said that it does not make people lazy; 9% said that it depends; and 7% did not respond. The most audible voices reporting khat's tendency to make people lazy do not represent the perception of the majority of the population.

Despite these accusations of laziness, however, what seems clear from the outside, and what the common people implicitly recognize, is that not only are there not enough jobs for the available manual labor market, there are not enough professional jobs available to make staying in school seem worthwhile. Jennifer Cole (2005) identifies similar dynamics in Tamatave, another coastal city in Madagascar. She observes that young men occupy the social status of "youth" longer than they had in the past because of the lack of available work that would enable them to occupy an adult status as provider. When finding paying work is not available as a symbolic and practical gateway into adulthood, the cultural period of youth, or emerging adulthood (Arnett 2006), lengthens, and for some, Cole argues, may never end. Many *koroko* idealize the life of a *jaoambilo*, a young man who lives off the earnings of a woman—often gained from prostitution or a longer term relationship with a foreign or wealthy man. The cultivated look of a *koroko* is of one who is stylishly dressed yet is well-to-do enough that he does not need to work. Despite this intentional devaluing of work, most *koroko* do, in fact, work—often in the informal market. Many are khat sellers.

One of Mbima's interviews with a group of six *koroko* illustrates this complex relationship between *koroko* and work: Mbima asked if life is difficult in Diego Suarez. This respondent, who works seasonally at the port and does odd jobs the rest of the year, replied in *koroko* slang:

> *diffcile ? ia faut qué môn* quoi ! *trav nada/ pésdés vrac–ny* tout ça là quoi ! *maro tsisy travy/ or qué ladéguizment bligé diffcile/ rabary café koroko déviendre mi–trav* la nuit *an* ! faire l'opération quoi *misy vendage khât/ sanamany dokr misy jaombl misy ka espécialité-nany tcholeur seulement/ ia/ à la fnac// to /faut que an/ faut que: trouvage* barbeaux *pose look at I am the girl comme ça que coûte que coûte* !

Difficult? Yes. You need money. There is no work. There are many unemployed people. That's what it is. Many young people are without work, even though you need money to buy clothes. It is difficult. That means that *koroko* must work the night! They must do operations (of stealing). There are those who sell khat. Some work at the port as dock workers. Some live off the earnings of women (*jaoambilo*). There are still others whose specialty is stealing at the outdoor market. Because it is necessary to find attractive clothing, whatever it costs. (Mbima 2006:618)

Khat is associated with male youth and unproductive inactivity in other global contexts as well. In Ethiopia, for example, Mains (2010) found that, when asking about unemployment in Jimma, Ethiopia, many people volunteered comments about how all youth are interested in is chewing khat and not working. Others argued that people chewed khat because they have few hopes for employment. Whatever their opinion, the relationship between unemployment and khat is close in people's minds. From the perspective of the youth, their experience of khat is similar to that which I found in Madagascar: It allows them temporarily to dream and make plans for the future in the context of chronic unemployment—for many, despite their formal education.

As for its association with fashionable youth culture, khat chewing in Madagascar appears to have much the same role as it does in other places, especially in the Horn of Africa. In southwestern Ethiopia, khat is associated with being *arrif* or *arada*, which could be translated as "cool" in the local youth slang

(Mains 2010:53). In Kenya, khat has also become *poa*, the Kiswahili word for "cool" (Carrier 2005a). As in Madagascar, a cheek full of khat has become cool in the same way hip hop, reggae, and brand-name clothing have become cool. They also speak a similar slang as *koroko*, called *sheng*. *Sheng*, spoken particularly by the young, is linguistically playful, mixing English words with Kiswahili grammatical structure, for example.

These youth slangs each have a well-developed vocabulary for khat. In Madagascar, words in *koroko* often change, and few have a stable meaning. In his brief visit to Diego Suarez, where he studied youth practices comparatively with Kenya, Carrier noted that some youth referred to khat and its effects as *yazzina*. *Boulitska*, from the French *boule*, referred to the wad of khat stored in the cheek. In his own study, Mbima (2006:265) found that *socobis* was a common term for a full cheek of khat. This is a humorous reference to sweet crackers made by the Socobis company that children often eat, stuffing their face and appearing with full cheeks. Khat itself is often referred to as *bontaka*, and to have a cheek full of khat is referred to as *mibontaka*. While in Madagascar there seems to be some bravado in the size of the wad stored in the cheek, in Kenya these tend to be discreet. Another difference with chewing in Kenya is the timeframe for chewing. People in Diego Suarez, if they had the funds to afford it, often spent afternoons chewing. By early evening, however, people tend to spit it out and eat a full meal. This contrasts with Kenyan youth culture, where people often chew through the night.

Khat is consumed differently in Kenya, Ethiopia, and Madagascar, but there is much about the consumption that is the same. Outside the traditional zones of consumption in Kenya and Ethiopia, khat is commonly chewed by youth, especially males, with little formal work. Within new contexts of consumption in Ethiopia, Kenya, and Madagascar, the khat trade is supported by the working poor and disdained by middle and upper classes.

Other Chewers in Madagascar

Counter-culture youth are not the only ones to chew khat in Madagascar. Until the early 1990s, consumption was mainly by the Yemeni-identifying community (known locally and self-identified as *arabou*) who chew khat regularly—even daily. They often chew it more frequently during Ramadan to stay awake later at night. These tend to be business people, many of whom are either well off or at least have a regular source of income. Within the *arabou* community, many are regular clients of major suppliers. One grower from Amber Mountain delivers khat directly to the homes of many of these regular clients, who pay by the month. They distinguish themselves from the *barbo* by their manner of chewing:

They chew indoors instead of on the street, and after they spit out the leaves at the end of the chew, *arabou* drink water, hot tea, or milk. The *barbo*, on the other hand, often drink alcohol to *mamono ny dosy*, or kill the effect.

Many *arabou* spoke with disdain about those who drink alcohol with khat. Most of the *arabou* are practicing Muslims and respect prohibitions against alcoholic drink. They also believe that drinking alcohol increases chances of getting sick and in engaging in anti-social behaviors. When people of Yemeni descent were asked why they chewed khat, they often said merely that it is the custom of *arabou*. Others mentioned the welcome feeling of alertness it provided and some mentioned the enjoyment of chewing it together with friends. Gradually, more and more non-*arabou* began chewing it. Many concur that taxi drivers were among the first non-*arabou* to chew khat in order to keep themselves awake while they worked at night.

Many people, both *arabou*-identifying and other Malagasy, chew khat while working. Many formal-sector laborers began chewing it on their job sites, even though it has now been banned in most. A high-level administrator at the port authority commented on why khat was banned from the workplace. He cited three main reasons. First, he said, many of the jobs require making parts that require measurements to exact industry standards. When chewing khat, workers do not concentrate as well and make errors more often. Second, it is hard to get people to start working when they chew khat, which means that it takes longer to get jobs done. Finally, workers tend to spend too much money on khat, not leaving enough for their families. The administrator also added that it is not good manners to chew khat in formal situations. When asked if there are any positive sides to khat, he said that once people get working, they work hard at manual labor tasks. "They work like cattle!" he exclaimed. Yet for him, the downside prevails: They are not as agile and their reflexes not as accurate. It is worth noting that this man is from the north and chewed khat himself for over twenty-five years. He does not uniformly condemn khat, as do many who are not from the region and have no experience with it.

Taxi drivers, security guards, and the self-employed chew it to stay awake and alert. They find it an effective tool to enhance stamina and concentration. Mains (2010) also found that in urban southwestern Ethiopia, in addition to unemployed youth, self-employed people, often in the informal sector, chew khat to enhance work and even to find creative solutions to specific work challenges.

Additionally, many Malagasy business professionals and laborers chew khat on their day off. Mostly men, they get together with friends and spend the afternoon chewing khat and often playing cards or watching television together. Sometimes married couples chew khat together on weekends. As Mbima (2006) noted, while there is much criticism of the *koroko* within the Malagasy community, there is also tolerance and even participation in its subcultural forms. He noticed that parents and grandparents may simultaneously chide their children for using *koroko* slang yet still adopt some of its vocabulary in their own speech. Similarly, concern about the behavior of youth does not prevent laborers and professionals from chewing for recreation.

Sometimes work and recreation are combined, especially in the entertainment industry, where the line between labor and leisure is blurry. Female sex workers who chew are part of a public youth culture analogous to the male *koroko* groups. They do not form a linguistically marked self-identified group, as do the *koroko* men, but the research of Betina Torbjornsen has revealed that they do share a common identity as sex workers (*makorely*) and have tight networks of friendships that are characterized by a high degree of mutual aid, exchanging money for food, rent, utilities, childcare, and clothing and shoes. The intensity of these friendships waxes and wanes. Relationships strengthen through positive shared experiences, but become strained by gossip or failure to reciprocate appropriately. Emotional highs of finding lucrative and satisfying relationships can quickly become contrasted with the lows of financial hardship, emotional depression, physical difficulties (e.g., abortions and fear of pregnancy), and alcohol abuse.

For these women, khat is an integral part of both community life and coping with the demands of having to stay up all night for several nights in a row, often dancing much of the evening. While they go to hotels and bars with their clients, they generally chew khat in their home or neighborhood, with their friends and fellow sex workers. Chewing khat is a characteristically local, or Malagasy, experience, and tends to be kept in the private spheres of these women's lives rather than the public sphere of the bars where they seek clients and conform to more Western forms of entertainment and inebriation, such as drinking alcohol. Even though the express purpose of the khat-chewing sessions may be to stay awake enough to work, the spirit of those sessions is often lively and sociable. Not all sex workers chew khat, however, and some only chew when they feel particularly tired. Others chew it several times per week or only when they want to relax with friends. Chewing khat is generally associated with men and masculinity. Women chew, and not just sex workers, but they are the marked category—the one about whom even khat sympathizers often worry.

In addition to urban-based khat consumption, many khat farmers in the rural areas chew it daily, often unceremoniously as they work in their fields. It is common to find men of all ages chewing khat in the afternoons, either by themselves or in small groups, after finishing the morning's labor. Many who chew claim that it makes them work harder. Not all chew, however, and some disdain the practice, saying that it makes farmers lazy—especially those who have become too accustomed to the easy money from khat. Many of those who do not chew have chosen not to grow khat and focus instead on other crops: vegetables, fruit, or rice, for example. When discussing this, they state that they value food production rather than nonfood crops. They also fear that the high earnings from khat are not sustainable and note that with the increased supply of khat, the possibility for high earnings has gone down.

Khat as Identity Marker

Khat serves as an identity marker on several different levels—for masculinity, youth, and as a Malagasy person of northern coastal descent. Khat is also strongly associated with a particular kind of masculinity—one associated with hip youth culture. Mbima's descriptions of the *koroko*, for whom khat chewing and selling is an important symbol of belonging, do not address gender directly, but they imply a masculine subject, when, for example, Mbima provides a general description of *koroko* as seeking a woman to support them. Transcripts of conversations he recorded suggest gender ideologies in which women are often sexualized. The most confident of the *koroko* see themselves as attractive to women because of their identity as *koroko*. Ironically, however, in keeping with their idealization of *jaombilo*, they are proud to not conform to dominant expectations that men buy things for women and give them money (see Chapter 5). This ideal *koroko* relationship breaks the pattern of "material reciprocity that structures intimate social relations" through which affect and exchange become mutually constitutive, as identified by Cole (2009). Reciprocity where the man gives money and gifts and the woman gives sexual access and domestic care has been a norm in rural as well as urban areas throughout much of the coastal region of Madagascar. Cole (2005:902) describes the *jaoambilo* as paradoxically embodying both a new kind of hypermasculinity—one associated with good looks and sexual attractiveness—and a certain emasculation associated with not being able to find work. She writes: "The jaombilo also seems to embody a kind of transgressive pleasure obtained from consuming without actually working, or at least . . . not working in the normative sense of the term" (p. 902).

Although the term "*jaoambilo*" traditionally has somewhat negative connotations, the *koroko*, and presumably some of the young men in Cole's study, proudly seek this status. One young man stated:

lemofale ity partie à lezabarile ima lexitale ity déjà défalquée par les koroko mércains drecs maman ! oy/ oy laona toute la cité ! pio ! lamnute seulment déjà payé par madamage l'hôtel l'argent de poche/ gum déjà dantsinment drecs barabony merci pour zawadi ledimale lelilahale an !

The woman, she goes to the market by taxi, and she is immediately deviated from her path by some *koroko*. That impresses the whole city! The good woman quickly pays for your hotel room. [She gives you] pocket money and chewing gum. And then you have sex with her! Thanks for the present, for the good legitimate meal, no! (Mbima 2006:510)

Living off a woman's earnings with little to no obligation to reciprocate is seen as the ideological ideal for a *koroko*, even though many men continue to contribute to the livelihoods of their female sexual partners from their earnings in the informal sector. Nevertheless, this ideology is undermining for women whose livelihood depends on contributions from the men they are involved with—and who may be the father of their children.

Despite the valuing of women earning money, many still see khat selling as the domain of men. This partly because of the association of khat with masculinity and sexuality, and partly due to the fact that khat brings in considerably more profit than nearly any other item sold in the market. In a group conversation, several men said that young women have no right to be selling khat. They should be in the market selling vegetables and other foodstuffs, they said:

A: même *ces gronz sur plat kakamitaly* maintenant *mi- tirav/ a::* vendage *khât io !*

Even (adolescent) girls with small breasts are out selling khat these days.

B: *ça/ ça/ cé pas l' métier dé kakamitaly pinoakables là la place-ndrô/ ça* là-bas/ à *la fnac/ vendage girda zabar/ tômtômate/ brbrède/* comme ça . . .

That is not a job for sexually active young women. Their place, it's over there in the market, selling tomatoes, greens, things like that. (Mbima 2006:585)

As an identity marker, khat most saliently marks a particular form of masculinity—one that often sexualizes women and casts them as an economic other. Economically, woman are often viewed as a potential source of money or as competition in selling a particularly lucrative and masculine substance—khat.

In addition to its link with gender identification, it can be argued that one reason why khat has taken root in Diego and why it is spreading in the coastal regions of Madagascar is that it forges a sense of community. Khat consumption is rising within traditional regions of consumption and worldwide, and not everyone sees it as culturally and socially valuable. As will be explored in greater depth in Chapter 3, much that is published about khat portrays it as a social problem, especially in the popular press. Even within the regions where it is chewed, such as Somalia, Madagascar, Kenya, and Yemen, many see khat as a barrier to economic and social development. In some places, especially Somalia, khat's detractors see it as a source of social discord that should be culturally and politically discouraged. Despite this, there is a counter-narrative that highlights khat's positive social and cultural role (Beckerleg 2006). Such a narrative is promulgated by consumers, producers, and traders, and by some outside researchers for whom khat consumption is seen as playing a positive role in terms of strengthening identity and forging social links.

People experience the psychotropic effects of the stimulant in social contexts, and in so doing they form and reinforce particular ways of seeing their place in the world. In a global landscape characterized by the weakening of traditional local identities and increasing poverty in marginal areas, new identities often emerge (Comaroff and Comaroff 1993), and khat is the pivot around one such identity in northern Madagascar. Mbima (2006) notes, for example, that the *koroko* groups have become a melting pot for individuals of different ethnic as well as socioeconomic backgrounds, with ethnicity and socioeconomic status having become a less relevant social marker than the *koroko* group itself. Mains (2010) and Ahmed (2010) make a similar argument for khat in northern Ethiopia, arguing that as the use of khat has spread after World War II, it is chewed by Christians and Muslims alike, especially in urban contexts—often in jointly attended khat sessions. Ahmed writes that "the khat ritual plays a integrative and cohesive social role in a country of ethnic, linguistic, and religious diversity" (2010:24). Mains explains it as an urban and generational phenomenon, writing that "young men in Jimma often claimed that their shared khat consumption was evidence that ethnic and religious divisions are not important for their generation" (2010:350). Gebissa (2010d) also observes that khat chewing in the traditional region of Hararge unites people of diverse ethnic groups and even integrates immigrants to the region.

Mbima states that *koroko* youth identity replaces outmoded forms of identity that are not flexible enough to navigate contemporary demands and transformations (Mbima 2011). *Koroko* identity is at once local—rooted in local neighborhoods—and global, as it sets its sights on other nations. Mbima explains how *koroko* discourse diminishes Africa, refers to France (the former colonial power) as disappointing (indexed in part by the fact that few *koroko* have the ability to speak standard French), and instead turns to the United States as an idle dream. He presents an emblematic *koroko* expression: "*Koroko gasy, barbo parle francais mais man merican*" (I am Malagasy, I speak French [slang], but I live like an American). Living like an American is marked symbolically through taste in music—especially rap and hip hop artists and clothing styles—modeled on that of hip hop artists and focusing on brand names, proudly displayed, such as Nike, Ray Ban, and Ralph Lauren—and an ideological appreciation of money and wealth, which they associate with the United States. One youth proclaimed: "*Fèmgé ne parle pas barbeau mi-raisonne dolls seulement man/*" (The FMG [Malagasy currency] is worth nothing. We only deal in dollars, man). This global identity, Mbima (2011) argues, exists amid poverty that these youth have little hope of escaping. Nevertheless, this pluralist form of identity and communication provides them with a way of appropriating the diverse influences that affect their lives and creating a new, local form of linguistic and cultural capital that they themselves master.

In all its contexts of chewing—on the job or with associates, and at any age—khat provides a common and enjoyable point of reference for people of diverse backgrounds in a politically and economically uncertain context. In this way, khat is a cosmopolitan substance in both the diverse rural and urban areas, where no ethnic group makes up a majority of the population.

On a national scale, khat symbolizes difference from the high plateau, where the capital city, Antananarivo, is located, and which is home to the wealthiest, most highly educated, and most powerful ethnic groups. Highlighting difference in this way builds on centuries' old animosities between the coastal populations and central highlands, when the Merina imperialist state often successfully sought to extend its boundaries to the edges of the island, much to the chagrin of local polities who desired to remain autonomous (Kottak 1980). The local Antankarana polity, whose members opposed Merina expansion throughout the nineteenth century, is one such group (Gezon 2006; Lambek and Walsh 1997; Walsh 2001).

This divide between the coasts and the high plateau extended into the colonial era, when the British and later the French favored the people in the high plateau by providing them with more access to education and professional opportunities. The stratification between these regions has resulted in an ongoing tension that occasionally makes a blatant appearance in the midst of national politics (Vérin 1990). The difference in status is also seen on a daily basis in that most Malagasy professionals on the coasts today remain of high plateau ancestry. While certain traits have long symbolically marked those of the high plateau as different, such as phenotype and dialect, khat chewing as a marker of coastal identity has emerged in approximately the last twenty years and is becoming more deeply entrenched as increasing numbers of coastal people chew it or associate it as a particularly northern coastal custom. The difference became more deeply engrained, for example, when people remember that the former president, Marc Ravalomanana (2002–2009)[2], of high-plateau ancestry, publically denounced khat as a detriment to the nation's development and entreated people to stop growing and chewing it. The symbolic strength of khat is rooted in the fact that it has become the backbone of the northern economy. The president's denouncement is, therefore, not only an affront to khat as an isolated cultural practice, but to what has become a total way of life and survival to many.

Global issues beyond the border of this island nation provide a framework for analyzing the symbolic role of khat. As president, Ravalomanana was strongly aligned with the West and to the United States in particular. Khat, on the other hand, represents, or at least suggests, an affinity with the broader world of the Horn of Africa and the Arabian Peninsula. While the common people do not express affinity for radical politics of any kind and are clearly not anti-Western in their attitudes, many are at least vaguely aware that outsiders associate khat with radical anti-Western political and economic activity in Somalia and Yemen. The alignment away from the high plateau may have its roots in history, but it remains fueled by contemporary issues even beyond the borders of the island nation.

Wherever khat is chewed, scholars have noted that it has served as an identity marker. In Kenya, for example, Carrier argues that khat has become central to a youth ethos and helps "forge an identity as young, modern and Meru" (2005b:210). In southwestern Ethiopia, "khat consumption connotes a certain amount of youthful rebellion" (Mains 2010:53). Among diaspora communities originating from East Africa, khat consumption is also seen as a practice that maintains cultural identity and social solidarity. Stevenson et al. (1996) report that in Australia, khat consumption "is proving to be important as an identity marker. Through their use of *khat* East Africans are able to assert their desire to preserve distinct identities within a culturally diverse community" (1996:80). Carrier (Carrier and Gezon 2009) reports that the sights, sounds, and smells of a chewing session in the United Kingdom is not much different from one in Mogadishu, save for the climate and temperature. Fellow partakers often watch Somali videos and listen to Somali music.

Several authors have noted that khat has been an important source of national identity in Yemen. Varisco (2004) writes that a strong national identity emerged in north Yemen after a revolution in 1962 and then with the unification of the north with the south in 1990. This corresponded with both a dramatic increase in the production of khat in Yemen. The reason, he states, is that khat is a social practice and a marker of identity. This interpretation is similar to Mbima's arguments for khat's role in Madagascar: the formation of newly relevant categories of identity and social networks. Varisco argues that khat rose in prominence as a marker of cultural identity "in a climate where Yemen was continually being disparaged by Westerners and fellow Arabs alike" (2004:111). In addition to reaffirming self-worth amid stereotypes of being poor and backward, khat chewing facilitated the establishments of social networks that could be mobilized in local development. Wedeen (2008) also points to khat chews as a central aspect of informal—and sometimes even formal—Yemeni political practice, as people spend much time commenting on, deliberating, and debating current events while they chew. Sometimes policy decisions even get made when high level officials are chewing together, which they often do. The openness of chews creates "minipublics," where ordinary people and politicians participate together in discussion. In many contexts where it is chewed, khat is an important part of contemporary identity expression that is both locally and globally relevant.

Khat and Health

This chapter has placed khat within its social and cultural contexts of consumption. The material provides a way of evaluating one aspect of khat's indirect effects as a drug, namely, its social and cultural effects, considering the quality of interpersonal relationships and labor productivity. In terms of interpersonal connections, khat has both negative and positive aspects. As a form of cultural identity, khat chewing has become critically important in establishing alternative forms of collective imagination, forming one axis of a cultural connection that unites people in new, entirely contemporary ways, replacing or supplementing identity by ethnicity or neighborhood. Khat, then, plays an important part in a modern local adaptation to changing circumstances. Not only does it unite people, it gives them a way of thinking about themselves in relation to the world: in relation to France, their former colonizer, to the United States, recognized as a world economic power, to Yemen as a location for drug-induced pleasure, to Africa as regressive (Mbima 2006).

Khat is primarily a masculine form of identification. While establishing positive connections with other young men in the community, khat may become a source of concern to those with whom khat chewers share a household or to their primary sexual partners. With the money spent on the khat-chewing experience, the time spent exclusively with friends, and the tendency to want heightened sexual activity—and not always with one who is socially recognized as the primary partner (a girlfriend or wife)—khat must be acknowledged as being associated with some interpersonal tensions. Many local people recognize it as often being the cause of detrimental spending and anti-social behavior. Mbima (personal communication) identified it as a problem when men and their friends spend hours chewing in darkened living rooms because the children and other household members may not feel welcome in their own homes. This possibility of alienation in the home must be taken seriously, especially given the recent phenomenon of children joining violent gangs in Diego Suarez. They call themselves *foroche*, derived from the French *force* or *féroce* (ferocious), and congregate in abandoned buildings. They are armed and have a reputation for attacking people in the streets. Even a *koroko* leader with whom I spoke told of avoiding certain parts of town at night because of this phenomenon. Men are not the only ones who chew, however. Many women also chew khat, and others actively approve of their partners chewing it. Middle-aged professionals and laborers chew as do underemployed youth, so a monolithic judgment of khat's social effects must be avoided.

In terms of labor, several factors must be considered. First, as a stimulant, khat actually helps many people get through tasks that are tedious or repetitive and require alertness. Second, the cultural context of chewing recreationally in groups encourages both an attitude of leisure and requires taking time in the middle of the traditional work day.

On the one hand, few formal-sector jobs are available to Malagasy. This point must be emphasized: Madagascar is one of the world's poorest countries. According to the CIA World Factbook (www.cia.gov [accessed June 6, 2011]), its GDP per person was about $900 per year in 2010, which put it 218th out of 228 recognized countries in the world—nearly at the bottom. To put this into perspective, it contrasts with the United States, where the GDP per person was $47,200 in 2010 and ranked 11th in the world. With poor infrastructure and little access to the financial or social capital necessary to develop profitable business ventures, people throughout Madagascar, and in the north in particular in this case, lack the ability to participate as full members in the global capitalist economy. The informal khat economy has permitted these people, on the margins of the global economy, to survive in conditions where they have little chance for upward mobility—or even basic survival. Khat has provided a local adaptation to challenges associated with entrenched poverty. Many do work in informal jobs that do not require traditional hours.

On the other hand, chewing khat may for some—especially the *koroko* youth—go hand in hand with an attitude that devalues traditional puritan attitudes toward accumulation through hard work. Whether that is the fault of khat is up for debate, but it would be hard to argue that khat holds sole or even primary responsibility for that attitude. Pharmacologically, khat is a stimulant, and a comparative look at stimulants (such as Adderall, tobacco, coffee, amphetamines [Weil and Rosen 2004]) reveals that they do not uniformly or predictably lead to lethargy and an unwillingness to work.

Some of the cultural contexts in which khat is chewed may encourage extended leisure time, and many recognize a "period of dreamy introspection" (Klein 2008:178) as following the high-energy rush produced by the stimulant. This culturally recognized period of lethargy exists for Somali diaspora communities in the United Kingdom, where chewers spend time in khat cafés called *mafrishes* (Klein 2008:179), in Yemeni-chewing contexts, and in Madagascar. It is worth noting that one facet of this attitude, particularly among new chewers who are urban, underemployed youth, may align with Baer et al.'s recognition that people often use drugs as a form of "self-medication for the psychosocial injuries of oppression" (Baer et al. 1997:158). Singer, who wrote the above with Baer, embellishes these ideas in his book *Drugging the Poor* (2008a), where he asserts that drug use "has functioned to pacify the poor and working classes (never completely, but often sufficiently) by diverting energies from collective action to individual palliative consumption and self-medication with solace drugs" (p. 231). This may also apply to the many young farmers and rural day laborers who chew in the khat-growing areas and who spend the majority of afternoons chewing khat with friends or alone by the roadside (see Figure 2.2).

A disdain for neoliberal global capitalism may be liberating on one level, but it also results in the perpetuation of unequal and unjust economic, political, and social relations. Khat chewing may, in Singer's words, perpetuate global inequality by "minimizing restlessness and rebellious resentment arising from the

Figure 2.2   Many people chew khat by themselves

experience of exploitation and relative deprivation" (2008a:230). In other words, a drug-induced deadening to an interest in work according to the standards of the global capitalist economy may be convenient for those who have little hope of success in that realm, and for those from above who desire a pacified population.

Mains (2010) points to the double-edged predicament of Ethiopian youth. He writes that: "In a social context of extremely limited economic opportunity, chewing khat provides a means of mediating the gap between one's desires and reality. . . . At the same time, the particular practices associated with khat use among the unemployed contribute to the reproduction of their joblessness" (p. 30). The value of a newly constituted identity, however, cannot be ignored. New urban identities, with khat as the symbolic center, defy traditional ethnic and religious divisions. Being innovative and locally embedded identities, they defy predictions of global homogeneity and prepare a new generation of urban youth for adaptation to changing economic and political contexts, where ideal-ized methods of getting ahead through formal education and other forms of participation in the global capitalist economy hold little promise.

In terms of the impact of khat expenses on household budgets, there is a com-mon perception that people easily and often spend so much money on khat that they do not have enough left for buying food. Although this certainly occurs, interviews with people (147 structured interviews in 2007, thirty in 2010, and many informal conversations over the past decade) suggest that most people monitor their expenditures on khat, purchasing it when either they have money or in the rainy season when the price is low. Many people speak of moving between periods of heavy to lighter use of khat for financial reasons. As with all dependence-producing substances, there is a continuum from highly dependent individuals, correlating with a likelihood of diverting basic needs expenses to the purchase of the substance, to consumers who are not dependent, correlating with the ability to evaluate critically how much they spend.

It would be misguided to blame khat for northern Madagascar's poverty, street violence, or interpersonal tensions. Khat may, however, point to and be symptomatic of larger social tensions, such as poverty and interpersonal discord. Eliminating khat would not erase global inequalities or interpersonal stress, however. The strong social networks and affective ties that it facilitates, along with the income that it provides for so many in this region, may, in fact, permit new and productive forms of adaptation to marginal economic and political conditions. This does not mean that the negative correlates of khat chewing—unemployment, feelings of economic hopelessness, gender and family-related tension—can be ignored or that they should remain unaddressed. Indeed, in addition to work being done to expand income opportunities, community mental health services, such as those being developed in places like Haiti

(BasicNeeds 2008; Diaz-Laplante and Schneider 2011) may provide strategies for people dealing with the stresses of poverty and deprivation.

In sum, on a global scale, khat chewing is an old tradition that plays different roles in different situations, but through time and across locations, it has marked an ethnic or cultural identity—from its roots among Yemeni elite, to new urban chewers in Africa, to increasingly globalized diaspora and youth cultures. Its contemporary contested status in areas of recent introduction and adoption by youth reflects the different interests of socioeconomic classes. Yet khat, like other drugs, plays a complex role in the political economy of Madagascar as we shall see in the following two chapters, which examine on-the-ground production and distribution practices.

Notes

1. Much of the cross-cultural content of this chapter is adapted from Carrier and Gezon (2009).
2. There was a coup d'état in March 2009, and the United States, as well as many other governments and agencies (such as the UN and the OAU) have criticized this move, eliminating all but the most critical humanitarian funding to Madagascar. The alignment of the government of Madagascar is less clearly Western now.

3

LEAF OF PARADISE OR SCOURGE?: DRUG EFFECTS AND HEALTH

As a drug, khat has direct effects on the physical and mental health of those who consume it. This chapter analyzes medical evidence of drug effects, as well as commonly held perceptions of its effects by local people (users and nonusers), considering contemporary ideas about khat in the context of the history of Western perceptions of it. A biocultural approach guides this analysis, recognizing that perceptions and actual effects are interlinked in a complex way. An important insight of the medical anthropology of psychotropic substances is that any evaluation of psychotropic substance effects must be culturally and historically situated. Because of the wide variety of possible effects, the label "drug" must be used cautiously, since it is a particularly emotionally charged term that suggests a priori that a given substance is harmful and its use should be controlled or prohibited. Academic studies of the effects of khat's active chemical properties serve as an important component in this investigation of khat's multifaceted effects on health. To this effect, this chapter reviews medical literature, exploring khat's immediate and long-term effects on mental and physical health. Additionally, cross-cultural ethnographic accounts and structured interviews report users' experiences, providing a broader cultural framework for considering health effects.

In keeping with a critical medical anthropology approach, I argue here that the political and medical contexts of a substance's evaluation are inseparable. In other words, medical evaluations of a substance's effects always take place within a political environment. Not only do political considerations shape the design of the studies themselves—the ways that researchers ask questions and analyze data—but political considerations also affect how policy makers distill the medical literature in making pronouncements about a substance's level of danger or acceptability. To this end, the chapter continues this discussion of health effects with an analysis of khat's placement within the World Health Organization's (WHO) schedules of controlled substances. It then considers the implications of this official evaluation for legalization or prohibition of khat both within Madagascar and in other countries. It explores local, national, and global discourses on khat, evaluating the inextricable interweaving of social, cultural, political, and health concerns. Another component, then, in a study of any substance's health effects is a critical examination of the political contexts in which studies are conducted and interpreted and in which pronouncements about health are made.

Khat's Effects: Physical and Mental

Khat, scientifically known as Catha edulis Forsk, was first described by a Western scientist, Peter Forsskal, in the mid-1700s. More complete botanical and chemical descriptions appeared in the second half of the twentieth century (Kalix 1992; United Nations 1971, 1975). Khat leaves get their potency from two alkaloids (cathinone and cathine) and tannins, with cathinone being the main psychoactive agent. Cathinone is unstable and breaks down into cathine after about forty-eight hours. Cathinone is a stimulant and is chemically and behaviorally related to an amphetamine (Al-Hebshi and Skaug 2005; Halbach 1972; Odenwald 2007). Kalix (1992) identified it as a "natural amphetamine," in contrast with amphetamines, which are synthetically produced for commercial purposes. In contrast with cathinone, cathine is derived from a different genus (Ephedra) and has been identified as being at most half as potent (Odenwald 2007). Scientific tests reveal clearly that cathine has a significantly milder amphetamine effect, is as much as eight times less potent than cathinone but has similar amphetamine effects (Nencini and Ahmed 1989).

Cathinone, like amphetamines, affects the central nervous system by releasing chemicals that transmit messages including arousal, positive reinforcement, and fight-or-flight responses to stress. Most importantly, it stimulates the release of dopamine in the brain and produces feelings of euphoria, often followed by a let-down in mood. Khat's maximum effect is reached about two–two-and-a-half hours after it is consumed (Cox and Rampes 2003; Odenwald 2007). It often produces feelings of optimism, general well-being, talkativeness, a reported increase in concentration, an increased ability to put thoughts together creatively, and heightened spiritual awareness. When the stimulant high wears off (as much as four hours into a khat-chewing session), the mood turns more introspective, quiet, and even depressed, nervous, tense, and lethargic. The following day, feelings of drowsiness and malaise are common (Nencini and Ahmed 1989). Because of this, some have described khat as producing emotional instability (Cox and Rampes 2003) in many users.

Physical Effects

Any evaluation of recreational drugs and the dangers thereof must take several factors into consideration. While there are many cross-cultural similarities in khat's effects that can be predicted by pharmacological studies, it is important to remember that the cultural context of use affects both perceptions of experiences and physical and psychological outcomes. One consideration is the route of administration (how it is consumed and the potency associated with it). Khat is generally chewed, with a plug of chewed leaves stored in the cheeks. The masticated leaves are generally spit out, but in some cases they are swallowed. In Madagascar, they are always spit out. The context comprises several other factors, including the novelty of the setting and experience, individual expectations of the experience, norms of consumption practices, the consumption of other accompanying substances, and potency of the substances.

State of mind, related for example to stress level and the novelty of the setting of consumption, also influences the physical effect of the substance. To illustrate this poignantly, a study of heroin users revealed that overdoses are more likely when a person takes the drug in an unfamiliar setting. In other words, given the same quantity of the substance, a person would be more likely to die of an overdose in an unfamiliar setting. This occurs because stress levels, triggering the release of chemicals in the brain to compensate, increase in unfamiliar settings.

Expectations also affect experience. The placebo effect, the likelihood that a pharmaceutical compound or treatment will be effective because people believe it will be, illustrates this. In deconstructing the placebo effect, Moerman and Jonas (2002) point out not only the role of inert pharmacological properties, but also the active role of meaning in the healing process. To understand the placebo effect is to accept that placebos actually do accomplish something, just not pharmacologically. They write: "To say that a treatment such as acupuncture 'isn't better than a placebo' does not mean that it does nothing" (Moerman and Jonas 2002:273). Similarly, Miller and Kaptchuk write that "the placebo intervention as a whole logically cannot be inert or inactive when it produces a real placebo effect" (2008:223). The key to its effectiveness is in systems of meaning, which

Moerman and Jonas (2002) name the "meaning response," and the social contexts of healing rituals (Miller and Kaptchuk 2008). Moerman and Jonas define the meaning response as "the physiologic or psychological effects of meaning in the origins or treatment of illness" (2002:472). To apply this to the context of drugs, we could simply state it as "the physiologic or psychological effects of meaning" in the experience of psychoactive substances. This understanding suggests that culturally based expectations will strongly affect both the physical and emotional responses people have to khat and other recreational drugs. It opens the possibility that negative physical and psychological symptoms may be more likely for some populations than others.

Norms of khat consumption behavior shape the substance's effects. Route of administration—chewed, consumed as a tea, or smoked—affects overall dosage and the rapidity with which it enters the bloodstream. Overall quantity and pacing of consumption are other important considerations. Odenwald (2007) points out that habits of khat chewing have changed in that there has been, across global contexts of chewing, an increase in the number of chewers—with more women and young people chewing, an increase in the quantity chewed, a khat-chewing session that lasts longer, and khat chewing at nontraditional times (such as earlier in the morning in some places). For example, one study revealed that over three-quarters of Somali immigrants in London, both men and women, chewed khat—on an average of three days per week, and 20% had only started chewing since they arrived in London. Many immigrants subjectively felt that chewing had increased since coming to London and attributed it to a desire to maintain cultural identity and to unemployment, which resulted in more time available for chewing (Griffiths 1998, cited in Cox and Rampes 2003:457).

The extent to which khat chewing is associated with other substances and behaviors—such as nutritious food on the healthy side, or alcohol and sleep deprivation on the negative side—also affects health. Caffeinated substances such as tea, coffee, cola beverages, or kola nuts may enhance khat's effects (Cox and Rampes 2003). It is commonly found that the spread of substance use to new groups without traditional cultural mechanisms to regulate its consumption can lead to increased cases of negative effects, often referred to as abuse (Coomber and South 2004b:13–26). It is possible that the most negative symptoms of khat chewing are associated more strongly with these new populations of consumers, but few medical studies have addressed this by incorporating questions of cultural and social context into pharmacological studies.

Plant potency is another factor affecting varied experiences related to khat chewing. The chemical agents present in any given khat leaf vary according to the physical environment of cultivation, the age of the plant, and the amount of time since harvest (Nencini and Ahmed 1989). The highest concentration of cathinone is in the young shoots; the bark and roots have none. Dried plants only have trace elements of cathinone. Even in markets where there are only fresh leaves for sale, plants vary in their cathinone content. One study found that the concentration of cathinone (as opposed to the much less potent cathine) varied by more than three times in leaves from different plants (reviewed in Nencini and Ahmed 1989).

Several reviews summarize what is known about the physical effects of cathinone (Al-Hebshi and Skaug 2005; Al-Motarreb et al. 2010; Cox and Rampes 2003; Halbach 1972; Kalix and Braenden 1985; Nencini and Ahmed 1989; Odenwald 2007). Khat users experience heightened heart rate, blood pressure, respiratory rate, and temperature (Al-Motarreb et al. 2010; Gebissa 2010d:64). Odenwald (2007) summarizes that several physical consequences seem to be confirmed, including heart disease, gastrointestinal problems, oral cancers, and reproductive issues (especially spermatorrhoea, or an involuntary ejaculation of semen). Al-Hebshi and Skaug's review (2005:303) notes the presence of constipation, anorexia, respiratory problems—especially bronchitis, low birth weight in infants with khat-chewing mothers, and urinary problems in women. They observe that the gastrointestinal problems seem to be due to tannins and not cathinone. Heart disease was found, but it seems to be confounded by smoking. Despite the reproductive issues associated with khat, Yemen's fertility and population growth rates remain strong. The most frequently mentioned side effects are insomnia. Recent research suggests a link with cardiac problems, especially when heavy and chronic consumption is combined with other cardiovascular risk factors (Graziani et al. 2008:772–773). Khat is also commonly linked to sexuality, being described both as an aphrodisiac and as inducing male impotence (Carrier 2007:209–210).

There is also some evidence of positive effects of khat, including "antimicrobial properties against some bacterial species" (Al-Hebshi and Skaug 2005:304) and cancer-fighting agents. Traditionally, khat has been used in Ethiopia and other places as a medicinal plant. Varisco (2004:105) notes that khat was used traditionally, since at least the 1700s in some cases, in treating nausea, indigestion, and epilepsy as well as in low doses to mitigate depression and anxiety. A report from the 1700s says that it helps digestion. In Harar, Ethiopia, over 500 medical uses have been found, including the treatment of depression (Anderson et al. 2007:182).

One of the most thorough and sound medical studies was performed by John Kennedy's research team, which conducted extensive surveys in Yemen on khat and health. After extensive research on the mental and physical effects of khat, Kennedy's team concluded that "even by the most conservative evaluation, the indictment of qat for the health problems of Yemen has been highly exaggerated.

... [T]he medical case against qat-use is much weaker than the literature would have us believe" (Kennedy et al. 1983:792–793). Several decades later, scholars (including Al-Hebshi and Skaug [2005] and Odenwald [2007]) still temper their analysis with a caution that there are few reliable tests, with many being based purely on clinical and anecdotal evidence. Al-Hebshi and Skaug (2005:303) note that many studies did not "cite controlled research to support their conclusions." Many did not control for preexisting conditions, the difference between heavy and moderate use, or the presence of pesticides—factors that may result in a false appearance of causality. In a recent study of a wide range of averse physical effects of khat, the authors conclude that "the evidence . . . is often based on limited numbers of case reports and only few controlled studies have been undertaken" (Al-Motarreb et al. 2010). The authors go on to identify the difficulty of isolating the effects of cathinone because of other properties such as tannins within the plant and pesticides that have been sprayed on. Despite these cautions, however, Kennedy et al. (1983) acknowledge that the risk to physical health should not be discounted, and Al-Motarreb et al. (2010) note that there are some clear trends of threat to several of the body's internal organs.

Dependence, Tolerance, Addiction

According to medical terminology popularized in part by WHO in the 1950s, khat is not physically addicting. In fact, few drugs are technically physically addicting according to their classification. Opiates and alcohol are considered physically addicting because of the way they operate on the body's chemistry and produce distinctive withdrawal symptoms of chills, fever, vomiting, etc. Under these criteria, even cocaine is not considered physically addictive, although it can be highly dependency-producing. This manner of placing cocaine and caffeine into the same category of psychologically, but not physically, addicting substances means that deciding how dangerous a drug is to individuals and society requires much analysis and social judgment.

Research suggests there is only a low level risk of dependency on khat (Graziani et al. 2008:771). In one study, central nervous system response was more pronounced in new users, suggesting that some tolerance develops among regular users. A confounding factor may be that people who had never chewed before were either already nervous or had not learned to moderate their dose (Kennedy et al. 1983; Nencini and Ahmed 1989:22). There is evidence of a mild withdrawal syndrome after heavy use, and consumers can feel a drowsy hangover effect the morning after a chewing session and sometimes experience bad dreams as the alkaloids leave their systems. Cox and Rampes (2003) report, based on clinical case studies, that depression is frequent following consumption and that it can, in rare cases, lead to self-harm.

Some researchers have determined that cathinone, if taken in concentrated doses, may be slightly more dependence producing than amphetamines because cathinone's action takes place more quickly, tolerance to its effects develops more quickly, and users experience fewer adverse effects (Odenwald 2007:10). Furthermore, when tested on primates, the animals voluntarily self-administered the drug continuously, making the drug's effects more similar to cocaine than to amphetamines, which have lower rates of continuous self-administration in a laboratory setting (Al-Hebshi and Skaug 2005:304; Nencini and Ahmed 1989:23). But keeping in mind the route of administration, cathinone intake by humans does not resemble that in the experimental contexts, because "the bulk volume of khat self-limits consumption" (Nencini and Ahmed 1989:23). Ingesting the cathinone by chewing khat leaves releases the active compound slowly, and it is far less likely to produce a strong dependence than amphetamines. Amphetamines (such as methamphetamine, speed, and benzadrine), which are produced in laboratories, on the other hand, are taken in concentrated doses and are associated with debilitating dependencies. Cathinone has had some limited success as a synthesized substance, used primarily in urban rave club scenes. While it may have enjoyed some short-term popularity, Anderson et al. (2007:186) report that it has not replaced existing rave drugs, because "the market is already saturated with well-established substances that have similar but far more powerful stimulating properties than khat and its principal alkaloids."

In Madagascar, heavy chewers claimed they missed khat and even craved it when they did not use it but did not experience physical withdrawal symptoms. One man, who used to chew it on weekends or on days off, said that the impulse to chew was strong enough that he found he had to come in to work on weekends to remove himself from a setting that would make him want to chew. Most, however, claim that they chew khat for pleasure and do not crave it when they do not have it. Weir (1985) notes that Yemenis stop using khat when they go overseas, for example, without any negative consequences beyond a mild craving. Weir makes an important point that the cultural context must be considered when evaluating whether people are addicted. People may experience withdrawal differently depending on the cultural discourse surrounding khat. But what appears to be addiction may be a highly compelling social ritual. In the Yemini context, Weir argues against popular analyses of Yemenis that claim that they spend time and money on khat because of their physical "addiction." For her, it is essential to assess the social and cultural impetus to chew. Indeed, the "qat party" is an important social institution for Yemenis, where friendships are strengthened, business contacts are forged, and political issues debated (Weir 1985; see also Kennedy 1987; Wedeen 2008). Given the foregoing, it is not surprising that so many people attend such parties, even those who are not actually enthusiastic about khat.

Psychological Effects

There is some discussion in the medical literature about khat's psychological effects and whether it produces negative effects. Most commonly reported is psychosis, which is characterized by a loss of connection with reality, hallucinations, and grandiose delusions and is evidenced by confused speech and agitated behavior. As with the physical effects, Odenwald (2007) cautions against assuming that association means causality. Complicating factors include preexisting conditions or stress related to other factors, such as poverty, unemployment, or immigrant status. Khat may, in fact, be a form of self-medication for anxiety and other traumas of life. Anderson et al. (2007:182) discuss a study of the mental health characteristics of khat users in one town in England that found that 25% suffered from significant emotional distress in their lives and that 72% had experienced some form of trauma. Mental health issues are common in refugee communities, and the Somali communities in the United Kingdom are no exception. Some of the troubles experienced are separation from family, unemployment, and experiences of violence. In other words, the correlation between khat and psychiatric disorders does not mean that khat is the cause—in fact, given the circumstances, it is likely the palliative.

Cox and Rampes (2003), writing for psychiatric practitioners, identify the main psychoses as short-lived bouts of "paranoid delusions, fear, a hostile perception of the environment, auditory hallucinations (frequently of a persecutory or threatening type), ideas of reference, thought alienation and a tendency to isolate themselves, or alternatively displaying aggressive behavior towards others" (p. 459). Symptoms of manic psychosis include "hyperactivity, shouting, pressure of speech, grandiose delusions with flight of ideas and tangential thought processes, and a labile mood varying from euphoria to anger" (p. 459). Psychotic symptoms tend be almost exclusively associated with heavy usage. Symptoms also stop automatically within days of ceasing khat consumption, without taking anti-psychotic drugs. Long-term health effects are not well known, and in their review, Cox and Rampes (2003) only cite alleged socioeconomic effects, such as "decreased productivity" and "family and marital problems"—factors that have been problematized by social scientists (e.g., Anderson et al. 2007; Beckerleg 2008; Gebissa 2004).

Beginning with Halbach (1972), scholars agree that incidences of khat-induced psychosis or other mental disorders are rare, that the studies that do exist have had considerable methodological problems, and that there is a lack of conclusive data. Underreporting is a problem in the case of clinically based studies, especially in countries where there are few psychiatric facilities and no tradition of Western psychiatry. Odenwald (2007) also notes that researchers rarely adequately isolate complicating factors. For example, they often do not take into account predisposition to psychosis or even distinguish the effects on heavy as opposed to more moderate users. He argues that "patterns of khat use, not khat chewing *per se* should be the focus of scientific studies. This implies that completely different research strategies should be used" (p. 17). This suggests that the cultural context, as well as the total individual, must become the object of study to truly understand khat's effects on mental health.

Assessing khat is difficult. It is complicated to isolate the pharmacological effects of the substance since the social and cultural settings of consumption, as well as individual histories of psychological response, strongly influence experiences (Cox and Rampes 2003; Odenwald 2007). It is additionally difficult because the use of psychotropic substances is highly emotionally charged. As Kalix stated, "the literature tends to either overindict the habit because it is strange and obvious, or to minimize its consequences in the view of its long-standing tradition and ethnological interest" (Kalix 1990:411, quoted in Odenwald 2007:17).

Convention on Psychotropic Substances Classification

WHO and the Convention on Psychotropic Substances, a UN treaty originally signed in 1971, play a strong role in labeling chemicals in socially meaningful ways. The convention categorizes psychotropic substances into "Schedules" according, first and foremost, to their medical usefulness, and secondarily to their "abuse risk" and potential for causing dependency. Many national governments, including the United States, have adopted them and base policies on their assessment of a substance's risk factors.

According to the convention's categorization, as a natural amphetamine, khat is the only member of its drug category, despite its behavioral and chemical similarity to synthetic amphetamines. WHO has determined that cathinone, has "high abuse potential," and was placed in Schedule I of the 1971 Convention on Psychotropic Substances in the mid-1980s (http://www.who.int/medicines/areas/quality_safety/4.4KhatCritReview.pdf; accessed January 12, 2011), although it did not explicitly ban khat. As a point of comparison, it is interesting to note that other drugs in Schedule I include narcotics, such as opium and heroin, and LSD. Coca leaves, crack, cocaine, and many amphetamines (including methamphetamine), in contrast, belong in Schedule II: drugs that have a high potential for abuse and addiction but also have safe and accepted medical uses in the United States. According to the convention, a drug is placed in one of four schedules based on its capacity to produce: "(1) a state of dependence, and (2) central nervous system stimulation or depression, resulting in hallucinations or disturbances in motor function or thinking or behaviour or perception or mood" (United Nations 1971:2). In the khat plant, cathinone transforms into cathine after a day or two, and cathine has been placed in Schedule III, which includes substances less susceptible to abuse and with acceptable medical applications.

A final ruling of the Drug Enforcement Agency (DEA) of the U.S. Department of Justice was announced in February 16, 1993 in the *Federal Register* (volume 58, number 9, 21 CFR Part 1308, January 14, 1993 [accessed September 22, 2011]), legally recognizing the placement of cathinone in Schedule I in the United States. It announced regulatory procedures that banned khat specifically, since it contains cathinone. The review by the U.S. Department of Health and Human Services (HHS) had begun in 1988, when the secretary of HHS asked the DEA to request an investigation (http://www.erowid.org/plants/khat/khat_law1.shtml; accessed January 12, 2011). In 1992, the assistant secretary of health responded with the recommendation that khat be placed in Schedule I for two reasons: (1) it was alleged to have similar abuse potential as amphetamine and methamphetamine, which are Schedule II; (2) it has no acceptable medical use in the United States and no procedures for safety under medical supervision have been identified, which conforms to drugs in Schedule I.

Attempts by WHO to identify khat as a possible drug of abuse date to the 1930s. The Advisory Committee on the Traffic in Opium and Other Dangerous Drugs of the League of Nations discussed khat in 1933 but took no action on it. In 1956, the UN Commission on Narcotic Drugs determined that more information on the chemical compound was needed before taking action. In 1964, that committee announced that problems with khat were similar to those of amphetamines and therefore there was good reason to consider regulation. In 1971, the UN Commission on Narcotic Drugs asked WHO to review khat and asked the UN Narcotics Laboratory to study it. It was during this investigation that cathinone was isolated chemically (DEA 1993 [http://www.who.int/medicines/areas/quality_safety/4.4KhatCritReview.pdf; accessed January 12, 2011]). In 1972, in the Bulletin of the World Health Organization, Halbach concluded that khat "can be considered as a drug of the amphetamine type" (1972:27).

From reading qualitative accounts of khat-chewing experiences (e.g., Carrier 2005a, 2005b; Kennedy 1987; Wedeen 2008; Weir 1985) or observing khat use in Madagascar, one would scarcely believe that its main active agent, cathinone, could qualify for such a radical placement in the WHO classification (keeping in mind that some Malagasy people find khat to be a serious social problem). To think that khat's effects are anywhere near as harmful as heroin, another Schedule I drug, is unreasonable. To identify it as similar in its negative health effects and potential for abuse as methamphetamine, crack, or even cocaine (all Schedule II drugs) seems absurd.

But the classification system analyzes cathinone in a laboratory setting, considering its potential for addiction. It is clearly not sensitive to context-dependent factors, such as route of administration. Consumed as it is in Madagascar, Yemen, and East Africa, chewed over a period of two–five hours, the release of its active ingredient is necessarily slow relative to other routes of administration—and hence the effects not so intense. Its concentration is much higher, and its effects much stronger, when the active property is synthesized and consumed in pill form, for example, as it has been for marketing in some recreational contexts in the West. Yet marketing cathinone in any form other than in khat leaves is difficult. Nencini and Ahmed (1989) criticize the placement of cathinone, stating that placing it in Schedule I "was nothing but a formality; since cathinone is difficult to synthesize and highly unstable, it is unsuitable for marketing" (p. 27).

The WHO typology has many weaknesses. For one, the schedules divide substances up into a limited number of categories that are designed for the medical community: There are multiple categories for substances that have medical uses, with several categories for varying amounts of abuse risk. For substances deemed to have no medical applications, there is only one category—Schedule I. This provides no category for substances such as khat, which have no medical applications but do not, in their leafy form, have high abuse potential. Similar substances that are consumed regularly in the West, particularly nicotine and caffeine, do not even fit into the U.S. DEA's adaptation of the WHO's schedules (DEA n.d.; http://www.usdoj.gov/dea/pubs/scheduling.html; accessed September 22, 2011). Neither does alcohol.

Second, analyses are performed under laboratory conditions, considering only the potential for abuse of the chemical in the abstract, under conditions of limitless supply. In other words, categories ignore not only the cultural context of chemical use, but also the route of administration: Coca leaves, for example, produce a very different effect than the highly processed cocaine. Khat as a leaf is quite different from the synthesized cathinone-based powder (methcathinone) that is synthesized in a laboratory, where there is no need for the khat plant, and which is consumed as a rave drug. As stated above, consuming natural cathinone in khat leaves provides natural limits to the amount an individual can consume. Most importantly, some of the substances, including khat, are not very well researched when they are given a schedule placement. There appears to be, for example, no medical use of cathine, despite its placement in Schedule III.

The placement into categories according to harmfulness has been critically evaluated by outside observers. Nutt et al. (2007), for example, published a rationale for evaluating the harm of drugs by potential misuse in *The Lancet*, a leading medical journal. Using measures under the general categories of physical harm, dependence, and social harm (including to self and society), Nutt et al. ranked twenty drugs, both legal and illegal ones. They then measured their own ranking against the drug's legal status in the United Kingdom and the classification of illegal or controlled drugs according to the U.K. Misuse of Drugs Act of 1971. They found, ironically, that two of the ten most harmful drugs—alcohol (ranked fifth) and tobacco (ranked ninth)—were not even classified, and marijuana (ranked eleventh) was considered less harmful than either alcohol or tobacco. Marijuana is a Class C drug in the United Kingdom (least harmful), but a Schedule I drug (most harmful) according to the U.S. Controlled Substances Act of 1970. Nutt et al. (2007) ranked Extacy seventeenth out of twenty in harmfulness, even though it is categorized among the most harmful substances by the U.K. Misuse of Drugs Act. Khat placed twentieth out of twenty (with cathinone a Schedule I drug), making it the least harmful of all. They conclude: "Our findings raise questions about the validity of the current Misuse of Drugs Act classification," and they affirm that "we saw no clear distinction between socially acceptable and illicit substances" (Nutt et al. 2007:1052). Their ranking was recently republished in a report on the war on drugs by the Global Commission on Drug Policy (GCDP), where the commissioners echoed their concern that "the categories of seriousness ascribed to various substances in international treaties need to be reviewed in the light of current scientific knowledge" (GCDP 2011:12).

The obvious disjuncture in the assignment of substances to categories in the WHO schedules and in national classification systems suggests that something other than medical knowledge is driving the placement process, and it raises larger questions about what might be driving this process. Nutt et al. (2007:1052) argue that "discussions based on formal assessment of harm rather than on prejudice and assumptions might help society to engage in a more rational debate about the relative risks and harms of drugs." As will be discussed in Chapter 7, some suspect that khat's placement is politically motivated (e.g., Armstrong 2008). Since placement in the schedules, policy, and effects on real people's lives are closely linked in many countries (including the United States), it makes sense to examine the possible political implications of such placements in order to identify the most rational approaches to policy and practice.

The next sections explore health issues from nonbiomedical perspectives, considering local perceptions in settings of khat use, and then a history of Western perspectives of khat's effects. It will consider both perception of health effects and opinions on legality, since they are so intricately linked.

Local Perceptions of Khat's Effects, with Implications for Legality

Local Perceptions of Khat's Effects in Madagascar

Drug Effects

Whether khat is or ought to be classified according to locally meaningful categories of hard drug (*drogue dure*) or mild drug (*drogue douce*) is a common subject of conversation among people in Diego, both within the khat production-distribution-consumption network and among professionals in town. Opinion tends to fall predictably along two lines, with those in the khat network arguing that it is not a hard drug and is no worse than caffeine. On the other hand, many professionals I spoke with, including a psychiatrist, a psychiatric nurse, and a judge, tended to believe that it was, or should be, classified a hard drug. Those in the psychiatric profession claimed that it made people crazy, especially when mixed with other drugs, such as marijuana. An inspection to the psychiatric hospital (a twelve-bed establishment with seven patients at the time of my visit) revealed that five out of seven were there for drug-related reasons. According to the judge, khat made people lazy and led to petty crimes, such as theft. Certain others, particularly practicing Christians and well-educated people far removed socially from khat-chewing environments, admitted they were not sure, but would not be surprised if it were a hard drug.

The confusion of the Malagasy as to whether khat is a "hard" or a "mild" drug is justified in part chemically, given the difference in potency in cathinone and cathine. But more poignantly, the uncertainty is based on a discrepancy between international discourse on the drug and on its observed characteristics. Because of its gentle effects relative to other drugs that they are familiar with, like alcohol or even marijuana, people in the khat network in Madagascar scoff at the idea that the drug could ever qualify for anything other than a mild drug. Khat users cross-culturally describe its effects in some similar ways, noting its ability to increase concentration either on one's thoughts, one's job, or the conversations one is having. Weir's (1985) description of the khat experience in Yemen as increasing concentration, endurance, mental attentiveness, and level of mood would fit with my observations in Madagascar and corroborate what others have written about it in other contexts.

In Madagascar, khat is a controversial topic locally, and people hold strong opinions on it. Its detractors say that it makes people lazy, its high purchase cost takes away from household budgets and results in poor nutrition, and it is associated with juvenile delinquency. Its supporters claim that, as a stimulant, it increases their work performance, increases sexual prowess, helps them forget about their problems and gain vision and inspiration for the future, engages them in animated discussions, and gives them something relatively harmless to do with their time. Few Malagasy in the general population of Diego Suarez find that it makes people lazy. In 2007, with a team of students at the Université d'Antsiranana, we conducted face-to-face surveys with 147 living in various lower working-class neighborhoods (*quartiers populaires*) in Diego Suarez. Many of our respondents chew khat, and all had people in their close social networks who did. Of the 140 who answered the question, only 9% responded that khat makes people lazy; 77% said it did not; and the rest were not sure.

In a subsequent study in 2010, I pursued questions of khat's health effects through structured interviews that were conducted by two male students at the Université d'Antsiranana in Diego Suarez. Each conducted fifteen interview sessions without me present. Several of them involved small focus groups and the total number of interviewees totaled thirty-seven. Those interviewed all lived in the *quartiers populaires* in Diego Suarez, where there is a high density of khat chewers. The students asked specific questions about khat and elicited open-ended answers. Only four of the thirty-seven in the groups reported that they did not chew khat. Nearly all the respondents were male.

Questions about khat were embedded in a broader survey about health care choices, and the respondents did not know at the beginning of the interview that khat was a focus of interest. Before khat was even mentioned, respondents were asked where they seek treatment for physical ailments, as well as what they do when they are having a hard time psychologically. Specifically, they were asked what they do when they have troubles or worries (*mijaly saigny*, which means "troubled psyche"). By way of a prompt, the interviewers suggested what they know to be common problems: trouble with a romantic partner, a wayward child, the death of a family member. In six interviews, people volunteered that they chewed khat to relieve these kinds of problems. One weekend chewer, a forty-year-old teacher who is the head of a household of five, said that he talks with friends, drinks alcohol, and chews khat. He said that khat does not clear the problem immediately, but requires several sessions. Another man, a twenty-seven-year-old mason, married and the head of a household of four, said that he first talks with his close associates, including his wife and parents. If that does not work, he chews khat and drinks a little alcohol. He said he only chews several times a year. A couple of young male taxi drivers said that chewing khat and drinking alcohol together makes them feel better.

When asked directly about the physical and mental health effects of khat, few (six, or 16%) mentioned negative physical symptoms. A few did mention gastrointestinal problems with digestion. Twenty people said khat has positive effects. A couple of people said chewing khat helps cure stomach aches, and an older woman said she drinks khat tea as a remedy against stomach aches as well as for fatigue. One mentioned that to prevent digestive agitation, he drinks milk with his khat. Aissa, a Muslim woman of Yemeni descent, stated that health problems associated with khat arise in large part from the manner in which it is taken: When combined with alcohol and poor nutrition, it causes problems. When taken the traditional Yemeni way—with milk, soup, or ice water—few if any health problems arise. Those in the Yemeni community (often self-identified as *arabou*), where khat chewing has been common since they arrived in Madagascar as dock workers in the early twentieth century, often decry the rise in use among the general Malagasy population, especially among young unemployed men. Some of their complaints mirror those of Aissa. The reason many chewers give for consuming alcohol is that it "*mamono ny dosy*," or, "kills the dose," referring to the frequent sensation of insomnia that accompanies khat chewing.

Khat is well known locally as an aphrodisiac, but its effects on sexuality are reportedly uneven. The Malagasy linguist, Pierre Mbima, in his research on urban youth slang, interviewed groups of youth. In one of Mbima's recorded discussions, one Malagasy youth explained that khat works well at helping men maintain an erection, but this only occurs when the effects are wearing off (Mbima 2006:584). They laughingly explained that people who try to engage in sexual relations while at the height of the khat high may actually find the opposite effect—temporary impotence.

In terms of effects on mental health, two respondents in 2007 mentioned dependence as a danger—one was a nonchewer, and one said its level of dependence resembled that of coffee. Most responded to the question of khat's health effects positively, mentioning either its benefit in terms of labor productivity or that it fostered satisfying social connections and helped them enjoy themselves. Several also responded to this question by stating that it boosts morale. Those who chew recreationally, including young and minimally employed men (the *barbo*), reported finding it an enjoyable way to kill time. They say they like the feeling it gives them of being concentrated on their thoughts (*concentré*) and of having the opportunity to share conversations with companions. Khat chewers say that it opens up thoughtful conversations on politics and current events and allows them to think about how to make more money or otherwise improve their individual lives. During interviews in March 2005, when rice was so expensive, many said that they still bought khat to chew because it enabled them to get rid of their worries (*mañadoso asa loha*) and strategize solutions to their problems.

Malagasy workers often said that they began chewing khat to keep themselves motivated and concentrated on the job as well as to inspire plans for improving their lives materially. At least eleven mentioned that a physical effect of khat is giving them the strength to work. Several occupations were represented, including student, entrepreneur/political leader (president of his *fokontany*, which is the smallest political unit, corresponding roughly to a neighborhood), night shift receptionist, odd jobs (*bricoleur*), and trades (baker, carpenter, artisan, mason).

It is interesting that no one mentioned that khat produces withdrawal—either depression or a hangover effect, as has been reported in other contexts of chewing (Cox and Rampes 2003). Recall that as an amphetamine-like compound, khat elevates mood, followed by a more introspective period of low mood or even depression. This low-mood phase is not generally recognized locally as part of the khat-chewing experience. In all my years of studying in Madagascar (since 1990, and since 2004 specifically on this project), I have not heard people discuss depression as a negative after-effect. The experience of low mood, if experienced at all, seems to be a more private affair. More research is needed on the actual manifestation of depressive symptoms associated with khat.

People focus almost entirely on the high-energy aspect of khat chewing, and these consumers would vehemently argue against khat as a substance that makes people lazy. In fact, in a much more comprehensive survey conducted in 2007, both chewers and nonchewers in the working-class neighborhoods in Diego Suarez were interviewed about various aspects of the khat experience. Only fifteen out of 154 people identified laziness as one of khat's effects.

So, why do people associate khat with laziness? I would argue that those well-documented medical effects of low energy at the end of a khat-chewing session are not what make its detractors think it causes laziness. It is, rather, linked to social and political reasons—including class-based anxieties. Nonchewers observe groups of young men on the streets chewing khat for long periods of time—for all phases of the cathinone's effects—in the afternoons, during the typical work day. What they do not realize is that many of these seemingly unemployed young men schedule their work doing odd jobs during the mornings so that they will have their afternoons free to chew khat with friends—giving the impression of complete idleness. Furthermore, these young men who work in the informal sector constitute only a portion of the total khat-chewing population. Many formal sector employees—from laborers to white-collar administrators—chew on their days off. Others—taxi drivers, those working at night (guards, receptionists, prostitutes), and self-employed entrepreneurs—chew on the job to enhance productivity and boost morale.

Accusations of laziness are commonly aimed at people of low status and often reflect a different set of work-related values and opportunities, rather than laziness. Recall that unemployment is high and there are few formal sector jobs available for young men. Several pointed out what seemed obvious to an outside observer such as me: There was a critical shortage of formal sector jobs, and this was the cause of inactivity, not khat itself. What I learned from the interviews is that the desire to have enough money to chew khat actually led to a vitalization of the informal economy, as young men engage in odd jobs—washing cars, running errands—to make money. In an economy with few options, where education does not assure a job, people have developed their own means of survival within the context of local constraints and opportunities.

From the perspective of medical doctors, many in Diego Suarez say that they do not have enough evidence as to whether khat is bad for people's health, but several mentioned gastrointestinal problems—confirmed by the medical research on khat and suspected to be due to its tannins and not cathinone or cathine, per se. Based on their clinical experience, it was hard for the Malagasy doctors to isolate khat from other potential causes of most of the ailments they treated. There were no strong, overwhelming correlations between khat use and physical ailments. Many commented that they would very much like more information.

In sum, Malagasy chewers do not identify many negative health-related issues with khat, and they identify it as having positive psychological effects.

Implications for Legality: Studying Up

As could be predicted, local users and their household members are not the only local people to have an opinion on khat's effects. This section focuses on local public opinion about khat by those in a position to influence or make policies. This analysis involves the methodological practice of "studying-up" (Nader 1972), or attention to the opinions of those with positions of authority. It examines discourses about khat that influence perceptions of health and opinions on legal policies. This analysis is based primarily on numerous interviews and casual conversations with public officials and civic leaders throughout my research.

While it is clear that public figures share no single opinion about khat, what unites them is a concern about the legal status of khat and what it does to or for people. Elected officials seemed somewhat ambivalent, acknowledging the important role khat plays in the local economy, yet showing concern for its effects on people and the economy. One prominent political official said: "Khat should be made illegal, since it is an impediment to economic development. It takes up land that could be used to produce food crops. People waste their money on khat and have no money left for rice." Another stated: "Khat is my great worry. It is supposed to give energy/force, but it tires people out. It is hard to have reflective conversations with people who have been chewing." And another reported: "I am concerned that khat is making the youth lazy and it is bad for people's health. I'm not sure what its legal status should be." A local judge held: "It is clear: khat should be made illegal because it is a drug."

This tendency toward condemnation that many political decision makers show is strongly shaped by national and international discourse denouncing khat. People with little exposure to khat, people with a higher level of Western-style education, and people not originally from the region tend to disapprove of khat based on negative stereotypes. The former president of the republic, Marc Ravalomanana (president from 2002 to 2009), is reputed to have publically criticized khat as antithetical to economic development. But many also reveal a genuine attempt to understand the issues and make thoughtful and wise decisions on how to handle it from a policy perspective. This is, in part, because they realize that khat is the lifeblood of the local economy. Public bureaucrats working in the economic sector, such as people in the Chamber of Commerce and in the tax office, recommended not only keeping it legal, but giving it a prominent place in the formal economy through taxation. The government has tolerated it at all levels, despite the suspicion that it renders people—especially youth—unproductive and therefore constitutes an impediment to development.

Perceptions of Khat's Effects Elsewhere

Wherever khat is chewed, its use is shadowed by strong voices denouncing it. Yet it is important to recognize that in some places it has been used for its positive medicinal and mood-altering properties for centuries. It has been integrated into work contexts throughout Yemen and the Horn of Africa to relieve hunger, thirst, and fatigue (Gebissa 2010d:74). It has been an important in ritual contexts as part of the observance of Ramadan, for example, in parts of Somalia (Anderson et al. 2007:65) and life-cycle rituals in Ethiopia (Gebissa 2004:10). In many of these traditional contexts, it is surrounded with an aura of sacredness. Well-identified chewing practices specify how much is chewed, how one acts when feeling its effects, and what to eat or drink in accompaniment. In many of these traditional contexts, alcohol is not consumed, but rather milk, soup, and ice water. Its overall social effects are generally to reinforce social integration.

Khat chewing throughout the Horn of Africa has expanded to nontraditional users—particularly in urban contexts, where it is often associated with male youth culture and increasingly with women. Carrier (Carrier and Gezon 2009) found that in Kenya, approval of khat seems strongest in the area where it is most intensively produced: the Nyambene Hills. Still, the earliest written accounts of consumption in the Nyambenes revealed concern over youthful consumption. These accounts were written by the explorers and hunters Chanler (1896) and Neumann (1982 [1898]), who visited the Nyambenes at different times during the 1890s. Chanler (1896:190) mentioned that Nyambene elders saw khat as something to be withheld from the young because it would cause them to stay awake at night and cause trouble. This idea of an earlier restriction of khat to Meru elders became important during colonial times. Some colonial officers accepted the traditional use of khat by elders; they were more alarmed by its increasing use by Meru youth and by anyone elsewhere in the country. They attempted various measures to shore up a restriction of khat to Meru elders, but none of them proved successful: Instead, khat became increasingly popular throughout the colony.

In Somalia, Anderson et al. (2007:56) note that its use has expanded to include all social classes, ages, ethnicities, religions, and genders. With its spread, the traditional contexts of use no longer hold, and new norms have been established. Some medical professionals and scholars express concern that these new contexts introduce patterns of consumption that could be labeled misuse because of their potential for negative health and social effects. Gebissa (2010d), for example, writes that new communities of users in Harerge, Ethiopia, chew either solely for pleasure, or instrumentally, for a specific purpose, such as working more efficiently. For the former category, "khat chewing is often followed by an alcohol drinking binge to counteract the stimulating effect of khat. The chewers also tend to refrain from eating. This pattern of khat use may appropriately be described as misuse" (Gebissa 2010d:73–74).

In many of these new contexts, other drugs often accompany khat, such as alcohol and marijuana. In Lamu, Kenya, people frequently take Valium to mitigate against insomnia (Anderson et al. 2007:106). Mains (2010) writes that in Jimma, Ethiopia, people drink alcohol to do away with the quiet, introspective period at the end of the chew—a phase that is embraced in many traditional contexts and considered an integral part of the khat party (Kennedy 1987; Weir 1985). In surveys they conducted, Anderson's team (Anderson et al. 2007:69–75) found that in Addis Ababa, 36% of the 212 khat users they queried agreed that khat is "very bad for health" (p. 71), 33% disagreed, and 31% were uncertain; 75% of the respondents were male. In Djibouti City, 28% of the seventy-four interviewed agreed that it is very bad for health, 27% disagreed, and 44% were uncertain; the sample was split almost evenly between male and female respondents. The high numbers in the "uncertain" category suggest a significant amount of ambivalence about khat's effects. The high numbers in the "agree" category point to a social concern shared by users that khat may not be healthy. These results indicate that chewers may, in fact, be receptive to a culturally sensitive, proactive public health campaign, based on scientifically based data about khat's effects, as has been suggested by Odenwald (2007). In Madagascar, in our survey of 147 individuals, of the 109 who responded to the general question "Is there any problem with chewing khat?," 83 (76%) responded in the negative and 26 (24%) responded in the positive. When asked more specifically, nearly half cited health and money concerns as a problem related to khat chewing. Almost none mentioned social problems such as crime or domestic distress.

In each of these contexts of consumption around the globe, there is a voice of opposition. Anderson et al. (2007), who did a broad study of khat chewing in East Africa and England, report the existence of anti-khat groups in Addis Ababa (Ethiopia), Lamu (Kenya), Uganda, and the United Kingdom. Social problems blamed on khat include crime, divorce, family discord, financial hardship, domestic violence, and prostitution. Detractors also present a medical case against khat, claiming it to not only be harmful in itself, but to facilitate the spread of HIV, TB (Anderson et al. 2007:78), and psychological disorders when combined with other drugs such as marijuana.

Several social scientists and their teams have come out strongly criticizing the anti-khat discourse that indicts khat for medical reasons. They point out its logical fallacies, its problematic factual nature, and political and social dangers of espousing it (Anderson et al. 2007; Beckerleg 2008). Perhaps the most significant problem is that people assume that a correlation between khat and some negative effect is actually caused by khat. However, research on the relationship between khat and both poor physical and mental health is "inconclusive and contradictory" (Gebissa 2010d:65). Gebissa (2010d:67–68) has also reviewed the literature associating khat and HIV and finds the connection to be unsupported. Further, none of the major studies has been able to identify a causal relationship between khat and psychosis. Exposure to clients with serious mental illness, who also happen to be khat chewers, has perhaps led certain clinicians in the United Kingdom to oppose khat, but this opposition is not based on scientific study (Anderson et al. 2007:192). Gebissa concludes that: "A glance at the history of the opposition to khat shows that moves to restrict the use of the leaves were driven by concerns over the alleged social effects of consumption rather than by medical evidence of harm" (2010d:79).

Shifting Western Perceptions of Khat

Since the beginning of contact with khat-chewing areas of the world, Western opinions of khat have shifted. As Weir (1985) notes, early accounts tend to be either descriptive or laudatory of khat's effects. Neibuhr, who was the leader of a Danish expedition to Yemen in 1763, compared khat chewing to the taking of snuff. A Frenchman who visited Yemen in 1837, for example, wrote that he "ended up getting great pleasure from its gentle stimulation and the vivid dreams which followed" (quoted in Weir 1985:55). It was only in the early twentieth century that Western accounts of khat more or less uniformly condemned it as a moral and economic vice to which the Yemeni were pathetically and unhealthfully addicted. One referred to it as "the most debilitating, time-wasting scourge of Yemen" (quoted in Weir 1985:58). Weir notes that much of the disapproval stemmed from an ethnocentric lack of ability to appreciate the aesthetic qualities of Yemeni life. One traveler in 1922 described the social setting of the small, enclosed, smoky room in which people chewed khat as "disgusting." Another referred to the act of chewing as "filthy."

Scholarship on khat in the 1960s tended to continue in the vein of condemnation, and it was not until the 1980s that the general opinion shifted again. Since then, scholars as well as development workers have often identified khat as a mild drug, incapable of the radically altered behavior, social disruption, and addictive disfunctionality associated with narcotics. Indeed, even a policy paper for the World Bank written in the late 1990s cited Kennedy et al.'s 1980 publication, saying that the harmful effects of khat are minimal (Ward 1999). A man I spoke with working for Catholic Relief Services, who had previously been stationed in Yemen for several years, spoke of it as an enjoyable and harmless social ritual so ingrained into Yemeni life that one could scarcely resist the call to join in on khat-chewing parties. Some recent journalistic writers have associated its use in Yemen as largely favorable and even quaint. Kevin Rushby, for example, has entitled his journalistic account of the delights of khat *Eating the Flowers of Paradise* (Rushby 1999), and Baron (1999), writing about his amusing experience at a khat-chewing party in Yemen in "A Memorable Experience" for the *British Medical Journal*, wistfully concludes that "every society has its own forms of chemical escape" (p. 500).

Negative aspects of khat came to the fore of the Western imaginary in 1992 with the U.S. invasion of Somalia. One journalist writing for the *New Republic* in November 1992 narrated his personal experience with those he thought of as crazed Somali khat addicts: "After taking the drug, restless adolescents become more and more agitated and less and less rational. A drug-induced insistence on personal supremacy turns pubescent energy into casual, cheap violence. Raw tempers are released in the form of reckless driving, senseless arguments, and the playful exchange of gunfire" (Stevenson 1992:2).

It is clear that evaluations of khat vary tremendously. Observers have identified it as everything from an Arabian delicacy and an enjoyable, mildly stimulating social ritual to a scourge that wrecks individual lives and causes social havoc. This vast range of opinions makes it clear that cultural factors play a significant role in the evaluation of khat's effects. The Schedules of the 1971 Convention classifications are based not only on pharmacological information on biochemical processes, but also on value judgments as to drugs' potential for harm to health and for causing social problems. According to a recent WHO Expert

Committee on Drug Dependence, for example, the effects of khat are not well known, but it is "believed to be dependence-producing" (WHO 2003:18). The committee implicitly legitimized its status as a Schedule I drug, adding that khat is "associated with a variety of social and economic problems affecting the consumers and their families" (WHO 2003:18), without acknowledging the methodological problems with that research. WHO reports, and Drug Conventions themselves, must be viewed as the cultural artifacts that they are—powerful documents with the authority to relegate any consumed substance deemed problematic to the realm of the pathological, subject to control within an institutionalized biomedical framework.

Significance of Health Research and Findings

What are the implications of both scholarly and popular discourses about khat? As discussed throughout this chapter, medical assessments of khat interweave in a complex way with stereotypes about its effects, which then become applied to political movements and policy decisions. Interpretations of health studies are central to discussions of the legality or prohibition of khat, and khat's opponents often make a strong connection between medical arguments and prohibition. While critics cite both social and health arguments, Gebissa believes it is the medical arguments that ultimately hold the most power of persuasion. In writing about Ethiopia specifically, he notes: "The prohibitionists realize the case against khat can marshal enough support only if the khat problem is defined as a medical epidemic" (2010d:77). Any discussion of khat's effects on health must take the larger context of potential prohibition into consideration.

Making khat illegal or ignoring it because of its marginal legal status has several negative implications. For one, it prevents open discussions about any of its possible health effects. Many people in Madagascar complained that khat causes stomach aches and digestive problems. But without further investigation, it is unclear whether this is due to some property inherent in khat or because of the way it is chewed, including the kinds of food, drinks, and other substances consumed before, during, and after chewing khat. As reported above, many chewers in other countries report health concerns. An important criterion for evaluating a psychoactive substance is its direct effect on health. A review of the literature reveals that negative effects are hard to isolate; they often occur in the context of other conditions and are context-dependent or involve medical problems that are coexistent with khat use. Despite the relative mildness of its effects, compared to substances like heroin, severe dependence-producing pain killers, or methamphetamine, concerns about health effects must be taken seriously. To this end, Odenwald (2007) concludes his review of mental health literature with a recommendation that future studies address the need to inform effective public health education efforts that are culturally relevant to specific contexts of use. He writes that "in order to find sustainable solutions, multidisciplinary research is needed, from economics to anthropology, medicine and pharmacology" (p. 18).

Second, making khat illegal would put both rural and urban livelihoods at risk in places where it is produced, increasing poverty and susceptibility to the diseases of poverty, such as infectious diseases and diarrheal diseases due to poor sanitation. Further, an overly strong focus on khat—to the point of obsession in some cases—can overshadow more serious health problems that a population faces. Varisco (2004) notes that although some minor health effects may be associated with khat, "the fact remains that the major health problems facing adult Yemenis are chronic diseases such as hepatitis, tuberculosis, schistosomiasis and malaria" (p. 104). Vilifying khat—whether it is legal or not—also has social implications for chewers and makes them vulnerable to societal disapproval and community sanction.

A final argument is that making khat illegal based on inadequate evidence of social and medical harm could be argued to be a human rights violation, infringing on people's quality of life and freedom of consciousness. Baer, Singer, and Susser define health as "access to and control over the basic material and nonmaterial resources that sustain and promote life at a high level of satisfaction" (Baer et al. 2003:5). As a recreational drug and stimulant, freedom of consciousness can be considered as integral to "a high level of satisfaction." In our interviews with consumers in the city of Diego Suarez, people overwhelmingly told us that khat makes them work harder and stay alert during tedious tasks—as do most stimulants. People also enjoy spending time with others while consuming this highly social drug and experience it as socially integrating. Throughout the history of humankind, people have been using psychoactive drugs to heighten experience and to enhance mental and physical health. Whether or not a particular substance is considered socially acceptable has little relationship to its health effects. Some of the most physically addictive and health-threatening substances known—alcohol and tobacco—are legal in most of the world. Caffeine addiction—a stimulant similar to khat—is a way of life throughout much of the world.

Movements to prohibit khat clearly point to important social problems. To reduce these problems to being caused by a mild stimulant not only unfairly targets users but misses the opportunity to examine larger social anxieties and experiences. The next section of this book (Chapters 4–6) examines indirect health effects of khat, presenting practices of production and distribution. Chapter 7 then picks up where this leaves off, considering the larger political and economic context in which discussions of health effects and prohibition take place.

4

GROWING AND SELLING KHAT

Madagascar is renowned for its unique and endangered biodiversity of flora and fauna, which has attracted the interest of scientists, tourists, filmmakers, and armchair travelers. Far less attention has been paid to the people of Madagascar, who are among the poorest in the world. When visiting the northern regions of the island, one cannot help but notice the vibrant economy associated with the marketing of khat, whose leaves are chewed for a mild stimulant effect. Khat is vital to the local economy and constitutes the largest change in land use practices in the far north of Madagascar. Its effects are multifaceted and complex, providing not only opportunities for local livelihoods, but also challenges to human health, the health of forests, and the functioning of the state.

Khat has multiple effects on health, both direct and indirect. The previous chapter identified direct effects of khat consumption on mental and physical health. This one focuses on an indirect facet of the relationship between khat and health: the impact of khat production on income in the region. It lays the foundation for analyzing khat holistically as a cash crop, considering the overlap between health and livelihoods. A holistic health systems approach, such as that taken in critical medical anthropology (CMA), considers poverty and control over resources as critical to evaluating states of health (Baer et al. 2003:5). A discussion of drug crop production raises issues of the ability to pay for health care, purchase adequate quantities of nutritional food, and engage in sustainable food production systems. This perspective reveals that issues of health go well beyond matters of direct drug consumption.

The chapter takes a political ecology approach to health, considering how the practices of production and distribution contribute to khat's overall health effects. This approach differs from many previous studies, which have emphasized impacts of the environment on health, focusing on such negative impacts as pollution, infectious diseases, and cancer (Singer and Baer 2007). Another way to integrate ecology and health is to consider nutrition. Baer et al. (2003) outline the relationship between subsistence strategy and nutrition, noting that food-producing societies—horticultural and agricultural—tend to have nutritionally inferior diets because of their reliance on a limited number of food staples that are low in nutrients compared to the varied diet consumed by foragers. Agricultural societies have the greatest disadvantages, partly because of the lack of nutritional variety, and partly because monoculture is susceptible to environmental disasters of floods, pests, and drought. Also, due to social stratification, the poorest in an agricultural society may experience more food shortages or nutritional deficiencies than those with greater access to resources. Baer et al. write: "Unequal access to food supplies contributed to the emergence of malnutrition and, as a consequence, greater susceptibility to disease among the economically exploited masses, particularly in urban areas" (2003:68).

In his exploration of the links between psychotropic substances and poverty, Singer (2008a) points out the relationship between poverty and health in general, noting that health status and income are correlated in stratified societies. The existence of high concentrations of poor people in one location is one factor that correlates with lower overall health. Pockets of poverty tend to correlate with reduced health-related service opportunities and violent crime. Another contributor to poor health is a sense of despair that often accompanies poverty. According to Singer, people who are both poor *and* who have a sense of hopelessness are more likely to use psychotropic substances, and, in turn, to suffer from drug use-related diseases, in addition to experiencing lower general health status.

The connection between health, income, and khat is complex. It is clear that however else khat may affect health (see Chapter 3), it does provide a significant source of income to many in the north. For many, it also lessens their sense of helplessness by providing a way to cope and even thrive in the midst of deep national and global political and economic crises. To this extent, khat production mitigates against the negative effects of poverty on health—by raising household and individual incomes, by raising the general well-being of the region, and by fostering a sense of empowerment in those who gain from it financially. Recognizing khat's indirect health benefits in raising the standard of living of farmers and traders does not preclude a negative assessment of khat as unhealthy for certain consumers and their families, however. It merely points to the multi-faceted and intricate nature of the situation.

A CMA that engages political ecology must be open to identifying positive as well as negative impacts of environment on health in today's globalized world. This is particularly important in areas where local people are carving out their own alternative modernities, in the face of a global capitalist economy where they cannot compete and where they have little hope of increasing standards of living according to the rules of that game.[1] The fertile volcanic soil and the source of water from Amber Mountain provide the people of northern Madagascar with a local resource that remains in their control and is therefore a positive environmental asset.

Social scientists and popular thinkers have focused on the increasing cultural, political, and economic homogeneity brought about by the processes of globalization (Friedman 2007; Giddens 1990; Habermas 1987). Many, however, have challenged this perspective by pointing out the enduring heterogeneity associated with global stratification and local cultural adaptation to changing conditions (Ong 2006; Tsing 1993). Escobar (2008) points to the work of a group of Latin American theorists (e.g., Castro-Gómez 2005; Quijano 2000) who challenge the Eurocentric hegemony of the theory of homogeneous globalization processes. They accuse such theories of being "blind to . . . colonial difference and the subordination of knowledge and cultures it entailed" (Escobar 2008:168). Recognizing colonialism as a force that underlies globalization opens up the framework to understand "the rearticulation of global designs by and from local histories" (Escobar 2008:169). Escobar writes that powerful global designs emerged out of the modern West after World War II, but that, "in the process of becoming a global design, however, not infrequently [modernity] was transformed into local projects articulated from the perspective of subaltern histories and interests" (p. 170).

The khat economy in Madagascar provides an important example of a local adaptation to globalization. Alongside the neoliberal struggle to incorporate all productive lands into a global economy, northern Malagasy farmers have developed a local economy that is not dependent on export earnings yet is not subsistence-based. They present a different model of survival in the global age—a form of economic adaptation based on local markets and local resources. It is worth paying attention to this phenomenon, since it is increasingly common in the global margins and it only comes to light when analysis is freed from the blinders of the assumption of global homogeneity. Khat has contributed significantly to farmer livelihoods overall, and while it has brought about some increased stratification, economic differentiation has been mitigated by the fact that khat is overwhelmingly produced by small-scale farmers.

The connection between health and production is twofold. First, khat's status as a recreational drug distinguishes it from other cash crops because of the high demand and the high willingness to pay associated with it. Second, as noted above, higher producer incomes may result in the ability to purchase better health care and nutrition. Although it is difficult to make any strong assertions about this, it can be suggested that based on what is known about local health care practices, higher income is likely to correlate with higher quality health care and better nutrition.

This chapter focuses on the dynamics of production and trade of khat. It presents the production side of the khat economy, revealing the conditions under which farmers have been able to grow it to their advantage. It begins with a description of contemporary production practices, focusing on the north and eastern sides of Amber Mountain. It then provides a history of agricultural production in this area, analyzing how colonial practices historically preceded and laid the conditions for contemporary khat production. It discusses strategies farmers use in making decisions to switch from one crop to another and the effects of recent shifts on rural stratification. The lens then shifts to processes of distribution, both from the perspective of rural wholesalers and urban vendors. I conclude the chapter with a discussion of the political ecology framework for considering these drug-related health issues, arguing for the advantages of a holistic, case method approach that reveals processes that can be observed worldwide.

Global Khat (Catha edulis) Production

Catha edulis favors an altitude between 1,500 and 2,450 meters and is found wild throughout eastern and southern Africa and Arabia, growing over 25 meters tall. The farmed variety is kept much shorter through constant pruning (see Gebissa 2004:15). Kennedy describes Catha edulis as follows:

> It is an evergreen tree with a straight and slender bole and white bark. The serrated leaves, ovate-lanceolate to elliptical in shape, are generally between 50–100 mm long and 30–50 mm wide. The plant has small petaled white flowers of yellowish or greenish tone. In Yemen the trees range from 2 to 10 meters in height, and some of them are claimed to be 100 years old. (Kennedy 1987:177)

In much of the production zone, high esteem is given to old trees: This is certainly true in Kenya, where old trees are reckoned to produce the finest khat (Carrier 2007:37–39). The actual harvested commodity varies from region to region in what is considered edible: In Yemen and Madagscar, often just the leaves and tender stem tips are chewed, whereas in Kenya small leaves and bark of stems are used. Ambiguity surrounds the substance, and it has accrued a wide range of contradictory associations. Some relate the substance to peaceful gatherings, others to Somali militiamen; some praise it as the economic savior of African and Yemeni farmers, others see its consumption as a drain on family resources;

Figure 4.1   A mature khat plant in Joffreville

defenders equate its effects with those of coffee, while detractors imagine it is closer to a drug with more dramatic effects such as marijuana or cocaine.

Khat is produced primarily in several countries, including Yemen, Ethiopia, Kenya, and Madagascar. Before the unification of North and South Yemen, South Yemen (formerly British Aden Colony and Protectorate) relied on imported khat, much of which came from Ethiopia in the 1940s and 1950s (Brooke 1960). While some khat is grown in northern Somalia (Somaliland), little is produced in the rest of Somalia and none in Djibouti. Another major production zone is in Kenya, especially in a mountain range to the northeast of Mount Kenya by subgroups of Bantu-speaking Meru (Carrier 2005a; Goldsmith 1999; Hjort 1974). Although some of the crop remains in these countries, khat is a major export crop for Kenya and Ethiopia and a major source of tax revenue for those governments (Gebissa 2004; Green 1999).

The Setting: Eastern Amber Mountain

Over the last twenty or so years, khat has become an integral part of the economy of the far north of Madagascar, with production focused in the rural areas east of Amber Mountain. Khat is a mainstay in the economy of the city of Diego Suarez, and it is important in Ambilobe, on the island of Nosy Be, and in other northern towns. It is in many cities throughout the country because dealers send it by air to their contacts, often to friends or relatives originally from the north who sell it locally and send money back to the dealer from Diego Suarez.

There are two main centers of khat production in the country, both on the eastern side of Amber Mountain, about 30 kilometers south of the regional capital of Diego Suarez on the northern tip of Madagascar (see Figure 4.1). Joffreville, on the northeast of the mountain, is closest to the city of Diego Suarez (32 kilometers); Antsalaka lies on the eastern side of the mountain, which is closer to the city of Ambilobe to the south and the highways leading to the rest of the island.

Joffreville was a colonial hill station and military base, which today is full of crumbling colonial buildings. Driving into Joffreville, one goes up a hill through the colonial center of town: a pot-holed boulevard lined with commercial buildings. Side streets pass by neighborhoods with scattered, once-stately homes—the remnants of dreams and hopes of building a town in France's own image. Some distance out of town lie the former barracks. The architectural town center is no longer the commercial center, though there are still shops that are open, signs for nearby hotels, and a few street vendors selling produce or prepared food on the road.

At the top of the hill, the road turns to the left, exchanging its concrete curbs and patchy pavement for a dirt road. It passes the multi-storied public school whose windows are broken and top floors no longer usable. A little way further, the dirt road comes to a junction. To the right, the road goes up the mountain for about 5 kilometers. Straight ahead, it dips into a dispersed settlement that is and always has been occupied by Malagasy people—originally by those who came to work for the French during the colonial era. It is at that junction that the taxies arrive to transport khat, other produce, and people to the markets of Diego Suarez.

This is the commercial center of the local economy for the distribution of its produce. The dispersion of the consumption and distribution centers, along with the physical dispersion of low population density settlements within Joffreville, contribute to giving the town the feel of a federation of villages without a strong centralized core. In 2003, there were approximately 1,500 inhabitants in the *fokontany* (the smallest formal political unit in Madagascar that has its own elected officers, including a president) of Joffreville, according to the president of the *fokontany*.[2]

Antsalaka, on the other hand, has grown from being a small village in the 1980s to a small town, with its hustle and bustle, population spike, and densely packed street activity. The population increased in the five *fokontany* making up

Figure 4.2 Antsalaka bustles with people every day

Antsalaka in just three years, from 2,855 in 1997 to 4,449 in 2000 (PCD nd). The population of the *fokontany* of Antsalaka Centre was approximately 1,800 in 2000 (PCD nd) (see Figure 4.2).

Antsalaka has the feel of a village that is beginning to outgrow itself: Individuals wealthy from khat have built cement structures side by side along the village's main street; less wealthy inhabitants have filled in empty spaces with homes; the road is clogged with vehicles at the taxi stop; vendors line the road most days, though especially on market day; small businesses have sprung up to service the khat economy, including small restaurants serving traditional Malagasy food (*hotely*), produce stands, bars, and small shops. The president of the *fokontany* in Antsalaka mused that every day is now like market day. Every day, the demand for meat is enough for butchering a cow, whereas before they butchered one perhaps once a week. The public infrastructure has not kept up with the growth. While there are some public water faucets, sanitary infrastructure is insufficient. There is inadequate access to clean drinking water, no public areas for washing clothes, no waste water disposal or runoff systems. The taxes that come in from khat are helping address these problems little by little, however. The local president's overall estimation of khat is that it has been good for the community. He says: *mampandroso tanana*, meaning it has brought about economic development.

Khat is perhaps more thoroughly integrated into the economy and ethos of Antsalaka than of Joffreville. It has been common in Antsalaka, for example, to convert rice fields into khat fields; there are more large-scale farmers of khat; there are more immigrants to the village who have the explicit goal of making money from khat-related labor (farmers, day laborers, distributors); the tax set on khat by the commune in Antsalaka does not exist in Joffreville; there is more visible wealth in the village center in Antsalaka; and Antsalaka has the reputation in Diego Suarez for having the most desirable khat. In and around Joffreville, on the other hand, many farmers have no interest in planting khat; some only plant a little in addition to other crops; and many vocally disagree with the practice of planting khat on irrigated land that could be used for growing food.

Both Joffreville and Antsalaka are villages of immigrants that began with the period of French influence in the 1800s. Some of the older residents' ancestors came from the high plateau regions of central Madagascar in the mid- to late 1800s, during or before the colonial era. Many people in the region continue to identify themselves as Merina[3] or Betsileo—prominent ethnic groups of the high plateau. There are a few individuals identifying as Sakalava and Antankarana, ethnic groups traditionally associated with the north. More recent waves of immigrants have come from the far southeast of the country, from the drought-ridden areas inhabited by people identifying as Antemoro or Antaisaka.

According to Sylvio, a *fokontany* president in Joffreville and border guard for the national park, the people from the south of Madagascar began arriving in large numbers in the 1970s and have continued to arrive to the present. At the time of the interview in 2003, Sylvio reported that about 70% of the population of Joffreville was Antemoro. The Antemoro and other southerners tend to form their own associations for mutual aid and for ethnically oriented celebrations. They collect money and lend to each other. Many families are quite wealthy, with several owning motorized vehicles. Residentially, they are concentrated in a certain part of the town. Incoming Antemoro—mostly young men—often work temporarily for established Antemoro families. This helps them become established in the community until they branch out on their own to either find land or move to the city. Sylvio, who is Antankarana and moved with his mother as a child to Joffreville from the northwestern town of Ambilobe, complained that the Antemoro keep to themselves and do not pay attention to him as president. Despite the relative independence of the Antemoro community, there is not a history of ethnic tension in the Joffreville area, and positions of political and community leadership, such as president of *fokontany*, have been occupied by Antemoro as well as others.

Land and Labor

There are several types of farmland on the northeastern side of Amber Mountain. The most productive land is flat and irrigated by canals, most of which were built during the colonial era. Another kind of land is on the slopes of the foothills of Amber Mountain. This is rain-fed land that is well suited to bushy perennials such as khat because khat's root structure mitigates against erosion. Many farmers with diverse holdings grow khat on the hillsides and rice or vegetables on their irrigated land. Some people, however, especially in the region of Antsalaka, have converted their irrigated fields into khat fields. The advantage of this is that, because of the increased access to water, these plants produce new, edible leaves year-round instead of only in the rainy season when the price is low. Another kind of land is that which is carved out of the forest on the edge of the Amber Mountain National Park. On this land, people cut and burn the existing vegetation, replacing it with rain-fed fields—often planted khat.

People have gained access to their land through various means. An important way of obtaining land historically has been to clear and claim communal lands. People have generally had to ask permission from local leaders to do this. Sylvio, the *fokontany* president in the early 2000s, said that some communal lands remain but that they are heavily sloped and not good for farming. These farmers do not always have legal, state-recognized titles to this land. There have been recent campaigns to encourage farmers to obtain land titles, but there are still many farmers whose land tenure is insecure, particularly in Joffreville. Another way to obtain land is through purchase or inheritance. Many colonists, for example, sold or gave land to their most loyal employees when they left the country in the mid-1970s amid the socialist revolution. Much of this land is fertile, flat land with canals. Most of these canals have not been significantly maintained since they were built during the colonial era and are no longer efficient. A number of farmers sharecrop, farming land owned by those with too much land to farm themselves.

Others have been farming land of absentee landowners for decades. The mayor of Joffreville explained that some of the foreigners who owned land during the colonial era (e.g., those of French and Indian descent) left without paying attention to how their land would be used. They technically still owned the land, even though they were not on it. In some cases, the Malagasy farmers have begun obtaining titles to these lands. Other cases are more complicated and contentious. In a recent case that has left many without access to productive land, the absentee landowner sold a large tract to a developer who has since transformed it into an ecotourist destination. The new owners have forced approximately 200 farmers to vacate the land—land that they had been farming for decades since the colonial era when the landowner allowed them to farm there. The farmers have protested, and this is currently a legal issue that has yet to be entirely resolved.

A final way of gaining access to productive land is through paid labor. Those without land may not want to undertake the full responsibility of sharecropping and work as laborers on other people's farms. This is especially the case for single women and young men without dependents. There are many such laborers in Antsalaka, where transitory migrants often come to seek their fortune in khat (see Figure 4.3). One wealthy farmer, Aline, said that it is better to pay workers by the day instead of by the month because they are harder working and you only employ them when there is work to be done. Some, however, work as full-time farm workers and/or guardians of khat fields—sometimes for landowners living in the city who pay their khat workers by the month to oversee their khat. For an active, on-site farmer like Aline, hiring day laborers make more sense. Hiring a full-time caretaker of khat provides options not only to wealthy or absentee landowners, but also to single women landowners who cannot undertake the major farming labor or who may not reside in the village.

Many households supply all the labor needed from planting to weeding to harvesting (and sometimes even to selling wholesale). Some larger landowners

Figure 4.3   Women, interviewed by Louis-Philippe, harvest khat in Antsalaka

take on live-in workers to help with khat and other farm labor. Usually, these are young male migrant workers who have come from the south and live with a land-owning family for a few years before moving on. Small-holder households with little available labor sell their crop to traders who harvest it as well. For the traders, this extra work ensures they get the best quality khat. A well-maintained khat field must be weeded about once a year, but other than that, labor input is minimal, so it is a good investment for just about any household that has available land. Khat plants become harvestable between four and five years after planting, then the new growth on the ends of the branches is removed once or twice a week since people consume only the most tender leaves. People all along the khat commodity chain are aware of differences between rainy and dry season quantities—and prices. In the dry season, it is mostly irrigated khat that makes it to market, and the price is double or triple what it is in the rainy season. In the rainy season, even the rain-fed khat grows well and yields an abundant harvest.

History of Vegetable Production; History of Diversity

Colonial history provides an important context for understanding the current place of khat on the slopes of Amber Mountain. The farmers on the northern and eastern slopes of Amber Mountain have a long history of crop diversity. Before the colonial era, Malagasy farmers grew rice on land with canals that they had dug and which they owned and maintained collectively. On nonirrigated land, they grew crops such as manioc, sweet potatoes, and corn. The French established control over the northern part of Madagascar in the 1880s, about fifteen years before the official era of French colonial governance was declared in 1896. In 1885, after having defeated the Merina army (aided by the British), a treaty was established, declaring the far north to be under the protection of the French. In 1886, the city of Diego Suarez and its immediate surroundings were declared a French territory. At this time, the French established a military base next to the deep harbor of the bay and appointed a civil governor to rule the territory. The north was the first significant military stronghold of the French in Madagascar.[4]

Documents from the colonial archives at Aix-en-Provence in southern France reveal that the French already wrote about their desire to undertake economic activities in Madagascar in the late 1700s. A document from 1775[5] discusses Madagascar in general, stating that cash crops such as indigo, sugar-cane, and pepper grow well there. There were also many beef cattle. Presaging colonization, the document states that the island could hold ten times the current population. Early explicit discussions of colonization begin to take place in the early 1800s. Madagascar was particularly of interest as a place to send delinquent members of the French-descended proletariat on Ile de la Réunion (previously called Ile Bourbon), colonized in the mid-1600s by the French as a stopover on the trade route to the East Indies. Sugarcane production has been its main economic activity. As one colonial document dated 1829 states: "It will be most important to favor emigration of a large number of individuals of the proletarian class of the colony and who have been here without means of living and who have become dangerous to property and the public peace."[6] The French had sent a number of early settlers to Ile Ste. Marie off the northeast coast of Madagascar.

In the late 1890s, legislative proposals reveal that the French hoped that Madagascar would turn into a settler colony as a way of relieving poverty in France and on Ile de la Réunion and also provide a living for former military personnel.[7] In places where settler populations were encouraged, farmers of French descent (called Creoles) from Ile de la Réunion grew locally traded cash crops (*la petite culture*) such as rice, vegetables, and cattle to support the urban and military populations. A letter dated 1887 from the newly appointed civil governor of the territory, M. Froger, to the Naval Ministry, explained that life was expensive in Diego Suarez because so many of their necessities had to be imported. Froger noted that a few colonists were trying to grow European vegetables, and that he wished them success. He expressed the need for more colonists to arrive to engage in general manual labor and farming activities.[8] In a report dated the same year, he noted that many products were imported from Réunion because they were cheaper, including dry grains, potatoes, dry beans, and fresh vegetables.[9] Despite the need for *la petite culture*, colonists were nevertheless also enticed by hopes of growing exportable cash crops (*la grande culture*), such as vanilla, cocoa, rubber, cotton, coffee, manioc, banana, corn, and even opium, and the possibility of raising cattle and exploiting timber resources.[10]

The French architects of the colonization policies hoped to enlist local people as well as colonists (both Creoles and those of direct French descent) in growing the crops that the French desired. A 1897 legislative proposal recommended that each military post in Madagascar have an agricultural village nearby to provision it, and that soldiers help in training local people to grow crops desirable to the French, such as fresh vegetables.[11] Early documents about colonization in general explain agricultural efforts idealistically as a way of uplifting the Malagasy people and encouraging them out of their laziness,[12] so that they could participate in the benefits of colonization. Another stated benefit of agricultural colonization, according to a letter from General Gallieni to the minister of the colonies in 1898,[13] was that it was an efficient way to pacify a region and transform the morals of the people.

The 1897 legal proposal suggested that only unoccupied lands be taken, but that land and infrastructure be prepared for colonial occupation. The land was given or sold cheaply to people whose request for a concession was granted. Many of those receiving concessions on the east side of Amber Mountain were Creole, and, in the 1910s, a few Malagasy individuals. This request for private property by Malagasy individuals became more closely scrutinized in the late 1910s, when local administrators raised concerns that locals were being put up to these demands by colonists who planned to monopolize the land and sharecrop it out to local people.[14]

Soon, those concerns turned from protecting the Malagasy to being fearful of indigenous expansion into lands that they thought ought to be reserved for colonists. One piece of correspondence from the capital Tananarive to an administrator in Diego Suarez in 1918 scolded the Diego Suarez administration for giving out concessions to locals. It warned them about being careful not to put too many locals on land that would have to be irrigated at governmental cost, and instead advocated reserving irrigated land for colonists.[15] The assumption behind these discriminations was that local people only need, aspire to, or, indeed, are capable of life in traditional villages and subsistence cultivation. A written response found on several requests for concessions from Malagasy people in 1918 illustrates this: "*Ces morcellements de terrains deviendront plus tard un sérieux obstacle a la colonisation, et il y a lieu de les éviter. Ne faisons pas de gâchis: l'indigène n'est pas encore mur pour coloniser sérieusement et utilement*" (This breaking up of the land will later become a serious obstacle to colonization, and it should be avoided. Let us not make a mistake: the indigenous person is not yet mature enough to colonize seriously or usefully). All requests for concessions by local people were recommended to be put off until they could resolve issue of developing *réserves indigènes*, where people could own land communally.[16] These reserves were never created. Local people continued in their customary practices of communal and private (but not legally recognized by the French) land ownership.

By the early 1930s, most of the colonists in the region of Amber Mountain either had timber concessions or were small-scale farmers. Concession holders engaging in *la grande culture* were located primarily around the village of Sakaramy, several kilometers from Joffreville on the road to Diego Suarez. They were not numerous, nor did they have large-scale operations. They mainly grew manioc and sisal.[17] There was much demand for agricultural products locally, though, because of the military bases, the growing urban population, and the European community in Joffreville, which served as a sort of hill station for Europeans seeking a more temperate climate.

This is how the land around Amber Mountain became dedicated to vegetable production—to meet the local European demand for produce. In 1940, a report from an administrative field visit noted that Frenchmen were engaged in small-scale farming:

> *La grand colonisation représentée par les sisaleraies de la CAIM couvrant 1 millier d'hectares a Antamotamo et Apparihy.*
>
> *La petite colonisation créole d'Antsalaka et Ansakoakely est extrêmement intéressante. On rencontre la des européens travaillants comme des paysans de France. La région est située entre 400 et 600 m d'altitude et permet le travail manuel.*

La grande colonisation represented by the sisal plantations of CAIM cover 1,000 hectares at Antamotamo and Apparihy.

La petite colonisation creole in Antsalaka and Ansakoakely is extremely interesting. There are Europeans who are working like French peasants. The region is situated between 400 and 600 meters in altitude, which permits manual labor.

A report from a 1941 field visit reported that vegetable production had become remarkably successful in the Antsalaka region:

> *Les cultures sont importantes et sans aucun doute en augmentation sur 1940. A Antsalaka, l'effort fourni par les colons creoles est a noter. Ils sont des a présent en mesure de fournir en légumes d'Europe la plus grande partie de l'approvisionnement d'Antsirane.*

Agriculture is important and is without a doubt increasing around 1940. In Antsalaka, the effort put forth by the creole colonists is to be noted. They are presently producing the largest share of the supply of European vegetables for Antsiranana [Diego Suarez].

These archival documents reveal that local people did not have substantial land holdings during the colonial era. They were encouraged to farm on communal lands and not seek individual titles. Many did, however, learn to plant vegetables as a cash crop either as workers for colonists or on their own plots. When the French left the country after a series of coups and a socialist revolution in the mid-1970s, many colonists gave or sold their land to their Malagasy employees or sharecroppers. Others just left, and Malagasy farmers occupied it according to customary law. The canals that the French built remain in use to this day, though they are no longer as efficient from lack of maintenance. When the French left, so did a large portion of the local market for the vegetables they were producing.

A development plan (Plan Communal de Développent, or PCD) for the village of Antsalaka, researched and written in 2002 by a Malagasy nongovernmental organization, presents a history of the village and a case study of the above dynamics. According to this report, the village was first founded by Merina farmers around the end of the nineteenth century. Soon after, the village became home to people of many ethnic groups, including ones from the far south of the country (Antandroy and Antemoro), the high plateau (Betsileo), descendants of African slaves (Makoa), and the northern Sakalava. From 1925 to about 1950, farmers from Réunion, many of them poor, arrived to colonize the region. They were attracted by the fertile soils and the market for fresh fruits and vegetables in the city and at French military base. Under French and Creole influence, Antsalaka grew in size. The PCD notes that in the 1950s, there was a dispensary, two schools, a Catholic church built of stone, and running water for the schools, the hospital, and several Creole homes. There was a restaurant and three large boutiques owned by Muslims or Creoles. The PCD laments that after the relatively stable first republic (*la première république*) after independence, the second republic (1975–1992), led by socialist president Didier Ratsiraka, ushered in a significantly decreased standard of living.

Cyclones ravaged the infrastructure (homes, fields, schools) in 1974 and 1984, and Antsalaka was never rebuilt to precyclone conditions. The population decreased, many of the businesses closed, the services declined, and the infrastructure deteriorated. Khat, therefore, has been a boon to this region, as a result of the general poverty faced by much of the island and because of this region's specific history of reliance on crops for which there was no longer a market. Revenue from the sale of khat has provided a living for many farmers, traders, and laborers and, through taxation, has also enabled attention to improving local infrastructure.

During the mid-twentieth century, farmers of Yemeni and Creole descent were the first to plant khat commercially in Joffreville. According to interviews, before they started growing it, they bought and sold khat on a small scale. Realizing the demand for khat would grow with the increasing size of the Yemeni population in the city, they asked for cuttings from people farming it on a smaller scale and began planting it on the temperate slopes of Amber Mountain. Around the 1980s and 1990s, the demand for khat began to grow among people of Malagasy as well as Yemeni descent. As this market grew, more farmers began to grow khat.

Crop Diversification

Understanding the colonial history of vegetable production provides a context for understanding why and how khat has become so popular among farmers. Yet most farmers value diversification and few rely on khat alone. In a survey of fifty-five farmers from Antsalaka and Joffreville conducted in 2007 with the help of students from the Université d'Antsiranana, we found that fifty-one (92%) grew at least some khat. The other four grew rice and vegetables. But we also found that almost half of the khat farmers (twenty-six, or 47%) also grew rice; twenty-four (43%) also grew vegetables; and thirty-five (63%) also grew bananas and/or lychee fruit trees. Farmers in the late 2000s articulated the need for diversity in crop production as an economic safety net, as a continuous source of income throughout the year as different crops mature at different times, and to meet different kinds of subsistence needs—including cash for purchases and food for household consumption. Despite the lower demand for vegetables (see also Minquoy 2006) and the dramatically increased demand for khat, many farmers still grow vegetables to sell in Diego Suarez. They also strongly spoke of a desire to produce more, especially in Antsalaka, the center of colonial vegetable production.

In Joffreville, many landowners express a strong ethic of growing food crops. In interviews, several Joffreville farmers responded rather incredulously to a question about whether they grow khat, replying that they wouldn't think of converting their vegetable or rice fields to khat because khat is not food and it is important to grow food—whether mainly for subsistence (rice in particular—most farmers do not grow enough to have a surplus) or for cash (as in the case of vegetables). They explained disapprovingly that farmers in Antsalaka actually convert irrigated fields from rice to khat production. Many Joffreville farmers continue to grow a wide variety of vegetables, despite the difficulties relative to khat—real or perceived—in increased labor requirements, inadequate transportation, diminished markets, and lower value. While a few grow only vegetables, many also grow khat, often on hillsides unsuitable for any other kind of cultivation.

In Joffreville, bananas and lychee fruit (Litchi chinensis) are principle crops that are also less land- and labor-intensive than rice or vegetables. In Diego Suarez, Joffreville is known for its fruits, and these have a good reputation for flavor and overall quality. Bananas require shade, and banana plantings have traditionally been a source of forest degradation around the edges of the protected area where people have cleared land to grow them. With greater enforcement of protected area boundaries, many farmers reported having to switch from bananas to other crops, including khat. Bananas produce regularly, bringing in small amounts of revenue consistently. Lychee trees take approximately six years to produce. Once they are established, they produce a harvest annually. Bananas and lychees are good choices for people who either do not want to or who do not have the land and/or materials for growing other crops. Bananas and lychees are also good choices for people with a homestead but no cleared farmland since they take up relatively little space, especially lychees, a tree crop. An older couple living in the center of the colonial commercial district in Joffreville also no longer grows rice, even though they own much land. The woman claimed that this is because they are tired now. They, like the wealthy Antemoro farmer mentioned before, grow lychees and bananas in addition to khat.

Interviews with farmers reveal nuanced understandings of farmers' planting decisions. Farmers are attuned to the seasonality and the overall timeframe of their crops: Khat and lychees, for example, take time to mature and produce. Khat may take three–four years from the time of the initial planting of a branch in the soil to be large enough to pick (*mitsongo*) fresh young leaves for sale and consumption. The main tasks in the growing of khat are weeding (*mikapa*), pruning (*migratay*), and, if one is lucky enough to have a water source, watering (*mirosy*). The final step is picking (*mitsongo*) the khat leaves for sale. Weeding is perhaps the most onerous of the tasks, and farmers report that there is a significant difference in the vitality and output of plants depending on how often the ground is weeded. Observation reveals that some farmers weed meticulously, while other khat fields are overrun by tall, grassy weeds. Those with the means to hire workers are more likely to have well-weeded fields. Also, those with the luxury of a water source will also tend to invest more in weeding. Another challenge to khat farmers is fighting insects. Many farmers spray pesticides on their khat—especially the wealthier and larger scale ones who can afford the expensive products. Men do most of the work related to khat farming, but women may pick the khat leaves for sale.

Khat farmers in all locations are acutely aware of khat's varying seasonality: Irrigated plants produce fresh new leafy growth year-round. Plots without a water source only produce during the rainy season. Some farmers in Antsalaka pay canal owners for water during the dry season, which cuts into their profits. In Joffreville, there are few canals, so there is little irrigated production. Many local people recognize the potential for increased water, given their location at the foot of a reforested mountain that supplies water to the urban area of Diego Suarez. Lack of water due to inadequate canals was one of the primary complaints of farmers in our interviews—especially those in Antsalaka.

Because of the large numbers of khat producers overall, and the large percentage of farmers with no water source (twenty-one, or 38% reported having no water source), there is a glut of khat for market during the rainy season and the price decreases considerably compared with dry season prices. Despite the relatively low price, khat still provides many farmers with a significant income, making it worth the effort. Only a few farmers reported that the income from nonirrigated khat would be too small to bother with. During the dry season, on the other hand, consumer demand remains high, but the supply is significantly down—being limited to the harvest of those with irrigated fields. This forces the price dramatically up, excluding many from purchasing khat. In sum, khat makes a few farmers especially wealthy—wealthy enough to own vehicles, for example—and provides a decent income for many others.

Few farmers if any grow only khat, and even wealthy khat farmers diversify. One successful khat farmer from Antsalaka, Aline, grows rice, vegetables such as cabbage and carrots, and legumes. She explained that it is important to grow a diversity of crops since they are harvested at different times. Because she has enough land and irrigation, she and her husband can grow vegetables during the rainy season, when most people's fields are growing rice. While many grow vegetables in their rice fields after the rice harvest, Aline is able to plant and then harvest her vegetables when the price is high because supply is down. She and her husband have two plantings: one in March, the rainy season, and one in October, in the dry season. She admitted that only farmers with plenty of water and land could take advantage of their strategy. A wealthy elderly khat farmer in Joffreville of Antemoro descent grows only khat, bananas, and lychees and no rice or vegetables, claiming that those crops take too much work.

Less wealthy farmers find it perhaps even more important to diversify. Some grow khat on the side and focus principally on food crops. Because of the shortage of canals and the low price of khat in the rainy season, most farmers realize that they cannot count on khat as a sole or even primary source of income. They also grow vegetables and fruits to sell for cash. They grow rice and root crops like taro, cassava, and sweet potatoes for household consumption if they have the land and materials. Those with regular sources of additional nonfarm income may choose not to grow rice, however, because of the work involved. Sylvio, for example, also works as a guard for the national park, and his wife Diana buys and sells khat and vegetables. While Sylvio used to grow carrots and rice, he now only grows khat.

Some landowners do not grow much or even any khat at all—especially in Joffreville. One hamlet to the southeast of Joffreville has a reputation as a center of dedicated vegetable growing. Local residents recount that the hamlet was founded around 1900 by a woman who was from Antananarivo and identified as Hova (Merina). Her husband arrived later and was Betsileo. In the early colonial era, they grew rice, peanuts, corn, cassava, and carrots. They later began selling potatoes to the *vazaha* (Europeans) when they realized that it was lucrative. There are now about eighty people in the hamlet—mostly descendants of the woman and her husband. They collectively own 150 hectares of land. This past year, they farmed about 6 hectares with vegetables and rice. They refuse to plant khat in their fields but plant a bit around the edges. When asked why they do not grow more, they claim first that it is not acceptable to plant khat in rice fields and second that the micro-climate of the area is not as good for khat as it is for those closer to the mountain. During my time there, their latest endeavor was to plant large amounts of potatoes. One farmer reported having grown about 6 tons in 2007. They created an association of potato growers and built a community storehouse for potatoes awaiting export to a new market in the nearby Ile de la Réunion. Another retired farmer living in Joffreville proper grows only vegetables and rice, claiming that khat is of no interest to him. People steal khat, leaving him without any reason to plant it.

Khat is an important crop in the Amber Mountain region. It has brought prosperity to many and helped many more meet their basic subsistence needs. It is not the only important crop, however, and farmers strongly identify with the desire and need to diversify their holdings.

Stories of Farmer Flexibility

Farmers change their practices and the crops they grow when they perceive it to be advantageous to them. As economic anthropologists have pointed out, farmers around the world are less conservative and less traditional than is often suspected. They make decisions based on economically and often ecologically based rationales. If their decisions seem illogical to outsiders, it is because the outsiders do not comprehend the farmers' culturally grounded opportunities and constraints (Durrenberger and Tannenbaum 2002; Sahlins 1972; Wolf 1966). Several stories farmers told me illustrate this. Sylvio, the president of the *fokontany* and employee of the National Park Service Agency (ANGAP) during the early part of the 2000s, grew carrots before he began growing khat in 1998. He switched to khat for several reasons: The cost of carrot seeds was considerable; there is considerable risk because the success of the harvest directly depends on how much rain there is; it takes consistent work during the growing season; and the harvest only comes two times per year. Khat is less work, less risk, and more a consistent source of income than vegetable crops. He said he phased out of carrot farming as the price of khat rose. He noted in 2004, though, that some people have begun growing more vegetables again because 2002 was a year of political crisis (Marcus 2004; Marcus and Razafindrakoto 2003), with few to no trucks arriving with supplies—including vegetables—from the fertile central plateau, where the capital is located. The scarcity and the corresponding high price of vegetables in the local market encouraged some people to grow more vegetables.

Sylvio's story was confirmed in interviews with several farmers in Joffreville who were increasing their actual and projected vegetable production for that reason. One national park employee with a home near the park entrance began growing vegetables right after the crisis of 2002 to supplement her income from ANGAP. In 2004, she and her husband reported having found it lucrative, and they planned to continue doing so. In one hamlet east of Joffreville, as indicated above, the farmers had recently found an opportunity to export potatoes to Réunion Island and began to increase production to three crops per year, orienting a large amount of their productive capacity to potato growing. They created an association of potato farmers to be eligible for donor funds and were in the process of building a storage house for the potatoes in 2004. Despite the success of potatoes, the villagers have continued to grow other produce and to sell locally as well as externally. The biggest and best potatoes, they said, get shipped to Réunion.

Another man's story provides insight into the experiences of Antemoro immigrants from the southeastern coastal region of Madagascar. Born in 1956, Rakoto arrived in the north when he was eighteen years old with the intention of seeking a livelihood (*mamanga/mitady vola*). He first arrived in the northeastern town of Sambava and worked in the vanilla industry. Rakoto then moved to Diego Suarez to be with family. He worked in Diego until 1986 doing manual labor. While living in Diego, however, Rakoto bought land in the Joffreville area from a Creole and from a Malagasy landowner. In 1983, he began growing bananas because he saw the profit that could be made. He began growing khat in 1987, a year after arriving in Joffreville, because he saw people getting money from it. He also grew more traditional subsistence crops of sweet potatoes, taro, and cassava, which he sold to vendors in Diego Suarez. Rakoto now grows only khat, lychees, bananas, and avocadoes—all less labor intensive and more profitable crops than the root crops he used to grow.

Another immigrant family from the southeast (Anteisaka)—now one of the wealthiest farmers in the Joffreville region—tells a similar story. An interview with co-wives (an uncommon practice in the north) revealed that their husband and the older wife arrived in Diego Suarez to work for the government in the first republic after independence, under President Tsiranana (president from 1959 to 1972). Later they moved to Joffreville because they heard there was land available. There were still Creoles there at the time, but there was much farmland available to be claimed, and that is how they got some of their land. They have since purchased numerous additional parcels. Like Rakoto above, when they first arrived, they farmed sweet potatoes, taro, and cassava and sold them to vendors in Diego. Later, they began growing bananas and lychees, but never vegetables. They stopped growing the root crops because of how much labor it takes to grow them. It has only been in the last ten years that they have begun growing khat, but they now have large stands of it. They began growing khat because they saw that it brought quick money. They have several workers: some by the day, and some by the month, who also live and eat with them. This latter category tends to be young male immigrants from the south who are looking to earn money to send back home. They generally stay two or three years before moving on.

The life history of a wealthy, elderly farmer, Solo, from Antsalaka also reveals flexibility in livelihood strategies. He told the story of how he was born in 1928 in a local village and moved to Antsalaka with his parents, who worked for Creoles, when he was seventeen years old. He went to school, and on vacation he transported things like letters between Joffreville and Antsalaka for the Creoles. He started chewing khat around 1940, when he asked a Creole farmer for some. His father was angry and rejected him because he "ate" khat, a local way of talking about khat chewing. Then he went with his brother and acquired some land just north of Antsalaka. There were no Creoles on that land, so they were able to occupy it. They planted rice and onions at first. The brothers had a double wedding in 1942. They reconciled with their father, who came to the wedding and then taught them how to grow vegetables like carrots and dry beans. They cleared more and more land—some of which had been forested. Solo got the idea to grow khat from a friend of his who worked in Joffreville. He suggested they grow just enough to eat: At the time, they liked to eat it once every one or two weeks. As khat began to grow in importance, they began to plant more and more of it. Now they have 13 hectares of khat in addition to many hectares of other crops, including rice and dry beans. They used to grow much corn from 1995 to 2000, when the brewing company bought it from them, but now the brewery buys its supplies elsewhere and so people are growing less corn. He and his wife have four adult children, who are now farming on the land and doing well financially. Between them they own several vehicles, including a tractor.

These farmers' stories present the broader socioeconomic context in which farmers make decisions about what to plant and illustrate their flexibility to change their growing strategies in response to changing market opportunities. One farmer, Aline, the wealthy farmer from Antsalaka, told me in 2007 that, given the sharp rise in the price of rice, some people in Antsalaka had even recently torn out their khat plants to grow rice.

Rural Stratification

Khat has intensified rural stratification, bringing considerable wealth by local standards into the hands of a limited number of farmers. Factors enabling such wealth are land ownership and access to canals for irrigation. Having capital to invest in labor and materials perpetuates and continues to widen the income gap in a synergistic way. Having land and canals permits year-round khat growing, which brings in far more money than having no canals. The greater profit allows the owner to hire workers and purchase materials such as vehicles for khat transport. Vehicles make it easier to get the crop out and permit farmer control over wholesale and sometimes retail trading. Aline, for example, transports her own khat to the town of Ambilobe, where she sells it directly from her car. Wealth and success often bring prestige, and Aline's khat also has the reputation for being the best, providing her with more business than her competitors—many of whom are simply traders who have purchased khat wholesale in Antsalaka and paid to take public transportation to the point of sale. In Joffreville, several of the wealthiest farmers own vehicles for such transport. In addition to investing in the means of production, wealthy farmers also spend on conspicuous consumption—most notably, satellite dish television. The wealthiest farmers almost always also have enough land to grow other crops, such as fruit (lychees and bananas) in Joffreville, rice, and perhaps also vegetables and legumes.

The poorest people in the area are day laborers who get paid for doing such tasks as weeding, picking, and guarding the khat. They may be migrants, moving in to take advantage of the khat economy, or single women and land-poor people with more longstanding ties to the community. Some may get a monthly salary as caretaker, especially if the owner is absent. Farmers who are present may prefer, as Aline does, to hire by the day because day laborers are reputed to work harder and are only employed when needed. For many of these laborers, work is irregular. There are also poor traders—mostly women—who do not have regular connections with farmers and therefore no dependable supply of khat. I talked with one group of women who were sitting by the side of the road waiting for people to offer khat for sale. Often, they purchased it from day laborers who had pilfered it from their employers. The poorest khat farmers are perhaps those who do not have their own land, who find some to clear, often in the most inhospitable locations—like on the forested slopes on the edge of the protected area.

While khat has been a boon to the local economy in general, its wealth is not evenly spread. As with most forms of capitalist development, some have gained considerably more than others.

Selling Khat

môn mi-rentre fo ? hom/ pas toujours mi-rentre ë! pasqué io commerce quoi mi-compr rams? barbeau mi-registre pertes or qué bontka ty tôkotro mi-rapporte . . .

Does money keep coming in? Hmm, it does not always come in. Because it is business, you know. Do you get it, sir? Sometimes we have a loss, but this khat here, it is expected to bring in money. (Mbima 2006:586)

Khat sells, and fairly consistently, albeit with seasonal fluctuations. Strolling through the streets of Diego Suarez in the summer of 2010, I exchanged pleasantries with the khat sellers I had come to know over the past few years. I was looking for one woman in particular with whom I had had a particularly engaging interview several years earlier. In asking about her, I met a khat seller who invited my friend, a Canadian master's student, to sit by her and learn to speak Malagasy. Amid cheerful banter, she went on to invite my friend to travel with her to the khat-selling village the next morning to buy khat and return to sell it with her in town. The Canadian student was not available, but I seized on this opportunity for myself. We made arrangements for the khat seller to get me at my hotel the next morning at 6 a.m. We squeezed onto a minibus full of khat sellers with the same destination. The khat seller I knew spiritedly bragged about me, her new friend, and passed out my university business card to all who would take one.

One and a half hours later, we arrived in Antsalaka, and the sellers fanned out through the village to find either regular suppliers or to seek the best deal from the many individuals walking the streets with khat to sell. My khat-selling friend had no regular supplier, and she stopped numerous people to ask what they were

Figure 4.4 A wholesale seller displays her khat in Antsalaka

charging. She heatedly bargained with them, sometimes sealing a purchase and sometimes walking on. She was not satisfied with the amount of khat she was able to get, so we sat by the side of a side road that headed toward the khat fields for some time, waiting for a frequent supplier she was hoping would arrive before it was too late (see Figure 4.4). At the last minute, a young man arrived—the one she was looking for—and she was set. She stopped by a relative's house quickly to cover her face with *masonjoany*, a yellow paste from a grated piece of wood, to protect her face from the sun. We returned to the minibus and crammed in for an even more crowded ride back to the city.

After production, distribution is the next important link in a commodity chain. There are different patterns for vegetables, fruits, and khat. Increasing numbers of people have begun trading khat because of its advantages: It is light weight, easy to transport, available year-round, and brings in a substantial profit. For vegetables, several women work as wholesalers in Joffreville, buying up other farmers' produce. Selling to wholesalers works best for farmers who may not have the means to transport it (e.g., an ox-drawn cart or a motorized vehicle) or who do not wish to use public or rented transportation. This may be because of old age, convenience, or perceived cost/benefit ratio. The most prominent of these local vegetable collectors sold her produce wholesale in the city of Diego Suarez to women who sell it retail in the city's markets. She and her husband own a taxi, which he drives, making this process more efficient and profitable. I learned in 2010 that she and her husband had switched entirely to khat trading because it was easier and more cost effective.

Another woman deals in smaller quantities of vegetables and sells the produce herself in the market, often remaining in the city for several days until it is gone. Other vegetable farmers transport their own produce, using an ox-drawn cart from their farm to the city of Joffreville, and then use public taxis to get it to market to sell wholesale in Diego Suarez. Since Antsalaka lies just west of the national highway, many farmers transport their produce by ox-cart to the main road, where it is purchased by wholesalers. Others transport it to the village center where they find a public taxi to take it to the one of the city centers: Ambilobe or Diego Suarez. As will be explored further in the next chapter, the roads in the villages are of very poor quality, making it difficult to transport produce, especially fragile crops like tomatoes, to their point of sale. Khat sellers tend to be women, and many interviews with farming households revealed a division of labor whereby the man grows the khat, fruit, or vegetables, and the woman sells it, generally in the city of Diego.

There are several steps to moving khat from the farm to the consumer: People first move it from the farm site to a central location within the village. This may be done by the farmers themselves, or by paid labor. Once at the central location within the village, traders—often women—buy it and transport it to the urban centers, where they either sell it on the street themselves or sell it to someone else who will. Some also go directly to the airport to send it to another Malagasy city. These traders compete with each other for the opportunity to purchase the khat arriving from the farm fields. To avoid the unpredictability of the taxis (which also carry passengers and wait around until they are full), several collectors often pool their resources and rent a vehicle, called a "special," to take them to the city—either Diego Suarez or Ambilobe (see Figure 4.5). Some deliver khat directly to wealthy consumers who pay by the month.

Some growers also operate as distributors, transporting their khat from the farm to the city, either in their own vehicle or in a taxi. The wealthiest farmers own vehicles, which enable them to transport it directly to the cities on their own schedule. They may hire people to pick the khat and transport it to the site of the vehicle, but they oversee the process from field to city-based wholesaler. Often husband-wife teams work together, with the husband taking care of the khat plants and the wife taking the khat to the city to sell it. Owning a vehicle is a significant advantage, considering both the efficiency of operation and the perishability of khat.

Figure 4.5 Khat traders have rented this vehicle to take them and their khat from Joffreville to Diego Suarez

Selling in Diego

The pulse of Diego's street economy is fueled by khat, with buyers, sellers, and chewers dotted along well-traveled streets. In one part of town, where the high-quality khat from the southern zone (Antsalaka) is sold, people told me that sometimes when the khat just arrives there is such a large crowd gathered around one would think it was a funeral or some other large ritual gathering if one did not know better. The sellers may have family ties to the growers, or they may just have a business relationship with them. Several profiles illustrate the diversity of sellers. Jao grew up in near Antsalaka and buys his khat from family members. He has lived the majority of his life in the city doing a variety of jobs. He sold khat for a long time, then got a job as a gas station attendant, and now sells khat again. Jao said that he doesn't make nearly the money now that he did before, partly because he lost all his regular clients and partly because of the changing nature of the khat economy: There are many more sellers now than before. Furthermore, individuals do not buy as much since many businesses have forbidden khat consumption on the job.

Although Jao has only loose ties to the khat growers, another family has a well-organized division of labor among the father and his adult children, enabling them to cover all functions in the commodity chain, including the selling of khat on the street. This latter family is reputed to be one of the oldest khat-growing families, and their khat is reputed throughout the city to be the highest quality from Joffreville. They own the tallest (about 30 feet high) and oldest khat bushes I saw (claimed to be forty years old), and their irrigated fields enable them to produce high-quality khat during the dry season. They did not tell me directly about earnings, but they use costly technology (pipe irrigation) and own cars, unlike most farmers, who use public transportation.

Some sellers have family in the khat-growing areas. Vola moved to Diego Suarez from Antsalaka as a single woman and rents a room locally. She receives a daily shipment of khat from her family members in Antsalaka and is flooded with customers at her post alongside other sellers of Antsalaka khat in one of Diego's popular quarters. Others from Antsalaka sell in the town of Ambilobe to the south. Since it is closer, many sellers and even some growers commute from Antsalaka to Ambilobe daily. Not all khat sellers have family connections in the khat-growing villages, however. One young man selling khat in Diego Suarez, for example, explained that he moved there from Antalaha, a city on the northeast coast of Madagascar. He began selling khat because he liked to chew it. Consequently, he began to know the network and to make runs to Joffreville to buy it wholesale. People move to Antsalaka to take advantage of the booming economy, and many of those without family get involved in some aspect of distribution.

Many young men associated with *koroko* youth culture (see Chapter 2) sell khat. The quote that opened this section was by a member of a *koroko* group, who was explaining ways of making a living. Selling as well as chewing khat is integral to *koroko* identity because the product is valued, and it is in the informal sector, where *korokos* can manage their own time and behavior. One young man, referring to *korokos* in the third person as "*barbeaux* (*barbo*)" or hoodlum, stated:

barbeaux/ barbeaux tsy mi-trav privé barbeaux ka tsy foncs laisse barbeaux mi-trav am' secteur'ny barbeaux! point c'est tout/ mec tsy mi-casse-couilles barbeaux comme ça fo/ tous les jours/ tous les jours

Us. We don't work in the private sector. We are not bureaucrats, either. Let us work in our own *barbeaux* sector! That's it, man. And don't come break our balls over it, like they do every day. (Mbima 2006:587)

They said they felt somewhat protective of access to the khat market, mentioning that young women ought not to sell khat. *Koroko* men acknowledge that they themselves do not dominate the khat market and that they feel marginalized even though they comprise a large percentage of overall khat sellers. One conversation revealed that there is a high level of distrust of *korokos*, and they do

Figure 4.6   Khat and kola nut sellers in Diego Suarez

not even trust each other. While not explicitly about selling khat, the following comment reveals this insecurity about control over one's conditions of living:

lépèpl/ irô tsy mi-respèk barbeaux barbeaux gagos respèk n'a point pour barbeaux mêm' entre koroko samby koroko/ khât helin'ny barbeaux-là ka/ mbo frapper-n'ny koroko ka misy l'occasion faut qué barbeaux tout temps mi-faire l'attention

People don't respect us barbeaux. We remain stoic. There is no respect for us. Even between koroko, when you have a little khat, someone will steal it from you at the first opportunity. We must always pay close attention. (Mbima 2006:588)

More specifically related to khat selling, several *korokos* complained that they are excluded from formal khat selling associations, even if they pay money to participate:

toujours comme ça/ silagam difficiles pour lui réglos l'OVKAC là/ ça sert à rien quatre ans l'organisation là debout/ depuis mars quatravingt-dix-sept/ letrizay

statut ty barbeaux mi-connaître statut ty l'anniversaire chaque mois de mars mônin'ny barbeaux fo l'anniversaire ty / téachbé cageons-cageons . . .

Malagasy people are always like that. It is difficult for them to act correctly. Hey, that Organization of Khat and Kola Vendors, that serves no purpose. It has been four years since that organization began, in March 1997. The statute, I know it well. Each month of March we celebrate its anniversary. It is the money of the *koroko* that they use to pay for the celebration. There are lots of cases of beer. . . .

pasqué barbeaux pas foncs/ koroko pas zinvités quoi résèb derrière net !

But since we are not bureaucrats, we are not invited. We are not respected. (Mbima 2006:588)

The more dominant khat sellers tend to be older individuals, many of whom are women. These sellers, who have a serious work and business ethic, control community-based organizations of sellers. All khat sellers expressed frustration at being taxed. While khat itself is not controlled or taxed, there are taxes levied on people as general street merchants. They complain that the taxes are so high that they can no longer earn a profit. The *koroko* complain of being pursued all day long by tax collectors. One older woman seller told me that she and other sellers just patently refused to pay the tax this year because it has become too high—up to that time without penalty.

Those who have been selling khat for a long time complain that despite the rise in the number of chewers, several factors have made it harder to make a living from khat now than before, including increased competition from

Figure 4.7   Khat sellers in Diego Suarez

other sellers and reduced demand due to a growing tendency for workplaces to forbid its workers to chew khat. Some sellers have regular clients, and some even take orders from regular customers. The spike in the price of rice in the December rainy season (in early December 2004, the price of rice increased by over 100% overnight and did not go down again until early March 2005) also had an effect on khat sales. I spoke with one prominent vendor in early March 2005, and she said that with the price hike, she had many fewer buyers and at times she does not sell all her khat. She was beginning to worry that she would need to find another way to earn more money. With the high price of rice, she explained, people did not necessarily stop buying khat, but they bought it in smaller packets.

Because the active property in khat transforms into a much less potent form after about twenty-four hours, khat is not very storable. The traders must generally sell their khat the same day or take a loss. Although khat can be continuously harvested throughout the year if there is enough water, ensuring steady availability, the price of khat is volatile and depends on both seasonality and social conditions. In 2010, fewer people were complaining about not being able to sell their khat, suggesting that either there were fewer overall khat sellers, a decrease in production, or, more likely, an increase in consumption (see Figure 4.7).

All khat sellers are aware of fluctuations in the market. During the rainy season, there is an abundance of khat and the price goes down. In the dry season, less khat is sold, but the price is higher. Khat also sells better on certain days of the week, weekends especially. One khat seller, Marie, explained that she generally took Monday off because it is a slow day. She admitted that, despite the fluctuations, khat selling was a lucrative way of making a living. She was hesitant to reveal to me how much she earned, making me promise that I would not reveal her earnings in my writings about khat. Marie has the advantage of having been in the business for many years, with a solid clientele in town and reliable sources of khat in the village where she buys it. Not all sellers, and certainly not many of the *koroko*, have this advantage. Many of the smaller scale vendors do not go directly to the villages to purchase their khat and must acquire it from wholesalers in Diego, thereby having to pay for this extra service. The stronger one's connections to khat growers, the more successful one is as a khat seller.

Thus far, this chapter has provided an overview of the production and distribution aspects of khat in Madagascar. Although some have become far wealthier than others from khat production, a notable characteristic of this economy is that smallholders can grow it profitably, and small-scale traders and vendors can break into the market fairly easily and make a profit. Khat consumption in Madagascar is centered in this zone on the northern and eastern sides of Amber Mountain, affording a means of survival for many farmers and traders. I now turn to a consideration of khat production in the larger context of ecology and health.

Political Ecology and Health

Understanding khat holistically as a psychotropic substance requires a multifaceted approach that considers it from many angles. CMA goes beyond issues of drug consumption to consider physical and mental health as situated within a political and economic context, often with a global reach. Existing critical studies of drugs consider the politics of availability, control, and repression (Chien et al. 2000; Singer 2008b), drug trafficking, and the global War on Drugs (GCDP 2011). From a political ecology point of view, an analysis of drugs considers differentiated access to productive resources, such as land and water. Being a psychotropic substance, per se, distinguishes it from other crops in two significant ways.

First, status as a recreational drug shapes the demand for and pricing of khat, making it different from other subsistence-oriented or cash crops. Demand is consistent, and, it being a commodity that is tied to salient forms of local identity and prestige, demand remains high even in relatively hard economic times.

Being a luxury commodity, people are willing to pay more for it and they accept that a higher profit margin on the part of producers and sellers than they would for a basic staple such as rice. Understanding basic changes in the human interactions with the environment, such as the recent increase in land dedicated to khat production, requires an understanding of how khat is culturally constructed as a psychotropic substance, related to issues of identity, status, and recreational consumption.

Second, substances labeled drugs are unlike other commodities in that they are often illegal or marginal and therefore surrounded with ambivalence. Khat is no different. However, there is no repression of khat in Madagascar and it is officially legal, which makes it different from other prominent drug crops, such as opium and coca. Nevertheless, there has been much speculation about whether or not it ought to be made illegal. The former president, Marc Ravalomanana (president from 2002 to 2009), is reputed to have publically denounced khat as bad for economic development and a source of laziness in the population. Even if they are not against khat as individuals, city and other local government officials tend to consider khat an unresolved issue in need of attention. Many told me that they are not sure what should be done about its legal status—they see it as a cornerstone to the local economy and a harmful drug at the same time. This official ambivalence shapes the ways people access and use resources, making it a viable livelihood option without threat of repression and without any kind of governmental intervention, either through direct taxation or agricultural development aid. Its illegal status in countries to which people have export access (Ile de la Réunion, for example, which is French) has similarly shaped land use and trading patterns by limiting the demand.

From a critical medical point of view, understanding drugs and health requires broader attention than on consumption alone. Following such scholars as Paul Farmer (2000), studying health requires attention to the effects of broad-scale political and economic forces on people's bodies. Khat challenges scholars to move beyond studies of drugs that conceive of them as a unified category of substances that renders users dysfunctional, damages users' health or unleashes globalized drug violence on growing communities (Baer et al. 1997; Singer 2008b), or, on the other hand, that dismiss drugs' harmful effects in an effort to combat the moralism of mainstream Western society (Bennett and Cook 1996). It also challenges scholars from a political ecology perspective to consider how drug crops shape access to land and productive resources and how they present unique constraints and opportunities to people as they make livelihood choices.

Considering that khat is a substance that—based on medical and social studies—has relatively mild psychotropic and overall health effects and is not subject to violent repression, it becomes important to consider how the khat economy has affected health and physical well-being in other, more indirect, ways—in particular, in providing access to higher incomes and a sense of economic accomplishment in the face of national and global crisis. Recalling Singer (2008a), higher incomes and a sense of well-being often correlate with healthier populations, both mentally and physically. The next chapter will more closely consider the specific effect of earnings on health care spending, but knowledge of production and distribution practices suggests that khat has had positive effects on many livelihoods, and by extension, on health.

Notes

1. For a critique of neoliberal economic development, see Escobar (1995), Ferguson (1990), and Goldman (2005).
2. The names of the political units—territorial and administrative—have changed frequently with different national administrations.
3. Those who recognize Merina descent tend to refer to themselves as "Boursane," a term that in some contexts of use is a pejorative way of referring to the Merina, who have been historically at odds with people of the northern coast of Madagascar (see Chapter 1). Despite this history of tension, Merina descendants living on the Amber Mountain are well integrated with people who identify with other ethnic origins.
4. The French have an even longer history of ties to the Ile Sainte Marie on the northeastern coast of Madagascar. In 1750, the Compagnie Française des Indes set up a base on the island, after having received permission from the Merina queen. The island was France's main port on the eastern side of Madagascar at that time. Later, in the early 1800s, the French sent colonists to Ile Ste. Marie. There had been other small French military garrisons in the early 1800s, including a small one at Fort Dauphin (Laillet 1884:109).
5. Document AX_FMSG_c150d207: Projets de colonisation 1775–1853.
6. Document AX_FMSG_c14d28 : February, 1829. Extrait no. 6 du register des process-verbaux des deliberations du conseil privé de l'Ile Bourbou.
7. Document AX_FMSG_425d1134 : Colonisation 1890s, proposition du loi et debats Proposition de loi relative a la colonisation de Madagascar N. 2747. Presenté par MM. Louis Brunet et de Mahy. 28 oct 1897; Proposition de loi ayant pour objet l'introduction gratuite a Mada de colons francais no. 2762. 4 nov 1897.
8. AX_FMSG_c188d332 : Economie 1887 26 april 1887. Letter from M. Froger (M. le gouverneur de DS et Dépendances) to the Ministère de la Marine et des Colonies.
9. AX_FMSG_c188d332: Economie 1887. 1887. Report from M. Froger, M. le Gouverner de Diego Suarez. "Renseignements commerciaux sur Diego Suarez."
10. AX_FMSG_c425d1135: Colonisation, 1890s. Flyer, officially printed, "Renseignements sur la Colonisation a Madagascar."
11. Document: AX_FMSG_c425d1134: Colonisation 1890s, proposition du loi et debats Proposition de loi relative a la colonisation de Madagascar N. 2747. Presenté par MM. Louis Brunet et de Mahy. 28 oct 1897.

12. AX_FMSG_c425d1133: Circulaire a propos de la Colonisation, 1890s. Instructions au sujet des principles de colonization a appliquer a Madagascar 22 Jan 1899. Gallieni.

13. Document: AX_FMSG_c425d1134 : Colonisation 1890s, proposition du loi et debats. Letter dated July 25, 1898.

14. Document: AX_MADDS_368: P de DS, Réserves Indigènes, 1910–1922, October 18, 1917. Correspondence from Administration en Chef des Colonies, Chef de la Province et Maire de Diego Suarez, M. Demortiere to M. le Gouverneur General de Madagascar et Dépendances—Affaires Civiles de Bureau.

15. Document: AX_MADDS_368 : P de DS, Reserves Indigenes, 1910–1922, Feb 6 1918. Correspondence from Tanarive, Le Gouverneur General de Madagascar et Dépendances to M. le Président de la Chambre Consultative de Diego Suarez.

16. It is hard to read this without thinking about Frances Moore Lappé and Joseph Collins's *Food First: Beyond the Myth of Scarcity* (1977), which ties contemporary poverty with colonial practices of discrimination.

17. AX_MADDS_369: Colonisation 1932–35. August 1933. List of concessions and activities at Sakaramy and the number of indigenous employees.

5

INDIRECT EFFECTS OF KHAT: CONSERVATION, FOOD SECURITY, AND ACCESS TO HEALTH CARE

To understand the health issues related to khat requires examination of both its direct and indirect impacts on the lives of those who grow, trade, and use khat. Chapter 2 examined the social and cultural dynamics of khat consumption, and Chapter 3 presented the indirect health effects of khat in raising the household incomes of producers and traders. This chapter considers other indirect outcomes: at the macro level, khat's effects on forests and food security; at the micro level, the effects of income. Each of these issues affects all participants in the commodity chain: producers, traders, and consumers—albeit in somewhat varying ways.

For example, forest health is important to human health both directly and indirectly for many reasons. Forests are important sources of medicinal plants (Harper 2002); they protect and nourish water sources used for drinking as well as irrigation; and they provide cost-effective building materials. Food security is directly related to nutritional status and to levels of stress and therefore is a health concern. The extent to which income from khat permits or inhibits increased access to nutritional food and to health care may be different for producers and traders, who have increased income and means of access, and for consumers, who may have diminished resources as a result of purchasing khat. The health effects of khat must be considered in a holistic cultural context, considering both direct and indirect impacts.

The previous chapter presented the mechanics of production and distribution on the east side of Amber Mountain. Contrary to popular opinion that farmers indiscriminately jump on the bandwagon of growing the vastly profitable khat plant, I argued that farmers are flexible in altering their farming strategies and growing different crops based on various criteria, including cost, labor, quality of infrastructure, desire for diversity, and personal choice. This chapter takes a more targeted approach to the question of farming strategies by addressing two specific concerns about the effects of khat locally, namely, the effects of increased khat production on the forests and on regional food security. Important questions are whether khat leads to deforestation or to a decline in food crop production. The first question raises concerns about the conservation of Madagascar's biodiversity. The question of food security raises issues of nutrition quality and regional self-sufficiency in food production. Each of these concerns is shared by many of the Malagasy people I met in the north, and, in fact, my pursuit of these questions in depth was driven partly by the extent of concern I witnessed.

I begin this chapter with a discussion of the macro-level considerations of deforestation and food security and end with micro-level effects on nutrition and access to health care. I investigated deforestation and food security in separate but overlapping processes. Conservation-related issues were addressed using both satellite image data and on-the-ground interviews. To look at issues of food security, I explored whether khat growing has been displacing vegetable production based on extensive surveys with farmers and urban buyers and sellers. The analysis that follows shows the connection between these issues in Madagascar and points to similar issues in other countries where khat is grown. I address the micro-level issues of the relationship between khat, nutrition, and access to health care based on participant observation, urban vegetable consumption surveys, and targeted interviews about health care behavior.

Forest Effects: Implications for Conservation

Madagascar has been a hotspot in global conservation since the 1980s (Gezon 1997b; Kull 1996; Marcus and Kull 1999; Pollini 2011). Natural and social scientists have flocked to this island nation, drawn by the uniqueness of its flora and fauna—70–80% of its approximately 11,000 plant species are endemic (Lowry et al. 1997); 95% of its 300 total species of reptiles are endemic (Raxworthy and Nussbaum 1997); and 100% of its nonhuman primate species are endemic. Concurrent with such biodiversity are threats from human activities, which have often been blamed almost exclusively on local people's subsistence practices.[1] International donor institutions such as the World Bank and USAID took an interest in funding conservation and development activities in the 1980s, especially after they received strong criticism for sponsoring environmentally insensitive projects elsewhere in the world. USAID opened its Madagascar office in 1983 and had a strong environmental program. By the late 1980s, the World Bank became the leading donor institution and coordinated the activities and policies of an association of donors (Gezon 1997b).

In 1984, the Malagasy government drafted the National Strategy for Conservation and Development, which is recognized as one of the first national environmental plans established in Africa. The government of Madagascar organized the International Conference of Conservation for Sustainable Development in 1985. In 1987–88, the government, in collaboration with donor institutions, developed the National Environmental Action Plan, to be executed in three five-year phases, beginning in 1991 (Gezon 1997b). During that time, the national park service (Association Nationale pour la Gestion des Aires Protégées, or ANGAP) was established to manage and eventually fund basic conservation efforts. In the first phase, conservation and development were integrated through integrated conservation and development projects. In the second phase, these tasks were split up, with ANGAP taking charge of conservation activities, and outside donors initiating development projects—sometimes (but not always) in collaboration with ANGAP (Gezon 1997b, 2000a).

My research began in Madagascar in 1989. The first project focused on the politics of managing the Ankarana Reserve protected area, which lies just south of Amber Mountain. That study revealed how local political processes intersect with regional ethnic, state, and NGO politics in the context of claims to the legally protected forest (Gezon 1997b, 1999a, 1999b, 2000a, 2006). The problem that guided this study was to understand how multiple actors negotiate jurisdiction over the rights to manage the protected area. Because of the difficulty in enforcing reserve boundaries, local sources of control were as important to compliance as the presence of outside enforcement agencies and agents. In some cases, rights to the land were delicately played out in the context of ethnic ritual events occurring within the boundaries of the protected area (Gezon 1997b, 2006).

While my previous study focused on the micro-politics of decision-making about protected area management, the study of khat emerged from a different point of departure, namely, the actual ecological pressures on a forested protected area. The focus for this study was the Amber Mountain National Park and Special Reserve, located about 30 kilometers from the city of Diego Suarez. Preliminary studies of the Amber Mountain region in northern Madagascar revealed that cash cropping, including khat and banana production, emerged as pressures of great concern to local people. Our own studies of the area suggested that logging and charcoal production were also serious threats to the region's forests, both within and outside the Amber Mountain protected areas (Gezon and Freed 1999; Gezon et al. 2007).

With a focus on khat as the fastest-growing cash crop in the region, I sought to go beyond local levels of analysis that merely focus on the proximate drivers of land use in and around protected areas. Instead of a narrow gaze on localized land-use practices and political debates, my study examined systematic links between localized land-use patterns and broader political and economic frameworks by tracing commodity chains of cash crops produced in and around protected areas to their points of consumption. In particular, this project explored the relationship between urban demand and protected area land-use patterns, focusing on the social and cultural factors in production for market (cash crops), distribution, and commodity consumption around the Amber Mountain protected areas of northern Madagascar.

On a practical front, a goal of this study was to identify what motivated farmers to make land-use decisions as well as to ascertain what the environmental implications were for making certain choices. My concern with health effects of khat production emerged in this context. First, I discovered that growing a drug crop made a difference in the unfolding of productive opportunities and constraints that farmers faced. Second, while khat brings wealth to farmers who sell primarily to markets, concerns for consumer health and livelihoods cannot be ignored. Indeed, these issues are contested and debated continuously in Madagascar.

This chapter focuses on the production side of the khat commodity chain, considering land-use choices and the implications of a drug cash crop in shaping the contexts of decision-making. The questions it explores are twofold: The first arose out of my original concern with issues of conservation and anthropogenic pressures on forests. It hypothesizes that people are cutting down forests to grow khat. In other words, I asked whether or not khat is a conservation threat. Answering questions about khat's effects on forests is a first step in understanding the overall environmental sustainability of khat production. The second question emerged in the early phases of research from conversations with local people—especially educated people in the city. They feared that khat was being cultivated to the detriment of food crops and therefore threatened the region's food security. What had been a region rich with rice and a major supplier of vegetables to the surrounding area was becoming increasingly dominated by khat production. This question brought to light a concern not for cash crops, per se, but for a cash crop not basic to essential nutrition—concern for a drug crop. So my focus expanded to inquire into the ways that land cover change informs broader discussions of food systems. My working hypothesis was that khat expansion had displaced food production and was therefore responsible for weakening the food security of the north by making it reliant on imports from other parts of the country.

Land-Use Patterns

The study of land cover change consisted of a focused interdisciplinary study carried out in 2004 by a team of researchers examining land cover change through satellite images and on-the-ground observations of trends noted on the satellite images, otherwise known as ground-truthing. For this, I collaborated with Glen Green and Sean Sweeney, remote sensing scientists from the Center for the Study of Institutions, Population, and Environmental Change (CIPEC), Bloomington, Indiana. In this, the earliest phase of the study, we acquired and analyzed satellite images in a university computer laboratory. With funding from the National Geographic Society,[2] we acquired nine Landsat images between 1972 and 2000. Sweeney and Green digitally processed the images at CIPEC (Gezon et al. 2005) and generated two-date multi-temporal composites, which means that they overlaid two dates to highlight the areas where there had been change over time—some of the changes were due to regrowth of vegetation, and others were due to the removal of vegetation. The composite image made it possible to observe these hotspots of change.

The three investigators (Gezon, Green, and Sweeney) then met in May 2004 in Bloomington to study the images and identify locations that had either undergone significant change or had remained basically the same throughout the north of Madagascar. We located twenty-seven sites for further investigation on the ground, including two in the heaviest khat-growing areas of Madagascar—one in the vicinity of Joffreville on the northeast side of the Amber Mountain National Park, and one in the vicinity of Antsalaka on the eastern side. We briefly described each of the locations of change based on what we expected to find, given the evidence of change in the digital information and our familiarity with the environment based on previous research; both Green and I had a long history of research in Madagascar (Kottak et al. 1994). For the khat-growing area from the northeast to the southeast of Amber Mountain, we noted that there was little digital evidence of change between 1972 and 2000 when compared with many of the other sites. The most dramatic change had occurred in one area close to the protected area of the Amber Mountain National Park to the south of Antsalaka on the east side.

Composite satellite images reveal whether there have been changes in the wavelengths of electromagnetic radiation, or spectral signatures, that identify objects. These spectral signatures reveal the presence or absence of vegetation and can even suggest something about the nature of the floral cover because soil and vegetation reflect differently, as do different kinds and densities of vegetation. Despite the ability for satellite images to make subtle discriminations, it takes ground observations to provide thorough botanical and geologic descriptions. During June–August 2004, we visited each of the sites directly relevant to khat production, with the intention of ground-truthing what we observed in the satellite data. Benjamin Z. Freed, a primate ecologist who studied the lemurs of Amber Mountain extensively (Freed 1996), also joined us to help assess the impact of human activities on the forests.

We took vehicles to the nearest access points and hiked to the exact locations we had identified on the satellite images using GPS technology. At each location, Sweeney and Green took GPS readings, photographs, and critical notes about landscape structure and geology to determine the nature and causes of land cover change. Freed conducted surveys of lemur populations. At each site he identified ecological and social data about crowned lemurs (*Eulemur coronatus*) and Sanford's lemurs (*E. fulvus sanfordi*) and recorded basic forest structure description (forest size, canopy height, dominant plant species, vertical stratification). This enabled him to assess the effects of anthropogenic pressures on lemur populations (see also Freed 1996). This data complemented the botanical and geological data we gathered, helping us interpret the ecological effects of land cover change on nonhuman primate species.

To learn about the social context of environmental change or stability, I gathered socioeconomic and ethnographic data by interviewing people we encountered along the way and by undertaking more structured interviews in villages at the investigation sites. The structured interviews focused on questions about migrations and residential patterns, social differentiation, road access, political and social organization, agricultural production and distribution, and histories of resource use. We supplemented this fieldwork with interviews of professionals in Diego Suarez and studies of gray literature reports, especially the Plans Communals de Developpement (PCD)—community development plans mandated by the donor community, which provided a socioeconomic overview of the areas they cover (for the full report, see Gezon et al. 2005).

Results

Our analysis of land cover change in this area relied most heavily on a qualitative interpretation of changes in spectral signature that revealed that khat was not the most important threat to the forests of the region, but rather that charcoal production and logging were responsible for the most extensive damage. These destructive practices generally occurred in classified forests—areas still under governmental control but with much less strict enforcement than national parks and reserves. Khat production was, however, an important activity on the borders of the national park and a potential source of pressure on its forests.

On the ground, we learned that in the Joffreville site there had been some forest degradation due to underplanting and clearing for bananas, but little to no damage from the expansion of other crops. Many small, isolated khat fields have been established in the zone peripheral to the national park, sometimes carved out of bare hillsides and sometimes replacing irrigated rice or other food crop fields—only sometimes as a result of forest removal. In Antsalaka (to the southeast), we determined that cyclone damage accounted for the changes we had seen in the satellite images and that people had indeed gone in and planted khat in the degraded forests in the aftermath. There was some minimal evidence of people cutting down forests in or near the protected area to grow khat.

In an interview, a senior official at ANGAP explained his perspective on khat's influence on forests: Expansion for khat production is more of a problem in Antsalaka and further south than it is in Joffreville. But it is less of a problem than other kinds of cultivation since khat protects the soil from erosion and gives farmers a reason to discourage fires. Khat fields can therefore provide a sort of buffer zone if planted up to but not within the protected area.

The rate of cutting in this area in general has slowed in the last fifteen years, partly due to increased surveillance by the national park service. But certain national park service officials fear that increased prices of rice and other food commodities, and a growing market for khat nationally, will provide people with incentives to diversify crop production to include subsistence as well as cash crops and to expand surface covered with khat. This would have the effect of expanding the amount of cultivated land—and the forest might become valuable as an untapped reserve of cultivable land. Khat is farmed by small holders, with most farmers owning less than 2 hectares of khat. The feared effect on the forest would be that numerous small-scale farmers would carve small fields of less than 1 hectare out of the forest.

The following story reveals the circumstances in which some people choose to cut down the forest. A recent immigrant from the southeast (Antemoro) in 1992, Radimy, lived in Joffreville for three years when he first arrived as a guardian for a house for a Karani of East Indian descent. He met another Anteimoro man who lived in the rice-growing village of Sadjaovato, near Antsalaka. The man sharecropped and grew rice there. Radimy recounts that he tried to be like him as a sharecropper, so he moved to Sadjaovato and became one, too. One day during the market at Sadjaovato, Radimy met a young Anteimoro girl from Antsalaka. He flirted with her, and then the girl said that he should come to Antsalaka to live better through working with khat. He fell in love with this girl and decided to work with khat, so he accepted right away.

When he first arrived, Radimy worked as a day laborer picking and transporting khat. Then his wife decided to sharecrop planting vegetables and rice. After six years of sharecropping, Radimy found forested land near the protected area, and he cut down 1.5 hectares of it. He started planting khat on this land three years ago. He said he didn't know whether his field was in the park or on public land, but that no one ever told him he could not farm there or asked him to leave. He continues to work occasionally as a day laborer for khat and rice farmers. With the money he got from khat, he has paid someone to help him dig a canal, and now his land has irrigation.

This story suggests that immigrants and other landless individuals opportunistically claim available land—forested or not. The advantage of khat is that it grows on hillsides, making more land available for cultivation than if one wanted to grow vegetables, which require flat, irrigated land.

During his research in 2009, Ben Freed reported that he found some evidence for khat cultivation having spread to the northwestern side of Amber Mountain. There, a well-established farmer planted fields that abutted the protected area. Freed felt, however, that this did not pose a threat to the forest, but rather acted as a physical and economic buffer against encroachment (Ben Freed, personal communication).

Significance: Khat Production and Environmental Change

These findings provide a historical and a regional perspective on the effects of khat production on land cover change and lemur species distribution based on empirical observation from above, using satellite images, and on the ground. This knowledge is critical for understanding and interpreting the environmental sustainability of khat production in this region. The relationship of khat production to forest and species integrity has ecological, economic, and political consequences. Given the country's commitment to conservation, an activity that posed—*or was imagined to pose*—a threat to the forests would be subject to (potential) repression. This is especially the case for activities carried out by local people, who are assumed in the common imagination to be the biggest threat to forests (as opposed, say, to formal sector commercial loggers or miners). Our results, however, show that khat production is not as harmful as it was thought to be and may even serve as a beneficial buffer between protected forest and farmland.

This was, in fact, one of the reasons I chose to investigate khat production: Mere perceptions of its destructiveness could have a negative effect on farmers. The small risks to the forest that do exist can be managed through conscientious agricultural planning and forest protection enforcement.

Food Security Concerns: Is Khat Displacing Vegetables?

The question of food security refers to the unintended health and security consequences of cash crop production, which affect the balance sheet of the health of an entire region, in addition to affecting individual farmers. Daniel R. Gross's (1971) study of conversion to sisal (from which rope is made) production in northeastern Brazil illustrates this. Sisal was introduced to this drought-ridden region in the 1950s as a way to both increase national exports and to protect farmers from cyclical drought periods. Many subsistence farmers replaced their squash, bean, and manioc with the perennial sisal plant with such a tenacious root system that it would make the fields difficult if not impossible to reclaim. Sisal is labor and capital intensive, and the unintended consequence was that a few entrepreneurs profited from processing sisal, lending credit and opening shops. The rest of the population became increasingly impoverished when the price of sisal plummeted in the early 1960s and they could no longer grow their own food. Gross found that nutritional levels had decreased for all but the wealthy few.

Similarly, khat production is thought to pose a potential threat to regional food security because of farmers' increasing reliance on a nonfood cash crop. People fear this because an increase in khat production correlates with a decline in vegetable production. This could leave the region in crisis if the normal supply of vegetables from the capital city, Antananarivo, were ever cut off again, since locals had recent memories of this occurring briefly during the political crisis of 2002, when the supply chain was cut off because trucks could not get through.

Preliminary research in 2003 and conversations with local people—especially educated people in the city—revealed deep concern over food security issues. What had once been a region rich with rice and a major supplier of vegetables to the region was becoming increasingly dominated by khat production. Thus, I began to inquire into the ways that khat production, as a form of land cover change, informs broader discussions of food systems. My working hypothesis mirrored the concerns I had heard voiced, that khat expansion had displaced food production and was therefore responsible for weakening the food security of the north by making it reliant on imports from other parts of the country. I set out to discover: (1) whether people were indeed substituting khat for vegetables (introduced in the colonial era) as a cash crop; and (2) whether people were planting khat on former rice fields, thereby replacing this subsistence-oriented food crop with khat and growing less and less rice (see Figure 5.1). In both of these scenarios, people who note the increase in khat production suspect that the high price of khat, combined with the lower labor requirements than for rice or vegetables, leads to the abandonment of other forms of cultivation.

Figure 5.1   Farmers have grown vegetables since the colonial era on the fertile slopes of Amber Mountain

To answer these questions, I used structured interviews, casual conversations, and a survey administered in 2007, toward the end of my research. With the help of Malagasy research associates, including students at the Université d'Antsiranana, I developed three sets of questions for the surveys on the production, distribution, and consumption of khat (Gezon and Totomarovario 2008). These more formal surveys supplemented informal conversations and observation throughout my study in the area. These surveys had two goals: First, they helped gauge the generalizability of the information received ethnographically from primary informants. Second, open-ended segments permitted discussion and revealed some new variables that I had not yet considered. The surveys were given face to face, with the researcher (either me or my research associates) asking the questions and writing down the answers. I conducted many of the production surveys myself, allowing me to engage in extensive informal conversation with farmers on their own land.

For each of the surveys, we asked for basic demographic information and general opinions about khat. We administered the production surveys in the two major khat-production areas: Joffreville to the northeast and Antsalaka to the east of Amber Mountain. We asked what people grow, how long they have been growing it, how they acquired the land for it, their labor arrangements, whether they chew khat themselves (making a connection to the study of consumption), and where and how they sell their crop (making a connection to the study of distribution). We also asked how they assessed the value of growing khat versus other crops and other open-ended questions about opportunities and constraints.

Constraints on Vegetable Production

Data analysis revealed that there is not a simple causal relationship between the decline of vegetables and the increase of khat. The reasons respondents gave have as much—or perhaps more—to do with constraints on vegetable growing as they do with the comparative attractions of khat. If the region is at risk of food insecurity, khat is not the culprit. As revealed in the previous chapter, most farmers would prefer to diversify, growing both vegetables and khat. The decline in vegetable production must be examined in its own right.

The problems with vegetables have to do with various aspects of their production and marketing. From the production perspective, farmers complain that seeds for vegetable crops are very expensive and often are not of good quality. One story people told was of a development project that had given them potato cuttings, which all turned out to be rotten. They claimed that the highest-quality seeds were not even sold locally, but had to be acquired at a high price through informal networks from Antananarivo, if one was lucky enough to get them at all. Another production issue is water: Most of the canals date to the colonial era and have not been properly maintained. This means that only a fraction of the potentially irrigable land actually receives water. The problem of insects also looms large for many. Several also complained that they lacked the material inputs, such as tractors beasts of burden, and plows to help till the soil. Without such materials, it was possible to grow only small amounts of vegetables, mainly for household consumption, not to engage in large-scale commercial vegetable production.

In some significant ways, however, farmers do consciously weigh the costs and benefits of khat versus vegetable farming and find vegetable farming wanting. Many khat farmers note that with khat, after the plant matures around three or four years after planting, one has regular income from the plants, especially if the khat is irrigated. Vegetables, on the other hand, only bring in money every three–six months. Some find that pest management is more difficult with vegetables than khat (though not all agree with this). Vegetables are also more susceptible to seasonal fluctuations in rainfall, suffering in years when rainfall is low. One farmer said that overall, khat brings in more money and is less risky than vegetable production. Many respondents also acknowledged that khat, although not labor free, requires less intensive labor than vegetables. One farmer, when asked why she grows vegetables despite the extra labor, echoed the sentiments of many: "*Samy am fotoany*" (Everything has its time). She, like many others, grows vegetables in the rainy season because the prices are high then. Although some find that vegetables are more labor intensive, they remain an important part of the overall production portfolio.

Some farmers chose to grow khat because they found it more lucrative than vegetables. One farmer needed to find an alternative crop to bananas, which had been his specialty. Since his banana plants were mostly within the reserve, tighter enforcement of the protected area meant he had to leave the forest. He chose to grow khat, because he noticed how much money people were making from it. Another man, an Antemoro immigrant from the south of the country, first planted root crops that are part of traditional Malagasy diets: sweet potatoes, taro, and cassava, but he switched to khat about in the mid-1990s because it was much less work and much more profitable than the root crops. He is now one of the wealthiest landowners in the region and the only man I met with two official wives.

Constraints on Vegetable Distribution

Related to the discussion of profitability are distribution-related constraints on vegetable crops. A major problem is that the condition of the roads is so poor in the rural areas that in some places people find it difficult to get their vegetable crops out to market. Either the roads are not easily passable—even by ox-drawn cart—or they are so bumpy that the crop could easily be ruined. Tomatoes, for example, are an important local crop that cannot withstand rough handling during transport (see Figure 5.2). During the colonial era, when vegetable crops were introduced, the roads were better maintained and sufficient to get crops out to the main road. Even where the roads are passable, however, transportation from the field to the main road is too expensive for many who do not own their own ox-drawn cart or other means transportation. It is in this context that the preference for khat must be analyzed. Khat is by far easier to transport because it is light and can be carried on one's back to vehicles that can transport it further. This leaves many undercapitalized farmers with little choice about what to produce.

Another distribution problem is that there is not a large local market for many of the vegetables that farmers have been cultivating since their introduction in the colonial era, and they have difficulty finding buyers for their produce. This was confirmed on many levels, including my own research and that of other scholars who have noted the same dynamics (Minquoy 2006). In my research, I learned of the paltry market for vegetables through interviews with farmers, interviews

Figure 5.2   Farmers must transport delicate tomatoes to the main road by ox cart

with sellers in local markets, and a targeted consumption study with thirteen people in Diego Suarez. One farmer—incidentally, a grower of many varieties of vegetables—scoffed, exclaiming, "Bah! Malagasy people don't eat vegetables. They only like greens. It is *vazaha* (white people/foreigners) who eat vegetables." Another commented that before, he could sell three large sacks of carrots in the same day to retailers at the urban market, but now the same amount brings in a lower price and does not sell as quickly.

Interviews with vegetable sellers at the market also revealed constraints at that end. One woman explained that it is risky to sell vegetables and that she often breaks even or loses money. She explained that her vegetable sales are directly tied to the availability of fish, especially tuna. When tuna arrives, people do not buy vegetables since they are accustomed to eating vegetables with meat, not fish. An interview with a second-tier seller further corroborates this: Mary sells a limited number of items at a stand connected to her house. She wakes up early each morning, goes to the market, and buys her produce. Her clients are people from the neighborhood who do not want to go all the way to the market. She has, in effect, a low-capital convenience store. What she typically sells are items that are central to a standard everyday local diet: greens, tomatoes, eggs, onions, garlic, dried beans, ginger, and pimento. She could not turn over vegetables such as carrots, cabbages, green peppers, green beans, eggplants, beets, or potatoes quickly enough. This list is what Malagasy people tend to refer to when they say "vegetables," or "*légumes*," adopting the French word. Greens do not generally fit into this list for them. Tomatoes may or may not be included, since they have been fairly well integrated into everyday local diets.

Vegetable Consumption Locally

Local cooking habits reveal the cultural logic of food choice. People eat rice with every meal, and a topping is spooned over the rice for flavor and added nutrition. Sometimes people have a plate of rice and then a bowl with the sauce, or topping, in the middle of the table, with each individual scooping out just enough topping for one or several bites of rice at a time. There are several categories of topping, with the most basic and inexpensive being a *roo mazava*, based on a clear broth. The least expensive meal consists of greens, salt, and water. Sometimes tomatoes are added. Other things cooked in the manner of *roo mazava* include dried beans, chicken, or beef. Vegetables such as those listed above (carrots, cabbage, etc.) do not fit in this list. The only way people cook vegetables in water is in a soup, which is generally eaten with bread, not rice, and is not a particularly common meal.

Another kind of cooking is vegetable oil–based. This is more expensive and richer, since people use large quantities of oil to cook these dishes. The oil becomes the base of what local people refer to as "*lasosy*," from the French "*la sauce*," in contrast with *roo mazava*. This is the main way people cook vegetables: in an oil-based sauce that is both too expensive and perceived as too rich for everyday eating. Another common style of cooking is with coconut, but this also does not generally include vegetables. People tend to cook dried beans, chicken, beef, or fish this way.

These observations about typical meals were further confirmed in the consumption study I conducted with thirteen local people who were selected through the intermediary of a local woman who served as a primary informant and research assistant. These were people she knew from two different neighborhoods. One neighborhood was a *quartier populaire* where she had lived for a number of years with her first husband. It bustled with activities of entrepreneurs in the informal sector. Some who lived there labored in formal sector enterprises or worked as domestic laborers in people's homes. The other neighborhood lies on the fringes of the rapidly expanding town, on the main road near the airport. Some of these people have the advantage of having more fruit trees locally, and perhaps even space to grow a kitchen garden. Socioeconomically, individuals ranged from very low income to quite comfortable. Of the lowest income, one was a teenager who had recently set up his own household within the vicinity of that of his parents, who cooked and ate by himself. Another was a disabled woman, her minimally employed husband, and their three children. Of the wealthier participants, one owned a boutique, and one lived off the wealth of his absentee mother in a large new cement-construction house (*tranovato*) near the airport.

I asked each of the thirteen individuals to record what they ate for each meal each day in a log, or a sort of food diary. When I dropped off the diaries, I asked them about general demographic information. When I picked them up between one and two months later (they had data for between twenty-two and forty-seven days of consumption), I asked them specifically about their food habits and preferences. When they were given the diaries, they did not know which variables I would be paying attention to. This experiment revealed interesting trends, confirming the above observations about diet. One man misunderstood the task and instead of writing down what he ate each day, he wrote his own general interpretation of Malagasy cuisine. He noted that when people have money, they buy beef, poultry, and fruit. He did not mention vegetables in any of his descriptions of what people eat commonly or on special occasions.

While thirteen respondents do not represent enough cases to draw reliable statistical generalizations, they do point to some general trends. Three of the thirteen respondents ate no *légumes* at all. Of those who did, seven out of ten ate potatoes, but no one ate them more than four times. Six people ate lettuce (all but one ate it only once); four ate cucumbers (all but one ate it either once or twice); three reported having eaten carrots (between two and four times); two had cabbage (twice each); and one ate green beans (five times). The one who ate the most vegetables did so far more often than did the rest. One woman, a boutique owner who was considered well-to-do by local standards, consumed *légumes* a total of thirty-two times, on thirteen separate days, or 38% of days reported. The median number of times *légumes* were consumed, however, was three times within the reporting period. In contrast, everyone ate greens, and over two-thirds ate them on at least half of the days recorded. All but one reported eating tomatoes, and half of them ate them on more than 40% of the days reported. These results suggest that *légumes* are not an important part of the diet of common northern Malagasy people, confirming what I learned through ethnographic observation and interviews. What this means for farmers is that because their primary market is local and local consumption is low, the price of vegetables is low. Some even claim that there is a great risk of farming at a loss with *légumes*.

Vegetable Markets beyond the Local

There is a market for vegetables beyond the local Malagasy population. There is an active port with ships needing supplies, and there are numerous hotels and restaurants, especially as tourism increases in the region. The problem with this market, however, is one faced by small-scale local farmers throughout the world: that of providing an adequate and consistent supply. The large-scale operations depend on wholesale quantities of produce being available dependably on a regular, year-round basis. They currently rely on regular deliveries by truck of high-quality produce from the region around the capital, Antananarivo. Local farmers cannot provide that. When I interviewed in 2007, several farmers in Joffreville talked about forming an association of growers that could coordinate efforts to negotiate with hotels and ship suppliers. As described in the previous chapter, one hamlet has formed a potato-growing collective for export to Réunion Island. But there is not much precedence of such cooperatives working effectively in this region. Furthermore, the farmers do not in all cases have the expertise or savvy to carry out this kind of negotiation. A senior official at the port authority acknowledged that it would be difficult to break into the ship chandler business because the supply chains are well established. He suggested, however, that the market seems wide open for exporting vegetables to the Comoros Islands. Thus, there appears to be the opportunity to expand the markets for local vegetables that could be exploited by local farmers. The existence of a market would only solve part of the problem for farmers, however: Attention to the entire agricultural system, including the refurbishing of market access roads and irrigation systems, would need to accompany this for a resurgence of vegetable production to be viable.

Difficulties of Khat Production

In addition to farmers' clear interest in vegetable growing, it is important to note that khat is not the panacea that many urbanites imagine it to be. Despite the stereotype that farmers prefer to grow khat because it takes less work to cultivate and requires no costly inputs, many farmers pointed out that they did not find this to be the case. To maximize productivity, khat needs weeding, water management (for the irrigated fields), surveillance, and harvesting. While wealthier farmers could afford to hire help with weeding and picking, the poorer ones could not. They must also deal with pests, which threaten to ruin the harvest. Some wealthier farmers purchase expensive pesticides to counteract this problem, but people are also afraid of the side effects of pesticides and are hesitant to use them. Cost and fear of health consequences limit the amount of pesticides applied, with the result that farmers risk a reduced harvest. In addition to farming-related tasks, theft is becoming an increasing risk and requires nearly constant surveillance. Especially for poorer farmers, khat does not necessarily provide a great relief from labor. For all farmers, the increase in overall production in the region has meant lower profits for individuals, especially in the rainy season. For farmers without irrigation, khat only brings income during the rainy season, leaving them without income for several months. Khat, by itself, does not meet farmers' needs.

The evidence presented above strongly suggests that khat production is not the cause of decline in vegetable sales among either poor or wealthy farmers. All farmers embrace diversification, and many would welcome the opportunity to increase vegetable production if the conditions were right. Khat production has indeed increased, and vegetable production has decreased, but increased khat production must be linked with both increased consumer demand for khat and decreased capacity for vegetable production and marketing. To an important extent, khat has filled a void left by the decreased viability of vegetable production. The old adage applies: Correlation does not imply causation. Also, the concerns about khat should not obscure the fact that most farmers have not abandoned vegetable cultivation and still produce a considerable amount each year. According to the PCD for Antsalaka (2001), 450 out of a total of 2,423 hectares were in rice cultivation, 256 were in tomatoes, and 150 were in corn, whereas 170 were dedicated to khat production. While the PCD report itself acknowledges that their numbers may not be exact, these numbers do suggest a proportional weighting of planting tendencies favoring production of food crops.

For those concerned with regional food security, implementing improvements in the local infrastructure would have the potential for increasing or at least stabilizing vegetable and rice production. This would include improvement of water delivery systems, road quality, and transportation; availability of high-quality seeds, fertilizer, and safe pesticides; and availability of mechanical inputs such as tractors. Targeting khat as the cause of lowered vegetable production obscures such local level issues and will only further impoverish farmers. This will not resolve the larger issues of food security.

The negative stereotypes held by khat's detractors about the farmers on the east side of Amber Mountain—that they are essentially lazy, want easy money, and are unwilling to put in the work required for growing vegetables if they can avoid it—do not hold up generally, even if there are some individual cases that support them. Like all stereotypes, they are oversimplified generalizations of a few cases that fit with a larger narrative. In general, the farmers of this area work hard to diversify production that is limited by structural constraints.

Comparative Anxieties

There has been debate about whether khat has supplanted other valuable crops elsewhere as well. In particular, people fear that khat has displaced coffee as a crop in Yemen and Ethiopia. Khat emerged as a viable cash crop in Ethiopia in the 1950s, and its growth coincided with the founding of Ethiopian Airlines, which facilitated its transport to Aden (Gebissa 2010d). In one of the major production zones in the Harerge highlands of eastern Ethiopia, production went up from 2,996 hectares in khat production in 1954 to 112,206 in 2000 (Gebissa 2010d:103). Production increased dramatically in Yemen in the 1960s, when the revolution of 1962 interrupted coffee exports (Cassanelli 1986). The production of khat increased further in Yemen in the 1970s when demand increased as Yemenis went to work in oil-rich Arab nations and began sending back remittances, giving people more disposable income (Weir 1985).

Gebissa (2004:66–70, 2010d) recounts that khat served as a solution to land scarcity in Ethiopia in a region that experienced population increase, land concentration, and government price controls lowering the price of coffee. Based on extensive empirical research, several authors in Gebissa's (2010b) edited volume, which is dedicated to examining the relationship between food and khat in Ethiopia, argue that as agricultural inputs such as fertilizers and pesticides increased in price, producer prices for commodities such as coffee declined. At the same time, demand for khat rose within Ethiopia and abroad as immigrant populations sought the leaf and transportation networks improved. The return for khat was many times higher than for any other cash crop, and the labor requirements were lower (Kassa 2010). Khat also permits intercropping with food crops, especially in the first several years as the shrub becomes established. An additional advantage is that khat is adapted to withstand the ecological conditions of frost and drought, and it is used as a conservation crop to offset erosion (Tefera and Start 2010:174). Overall, the intensification of production, with khat at the center, has been necessary where population density is high and where land holdings have become increasingly fragmented with each generation.

In Yemen as well as in Ethiopia, khat production has been in competition with coffee, and farmers often prefer khat because it requires less work and yields a much higher profit than coffee (Carrier 2005a:540; Gebissa 2004:73, 2010d; Kennedy 1987; Varisco 1997; Weir 1985). For Yemen, Kennedy reported that khat's detractors, often foreign planners and Yemeni officials, blame khat for displacing coffee and thus for being harmful to the country by being a barrier to export earnings, since most of Yemen's khat is consumed internally (1987:159). Kennedy argued effectively that this case has been dramatically overstated, with little evidence to back it up. He noted that coffee and khat grow in different micro-ecological zones (see also Ward 1999); that khat occupies less than 5% of arable land; and that though coffee production had declined, it had not been replaced with khat. Weir (1985:34–37) makes similar arguments, writing that khat has more likely displaced grain crops, which were costly to produce and, thanks to inexpensive imports, cheaper to buy.

In Ethiopia, on the other hand, khat has in fact displaced coffee in many places, primarily because of the declining price of coffee. Between 1999 and 2004, for example, Ethiopia's earnings from coffee went from 70% of exports to 35% of exports. During that same period, khat production doubled and became 13% of gross domestic product. In comparing prices, khat rose to about $8 per kilogram, while coffee fell from US $3 per kilogram to US $0.86 (Hailu 2010:129).

In addition to fears about khat supplanting coffee as a cash crop, there has been concern that it displaces food crops and thus contributes to household, regional, and national food insecurity. Despite massive Ethiopian government-led agricultural assistance encouraging food crops, including extension services, improved seeds, and subsidized credit, few farmers have found it beneficial to switch from khat to food crops. At the household level, those who grow khat tend to have higher incomes, enabling them also to invest in food crop production by purchasing costly fertilizers and pesticides. It also provides income for purchasing food if they do not grow enough to be self-sufficient. Gebissa (2010a) writes that before population pressure and land scarcity required increased intensification, farmers showed distinct preference for growing vegetables and food crops and for keeping small livestock alongside khat. Khat was also planted on marginal, otherwise nonproductive lands. Only recently have the most intensive khat cultivation regions moved to a khat monocrop regime, with khat displacing food crops (Gebissa 2010c:93).

Despite its advantages, khat does have its drawbacks. Tefera and Start (2010) point out that it is susceptible to frost and variability in market price and it ties up the land as a perennial bush, reducing flexibility in land-use decisions. On a national level, as diversification lessens and khat becomes a monocrop, food security for the nation does indeed become threatened. An additional concern about khat is the amount of water it uses (Date et al. 2004; Milich and Al-Sabbry 1995), which may threaten khat as an agricultural system. Ward (1999) writes about Yemen that "the unfavourable impact on groundwater resources of khat . . . obliges the nation to explore water saving possibilities in the khat business" (p. 24). Another is an environmental health issue pertaining to the effects of pesticides on khat chewers (Date et al. 2004; Milich and Al-Sabbry 1995).

Despite all these concerns, governments enjoy considerable tax revenues from the crop (Hailu 2010) and recognize the extent to which it has reversed some rural poverty and stimulated the economy as a whole. Governmental attitudes toward khat are therefore ambivalent. One way this ambivalence is shown is in the lack of agricultural extension activities associated with it. Despite the large-scale agricultural policies of the current government in Ethiopia, khat has received virtually no attention (Gebissa 2010d). Milich and Al-Sabbry (1995) note that even though donor nations have not sought eradication, as has been the case for coca in South America, donors have not been quick to develop initiatives to make khat production more efficient. They argue that this must be changed; otherwise, khat's negative effects will not be checked and reversed.

Income and Health

In discussing indirect effects of khat, it is important to consider the effect of increased income on the standard of living of farmers and traders. In Ethiopia, Tefera et al. (2003) found a correlation between production of khat as a cash crop and several indicators, including food security and the long-term positive nutritional status of preschool children. Khat cultivation clearly correlates with a higher standard of living, as measured by the presence of irrigation, use of fertilizer and improved seed varieties, ownership of cattle for diary and oxen, ownership of small shops, and receipt of remittances from educated children (Tefera and Start 2010:175). What I found in Madagascar is only suggestive, but it was clear especially in the khat-producing village of Antsalaka that ownership of khat fields correlated with the building of homes made of durable materials, such as cement, ownership of luxury items such as televisions, use of satellite dish service; and for some, even ownership of vehicles.

Interviews with people in Diego Suarez, many of whom are khat chewers, revealed general attitudes about health care that can be presumed to be shared by many rural residents, given the highly fluid movement between the city and villages. These interviews reveal both the health advantages of higher income for farmers and traders and disadvantages for households of consumers. Data from interviews suggest that being able to acquire high-quality Western biomedical health care services is a cultural value, and the ability to afford it is an important symbol of wealth and status. Educated, salaried professionals and others with sufficient income tend to go to private clinics, as opposed to the public hospital, which is not only less expensive but also seen as providing a lower quality service. People of all strata agree that having the money for purchasing pharmaceuticals is a major obstacle to good health, and people put their money toward medications when they can. In the village study I conducted in the 1990s, people would even sell cattle to afford hospitalization and pharmaceutical medications.

Many people combine Western medicine with traditional forms of healing. Religion correlates to some extent with choice of health care, with Christians being most likely to prefer Western medical interventions, including doctors, hospitals, and pharmaceuticals. Although many non-Christians also prefer these options, a certain number embrace the use of traditional healers and medicinal plants, and a few prefer them to Western medicine. Some say these are cheaper options, while others say that they can also be costly. Many use a variety of health services, depending on the type of ailment. For a broken bone, for example, they will tend to see a local healer. Many doctors feel that people tend to go to local healers first, waiting too long to see Western-trained doctors. The consequence is that Western pharmaceuticals and treatments are less effective. An additional consequence of using traditional healers, they say, is that the healers often engage them in bogus treatments that can be ultimately harmful. As suggested earlier, those with money will tend to consult Western-trained professionals sooner than those whose resources are more limited. Those with money also engage traditional healers effectively and consistently.

The interviews, as well as years of my own observation, suggest that higher incomes translate into higher quality health care, since it is held as a cultural value. Lower incomes result in a more opportunistic use of available services and a tendency to rely on ineffective traditional healers for a longer period of time before consulting a Western-trained health care professional. Considering the data on vegetable consumption presented above, it is also the case that higher incomes result in increased purchase of vegetables, because they are culturally valued symbols of wealth and are seen as healthy. What this means for khat is that higher incomes for traders and farmers likely translate into a healthier and better nourished population. For khat consumers, however, it may result in lower indicators of health and nutrition if resources are diverted from needed food and health care to purchasing khat.

The Nature of a Drug Crop: Implications for Critical Medical Anthropology of Drug Production

Critical medical anthropology (CMA) distinguishes itself by paying attention to the broader political, economic, and cultural dynamics shaping health care systems and access to them. CMA of drugs examines the structural conditions shaping the entire commodity chain—from the production, through the trade, to the consumption of psychotropic substances. In the case of khat in Madagascar, conditions favoring khat production include the general poverty of the country and, more specifically, the decline of the market for commodities produced since the colonial era. In addition, the crumbling of the agricultural infrastructure has inhibited the pursuit of new markets. Further encouraging production is the attractiveness of this recreational drug that has caught the imagination of adults as well as youth of the region.

Khat is lucrative for many farmers and traders. Evidence suggests that where it has supplanted food or formal sector cash crops, there has been a strong market and subsistence logic in this decision-making process. In all locales, price structures provide incentives for people to grow khat, food crops, or cash crops such as coffee. Nor has khat been a major source of deforestation in Madagascar. In some places, including Ethiopia and Madagascar, it is even credited for being ecologically beneficial in preventing erosion. The challenges of khat production that do exist—such as pesticide use and the need for water management—must be dealt with through agricultural extension interventions. As many scholars argue (Gebissa 2010d), khat provides too much good to peasants and traders to justify prohibition without a viable substitution.

Considering khat's high value as a recreational drug, which has a significantly higher consumer price than other agricultural crops, it would be difficult to find a substitute. A critical reason for khat's success locally is that it is a mood-altering crop that has become important in the individual pursuit of pleasure as well as in marking new cultural identities. Willingness to pay is high, as consumers seek out khat as a luxury and prestige item and as certain segments of youth subculture revolve around the acquisition and consumption of khat. As many scholars point out, drug production provides a living for many impoverished rural farmers throughout the world.

Drug studies in CMA focus not only on the medical effects of drug use on individuals but also on how drug crops may face a unique set of impacts compared with other kinds of crops, such as subsistence, or formal economy cash crops, in that they tend to be lucrative and yet stigmatized to one degree or another. This opens the door to cross-fertilization between CMA, which exposes the health effects of khat on producers and consumers, and political ecology, which exposes the political and economic conditions of production.

Notes

1. For a critique of this perspective and an overview of conservation in Madagascar, see Gezon (2006:31–43), Gezon and Freed (1999), Jarosz (1993), Kull (1996, 2004), Marcus and Kull (1999), and Sussman and Green (1990). For a more recent overview of conservation initiatives in Madagascar, see Pollini (2011).
2. Research funding from the National Geographic Society (Grant Number 7413.03) supported this research.

6

INTIMATE LIVELIHOODS:
GENDER AND SURVIVAL ON THE MARGINS

Le coeur a ses raisons que la raison ne connait point.

(The heart has its reasons that reason knows not.)

—*Pensées* (Blaise Pascal)

In this chapter, I present the on-the-ground workings of the khat economy by looking at actual relationships among real people. Such an examination reveals that the motive for economic gain is always constructed within a cultural context, and the cultural logic for decision-making lies embedded within and is indeed inseparable from economic rationality (Sahlins 1972). Important to such a cultural analysis is the understanding of the social networks through which people make a living as well as how those relationships are imbued with local meanings. In this case, I specifically examine how the local khat economy is marked at every stage by gendered "affairs of the heart." Throughout my study, I observed that socially and culturally marked sexual and affective relationships significantly shaped decisions about when, where, and how to engage in the khat commodity chain. And for many, the khat economy lies at the heart of everyday material and social exchanges and experiences.

Medical anthropological approaches to women have focused on women's health care issues, as identified by Marcia Inhorn (2006) in her review of the literature. Inhorn makes the point that medical anthropology has much to contribute to traditional medical approaches to women's health. Anthropologists consider health in a holistic perspective, seeing organic processes as intimately connected to social and cultural dynamics of health experiences. Anthropologists have contributed much to an understanding not only of traditionally female health concerns such as family planning and menopause, but also to the broader structural contextual aspects that shape both women's and men's lives.

One of the first indications I had of this connection between health, livelihoods, and affairs of the heart came from the story of Maman'i Vola who had lived her entire married life in Joffreville. She had several children and even several grandchildren. She made regular trips to Diego Suarez to sell khat, sometimes staying overnight in the city. In what seemed like a sudden and unexpected move, she decided to divorce her husband and move to Diego Suarez to sell khat full time. Maman'i Vola made weekly trips to Joffreville to buy khat both from her ex-husband's small nonirrigated holding and from others. She has been the subject of much gossip and speculation about the circumstances of her leaving her husband: Was it because he was having an affair and she was heartsick and could not stand it anymore, as she claims? Or had Maman'i Vola taken a younger lover with whom she moved to the city, abandoning her childcare and household

Figure 6.1   Many of the khat sellers are women

responsibilities, as many report? Whatever the case, it is clear that the opportunity to sell khat has given women a significant amount of autonomy in this region (see Figure 6.1).

As the example of Maman'i Vola shows, the khat economy is mediated and shaped by gendered interpersonal relationships. They provide the framework for interpreting opportunity, risk, responsibility, and expectations. I quickly learned that in northern Madagascar, the language of partnership, companionship, desire, affect, attachment, and sexual norms strongly shape this framework. This chapter draws on insights into the inextricable relationship between emotion, affect, and economics.

Elizabeth Povinelli writes that "love, intimacy, and sexuality are not about desire, pleasure, or sex per se, but about things like geography, history, culpability, and obligation" (2006:10). Eva Ilouz similarly argues that "emotional and economic discourses and practices mutually shape each other, thus producing what I view as broad, sweeping movement in which affect is made an essential aspect of economic behavior" (2007:5). Kathleen Stewart also notes the centrality of affect in the on-the-ground practices of neoliberalism and globalization (2007). Affective relationships provide the force behind global practices as they are carried out on a daily basis. Stewart challenges deterministic models of human behavior that look to rationality and predictability to explain actions. In embracing the subtlety of ordinary expressions of affect, however, she does not reject the importance of structural factors that shape choices. In writing about agency, for example, she stresses that the ability to make decisions about one's behavior does not equate with unfettered free choice:

> [T]he potential to act always includes the potential to be acted on, or to submit; that the move to gather a self to act is also a move to lose the self; that one choice precludes others; that actions can have unintended and disastrous consequences; and that all agency is frustrated and unstable and attracted to the potential in things.
>
> It's not really about willpower but rather something much more complicated and much more rooted in things. (Stewart 2007:86)

In her work studying American women's career choices, Dorothy Holland (2002 [1992]) and her colleagues studied how cultural ideals of romance shape female U.S. college students' career and educational goals. She found, much as I did, that women spent far less time talking about their careers (or their khat-related economic strategies, in my case) than about their relationships with men. Holland drew on cognitive psychology to identify culturally salient models of male-female relationships and to problematize the extent to which behavior is motivated by these perceptions. She argued that experiences of identity, selfhood, and identification with cultural models coevolve as people learn to interpret their experiences in terms of increasingly compelling cultural models. Following Vygotsky, Holland argues that "thought and feelings, will and motivation, are *formed* as the individual develops" (Holland 2002 [1992]:350, emphasis in original) in the context of social action, through which cultural meanings become salient.

Cultural models "shared, conventional ideas about how the world works" (Holland 2002 [1992]:368) emerge through social interaction (Quinn and Holland 1987). Holland points to cognitive anthropologist Mel Spiro (1982), who identifies levels of cultural salience, arguing that individuals vary in the extent to which cultural models are salient. Only at the highest levels of salience do cultural models guide or instigate action. While the lower levels focus on knowledge acquisition (e.g., how to be attractive to the opposite sex), people at higher levels of mastery engage more creatively in proactively emulating or even challenging cultural proscriptions. Identification with and internalization of a certain cultural model are partly functions of individual choice and partly products of an ineffable process of enculturation, social learning, and mutual accommodation. It would be a mistake to take any cultural model as a thing in and of itself. It is, rather, a framework of meanings on which individuals can draw (Duranti 1997). Cultural models represent patterns of interpretation of lived experiences that emerge through social interaction.

This work on cultural models informs understandings of how lived experiences of culturally mediated desire and attachment provide a framework within which people make economic decisions. Cultural understandings of desire, intimacy, attachment, and parenthood become increasingly compelling as people interact with others who share these frames of interpretation. Cultural models of affect, intimacy, and desire not only shape economic rationality, but actively influence the contours of the economy.

In the case of northern Madagascar, the following sections reveal that no single, uniform set of cultural models of intimacy exists. Western, Christian models promote the nuclear family as the ideal moral as well as economic arrangement. This contrasts with the lived experiences and ideologies of so many women and men in the city and rural areas, who have a great deal of autonomy to divorce, take on lovers, and live as single heads of household. Even within the common population of the north, there are differences and internal contradictions. Most obvious is what may be referred to as a double standard for men and women, where men are free to take on lovers but women are not. Women generally adhere to this dominant cultural proscription, but many do not agree that it is fair. Much of the vitality of the households in northern Madagascar stems from a vivacious interpretation and negotiation of these various and often contradictory cultural models. On-the-ground decisions about involvement with khat are situated at least partially within those debates. Intimacy is not only political but also economic.

The next passages identify cultural models of desire and attachment, with a particular focus on how they shape economic strategies. While many changes related to globalization negatively impact women (Gunewardena and Kingsolver 2007b), khat has provided expanded economic and relationship opportunities for many women in Madagascar. Earlier chapters revealed that one of khat's indirect effects on health is to raise household incomes of producers and traders, while taking money away from consumer households. Income-related health effects include the ability to purchase health care services, medicines, and nutritious foods. Khat has provided an opportunity for financial autonomy for many women producers and traders and constrained the budgets of others who live in a household with khat chewers—generally sons or husbands. Women deal with these opportunities and challenges through a flexible adaptation to changing conditions. The khat economy has grown in the cultural context where it has traditionally been permissible for women to engage in farming and trading and where women have had autonomy in making decisions about marriage, divorce, and sexual relations as single women (Gezon 2000b).

Vadiana: Socially Recognized Partnerships

Marriage (*vadiana*) in northern Madagascar is recognized as an arrangement that symbolizes not only rights to the sexuality of the other partner but also an economic partnership (Gezon 2002). Marriage, as a socially recognized state, may involve merely living together and combining resources. Often it includes formally presenting the partner to one's family, performing a family-level ceremony asking the blessing of the ancestors (*fomba gasy*), or obtaining a marriage certificate that legally recognizes it.

The more subsistence-oriented and geographically isolated areas of the north practice forms of marriage and sexual partnership that provide an important part of the framework for understanding marriage norms generally throughout the north, whether in villages or urban areas (Gezon 2002). Even where these patterns are not practiced, people tend to point to them as a normative reference. I first learned of these norms and practices in my research in the rice-growing Ankarana region begun in the 1990s. First marriages are often arranged and involve a bride price. On the western side of the Ankarana massif, where I conducted research throughout the 1990s, young men and their parents would identify a suitable young woman (in her early to mid-teenage years)—often chosen for her likelihood of sharing values of hard work and cooperation. They contacted her parents, and, with their consent, the prospective parents-in-law arranged a formal meeting between the young couple in her home. Based on this brief encounter, the woman could approve or reject the match. If approved, the prospective parents-in-law arranged a bride price, consisting of a head of cattle and money.

On the day of the marriage ceremony, or the day the bride is brought to live with the husband (*magnenga*), the groom also traditionally presents the bride with fine clothing and gold jewelry. Her parents provide her home furnishings, including a wooden bedstead, chairs, and kitchenware. The ceremony consists of the groom's arrival in the woman's village, accompanied by numerous family members and a means of transportation for getting her goods back to the nuptial home. The woman, scared and often crying, has been prepared to meet her husband by her female kin and one or two representatives of the groom's female kin. They bathe her and braid her hair in a special way on this day. She dresses in fine clothing and jewelry and covers her face with a cloth. The groom's family takes her away, and she then formally leaves her parent's household. When she arrives at her new home, she and her groom ritually share their first meal.

Despite the major material and emotional investment in this marital arrangement, a woman's obligation to stay married and keep her bride price and marital gifts is only one year. One young woman, Grace, who was fifteen at the time of my first research in the mid-1990s, told me of looking forward to the prospect of her first, arranged marriage because of all the goods she would get. She considered it shameful and unfortunate that her cousin had gotten pregnant before she was married and would never have the experience of a formal marriage. Grace was not afraid of ending up with someone she did not like because she realized she could leave. When I returned one and a half years later, she had indeed gotten married, borne a child, and divorced. She had left her husband's village to return to her father's compound. These marriages are often stable, however, and some couples stay together for decades. This practice of a negotiated and openly celebrated first marriage remains strong in many of the most rural and agriculturally self-sufficient areas of northern Madagascar (Feeley-Harnik 1991:277–297).

After a first marriage and divorce, and for those who never went through the traditional marriage rituals, it is socially acceptable for women to set up their own household, either alone or with the children they are caring for. If the father recognizes a child as his own, he may take the child to live with him and his patrilineal relatives. This happened to Grace, whose first child left her home to live with his father's family after he was weaned. By the early 2000s, Grace was raising her brother's child and one of her own.

Despite the social acceptance of singleness for women, many of the people I met in the course of this study of khat were married by local custom, though very few had had their marriages recognized legally by the state. One woman acknowledged that her husband had gone to her parents and given them money because he was not interested in an official legal marriage. Her interpretation of this was that it was difficult to get a divorce with a legal marriage. Another man corroborated this, saying that he and his third wife do not trust each other enough to commit to something so binding.

Many of those in the urban area of Diego Suarez and the rural Amber Mountain khat-growing regions have participated in a traditional form of marriage ritual, even if they are migrants to the city from different ethnic groups and their parents live elsewhere. An interview with one farmer in Joffreville revealed that he and his wife came from different northern cities and had met in Diego Suarez. He had asked her parent's for the right to marry her. He provided a bride price of money but no cattle. They commemorated their marriage with a small feast in Diego Suarez. Roberto explained that he had met his third and (at the time) current wife, Katia, in Diego Suarez at a disco. He told her about Joffreville and she was interested in checking it out. She liked it and stayed. They have three children together. After living together about two years, they visited her father in a different northern city (Vohemar). While they did not perform any traditional rituals, he said that he did give her father some money as a way of asking him to recognize their marriage. For another couple, recently divorced, the man came from the south of the country and the woman from Joffreville with parents of Merina (*boursane*) ancestry. He asked her father if he could marry her, gave money, and they performed the father's family marriage ritual.

There is great fluidity in the movement of people between the cities and the rural areas, and marriage is a primary mechanism for this. Several women interviewed revealed that they had moved to Joffreville (a khat-growing village with many immigrants) from the more isolated rural areas with the intent of finding a husband. All had been successful. Some moved to Joffreville; others took their husbands to live in their rural hamlets. A young man of around twenty years living just outside Diego Suarez on the road to the airport was divorced, but he and his wife had had a traditional marriage ceremony (*mangenga*) similar to that described above. He had given money but no cattle as a bride price. They were both from the same township. At the time of the interview, he was in the process of getting remarried to a young woman from near Joffreville—a woman who was kin to his older brother's wife, who had also grown up in and around Joffreville. An older woman, Mary, grew up in the khat-growing area of Amber Mountain, but was married in a traditional way to a man from Diego who came to get her with in a dramatic display with two vehicles. He treated her poorly, and they were soon divorced. Since then, she has had a total of nine husbands and has gone back and forth from living in Diego to rural Amber Mountain to the island of Nosy Be. At the time I met her, she was living in Diego with her ninth husband.

These stories reveal the fluidity and instrumentality of marriages in khat country. People meet in a variety of ways, from arrangements by parents to casual first encounters at the urban disco. There is great fluidity in the movement of people between the city and the nearby rural areas to take advantage of economic opportunities. Immigrants are often incorporated into the local economy through these flexible marriage alliances.

The Ideal: *Fanaraka Anjara*

One particularly pervasive cultural model of intimacy lies in the concept of *anjara*, translated as fate, or destiny. People conceive of their *anjara* in an integrated context of *vadiana*, love (*fitiavana*), procreation, and material success. Feeley-Harnik (1991), writing about rural Sakalava in northern Madagascar, found a similar phenomenon. She writes: "There was a sense in which searching for a spouse epitomized searching for a destiny (*mitady anjara*)" (p. 277). In my own research, I learned that an appropriate way to ask someone if they had a "good" relationship (*vadiana*) was to ask if their destiny coincided with that of their partner. "*Fanaraka anjara izihay*" (Our destinies coincide [or go together, or follow alongside each other]) was the mark of a successful relationship. For men and women alike, it was indicated by the presence of offspring as well as material evidence of financial success, often in the form of property ownership and the construction of a house. Getting to that point of success through complementary livelihood strategies was the ongoing process of couple-dom. Many said that they would be capable of achieving material success by themselves, but that having a monogamous partner, a complement, was the ideal.

This ideal partnership provides insight into local modes of survival as well as local concepts of economies of scale and efficiency. This connection between the economics of survival and the cultural context of marriage and sexuality reveals the ground-level workings of the local economy. Not all the examples below are about khat, per se, but they reveal a set of ideas that frame economic as well as interpersonal relations. Roberto and Katia, for example, have what each of them described separately as an ideal marriage situation from an economic standpoint. Roberto worked for the national park service and grew khat. Katia purchased khat wholesale locally and combined it with her and Roberto's own khat to sell in the city of Diego Suarez. They have what many consider to be an ideal marriage situation, where a couple's economic activities complement each other. Another local woman had a similar arrangement with her husband. She collected vegetables in Joffreville and used her husband's *taxi brousse* (a small truck with a cover over the back for transporting people and goods) to transport her produce. Since transport is the major hindrance to moving goods out of the rural areas, this arrangement worked well.

Farmers expressed an appreciation for the marriage partnership. They said that farm work gets done more quickly when there are two, and if one gets sick, there is still someone to look after things. In the rural khat-growing areas, it is common for the husband to undertake most of the growing tasks while the wife takes the khat to market to sell. This kind of partnership increases household profit by eliminating the money that would normally go to wholesale traders. Several expressed appreciation that they and their spouse share the same attitudes and values and that even when they disagree and argue, they can work things out to come up with the best plan. People engaged in entrepreneurial pursuits either in the city or village also have an appreciation of partnership. One man living in Joffreville who owns a bar said that he could not do it without his wife, and without the bar, he would not be financially successful. A spice seller in the market shared that she and her partner each work independently, but they pool their money to buy things of value, such as land and a house. She said that as long as people work well together, they stay together. One woman who worked as a prostitute with primarily foreign clients also had a relationship with a local man, whom she referred to as "*love-anaka*," or "my love." She explained that they each get money where they can, and he understands what she needs to do to earn money. Each of these is an example of frequently heard stories.

There are also sources of tension that threaten this fragile state of *fanaraka anjara*. While some marriages last decades, many more end quickly. Serial monogamy is the norm. Sources of tension are often children from previous relationships, who are seen as impeding efforts at getting ahead. This is especially the case with the man's children, whom his wife will be obligated to care for. In addition to the economic and time burdens, feelings of jealousy arise either on the part of the new wife or the child's mother. In Roberto and Katia's case, for example, one of his children by another woman lives with them. Roberto reported that Katia is convinced that the child's mother wishes her ill and uses sorcery to curse her.

Another source of tension often noted in the city is that one of the two, either the husband or wife, likes to go to the disco and socialize with friends (*misoma la vie*, or play at life), where they spend money and possibly engage in extramarital affairs. This is particularly the case for young married people. Some men also have the sense that women only care about their money and do not love them.

Similarly, some men feel that women are too demanding and too expensive to keep. In one interview, a woman complained that many men do not even want a wife in the house. Her husband responded that it is because women are demanding and expensive. He stated that it is more expensive to have a woman in the house. She disagreed, stating that a woman will not ask for things each day if they live together and they begin working together in a complementary way. The husband then revealed that many of his friends would rather spend their money on alcohol and casual encounters with women at discos than have a wife. Some men who are married still sneak off to go to the disco, meeting up with friends and sometimes other women.[1]

Deuxième Bureau: Extra-Partnership Affairs

Another cultural model, at times at odds with that of *anjara*, provides a framework for thinking about and engaging in extramarital sexual relationships. Perhaps the greatest marital tension is the male tendency to have another woman. Sexuality is gendered in that women's rights to men's sexuality are far more tenuous than are men's rights to women's. For men, having multiple sex partners after marriage can be a sign of prestige and material success, even though men tend to keep their affairs as secret as possible. Men may either engage in casual sexual liaisons or, more commonly, develop a more steady relationship with a particular woman, who is referred to as a *deuxième bureau*, or second office. When speaking either abstractly or in terms of their own experiences, nearly all people—especially women—cited the *deuxième bureau* as an important cause of tension and breakups. Many women state that it is nearly inevitable that a husband will have extramarital affairs. Katia noted, as did many people, that men tend to see other women if the men have money. She noted that she knew that her husband did this.

In local understandings, what makes a man's extramarital affairs tolerable is if he provides material compensation to his wife. Katia said that Roberto had bought her furniture to make up for it. This practice is so common and considered so thoroughly to demonstrate the man's love and compensation for his dalliance that women and men alike often consider a woman to be in the wrong or unwise to leave a man who materially compensates her for his transgressions. In addition to being compensated, women and men alike acknowledged that men with regular employment often give their salary to their wife and use any extra money they earn for their *deuxième bureau*. One woman, for example, said that her deceased husband used to steal paint from his employer to make his extra money. A retired woman in Joffreville explained that she had her husband prove to her that he was giving her his entire salary; if he found other money and had a *deuxième bureau* that was his business. She knew he had had *deuxième bureaux*, but since he was discrete about it, she paid no attention.

Some men do not compensate their wives, however. Some women tolerate this, but others divorce. One older woman, a khat seller in Joffreville, explained that her ex-husband had many *deuxième bureaux* but he was a poor farmer and did not have any money to give her. He would leave her for up to three months at a time, and she kept taking him back. She did eventually divorce him when he became mentally ill. Another woman living in the rural zone surrounding Joffreville described her first husband and their eventual divorce. She had never seen her husband before marrying him in the traditional way. He had many women and did not give her clothes or money. She said that she was embarrassed to go to ceremonies because of her clothes, so she had to borrow some from others. After three years and one child, she decided to leave him one day when he had left for Diego. She took their child, but he came to take the child back and told her she could either come back or he would take the child permanently. She left him and lived with her grandmother, who had raised her, and helped with the farming. Three years later, she married her current husband whose father owns 160 hectares of land here on which they grow khat and other crops. She said they have a good relationship and she likes that he asks her opinion on things.

Despite the general tolerance for a man who can properly manage his *deuxième bureau*, some women leave their husband when they find out he has been unfaithful. Razoky, for example, an older single woman who worked as a domestic, told me that she left her husband because he always had a *deuxième bureau* and she got sick of it. As mentioned above, Mary was on her ninth marriage. She exclaimed, as she made a kicking motion with her foot: "As soon as he goes with another woman, I kick him out!" Her first marriage was to an older man in an arranged marriage. She told me that after the birth of their first child, he began an affair with their laundress. The woman, being considerably older than Mary, began to treat her condescendingly. Mary eventually left out of fear that the woman would use black magic to kill her. At first her mother told her to return to her husband. Only after Mary revealed the extent of her fears did her mother understand.

These affairs are meant to be kept secret from wives and from any public acknowledgment. Very few men were willing to acknowledge to me that they or anyone they were willing to name had ever had a *deuxième bureau*. Some even expressed personal distaste to me, as a foreign female researcher, at the idea of having one. One retired petty bureaucrat living just outside Diego Suarez implied that he had had them but was tired of it. He explained that it is *mavesatra*, or heavy to have one. "*Ndre pont tsy mitsaka*" (You can't even cross a bridge), he explained.

I assumed that meant that it was a constant hassle juggling several women. At the time of the interview, he had been married to the same woman for twenty-five years. Another man from the rural area surrounding Joffreville said that having a *deuxième bureau* makes children disobedient and jeopardizes their future. In another interview, a Joffreville farmer stated his formal opinion that men should not have a *deuxième bureau* because it is disrespectful to the wife. Another man in the house, someone visiting who appeared to have been drinking heavily and was therefore perhaps less guarded in his speech, piped up and insisted that as long as the woman in the house gets money, she shouldn't care about *deuxième bureaux.*

While some men expressed disapproval at the idea of having a *deuxième bureau,* others discussed its allure. They explained that having a *deuxième bureau* was a sign of success. One group of young men explained to me that there is a popular song with the lyrics: "*Mampirafy donia izio, tsy mampirafy soboko.*" The song tells of how good it is to have more than one partner: You enjoy life when you have more than one partner, whereas you just sit there if not. It assumes that "*misoma la vie* (playing at life, 'partying')" is a good to be cultivated. People generally recognize that only people with money have *deuxième bureaux,* and having money is a sign of success. A group of young men told me that among themselves, men brag about having *deuxième bureaux,* which encourages and sanctions this behavior.

While men's affairs are officially secret, they are also highly condoned among men and generally socially tolerated. Women's affairs, on the other hand, were more uniformly condemned and regarded as shameful and harmful to children. They were much more likely to end in social censure and divorce since there is no form of socially acceptable compensation. Some called on a moral injunction, linking a woman's sexual responsibility to that of motherhood. Many felt that a woman should stay with the father of her children. Maman'i Vola, for example, whose story opened this chapter, was suspected to have had a *deuxième bureau* and to eventually leave her husband because of this. People often commented on her actions as frivolous, irresponsible, and selfish.

On a pragmatic level, having multiple "spouses" allows men to diversify their economic opportunities. At one point, one man had a wife in the city and a *deuxième bureau* named Panda in the rural area near the forest in Joffreville. Since his work took him between the city and Joffreville, this was convenient for him. His wife in town provided a base for managing the taxi they owned and their investment in real estate (they built a home out of corrugated tin in the expanding southern part of town), and the one in Joffreville helped manage their plans of investing in ecotourism locally. Eventually, he left his city wife and moved in with the woman in Joffreville and continued to build on their ecotourism activities. It is not infrequent for men to use their *deuxième bureau* as a base for diversified economic activities.

From the perspective of a married woman, their husband's extramarital affairs make emotional and financial security more precarious. The ideal of working together to invest and get ahead financially is jeopardized by the threat that the man will either leave for another woman, or perhaps worse, drain the household budget to finance his relations with other women. This is a source not only of practical insecurity, but also of frequent and often intense emotional trauma. The women in the above anecdote, Panda, for one, frequently wept in despair about the fact that her partner kept telling her that he'd left his wife in the city, only to learn that he had not done so. The formality of the interview format disappeared as her sister, Panda, and I shared a bottle of wine in her home late at night, as she revealed the depth of her anguish. She and countless other women routinely visit diviners who read their fortunes and give them herbal remedies to rebuild their sense of well-being (*mangamboatra saingy*) and attract the attention of those they are in love with through herbal remedies. The economic side of *vadiana* (loosely, marriage) is intricately interwoven with the affective experiences that powerfully color the daily happenings of social life.

Panda's case reminds us that it would be naive to forget that women also participate in extramarital affairs as lovers, as *deuxième bureaux*. From this broader perspective, the option not to be married, combined with the opportunities women have to be proactive in entrepreneurial pursuits, gives women livelihood choices and options for autonomy. Katia, for example, was aware that staying with her philandering husband was her decision and that she had the ability to make a good living without him if she needed to. Maman'i Vola also divorced her husband in part to be able to base herself in the city, where she preferred to live, and where she sold her khat daily.

The seemingly contradictory cultural models regarding intimate partners—that of *fanaraka anjara* and *deuxième bureau*—bring about a great amount of interpersonal tension, but they also lay the foundation for a high degree of livelihood flexibility, opening up spaces for economic innovation and experimentation. The khat economy has perhaps grown as quickly as it has in part due to these flexible affective-economic relationships. The next section continues this discussion, focusing specifically on the opportunities and constraints for single women.

Being Single

Being a single woman is socially acceptable in both rural and urban areas of coastal northern Madagascar. An unmarried woman may have one of several kinds of relationships with men. On one end of the spectrum is the *mangangy tovo*, which loosely translates as a sexually active unmarried woman with no ongoing commitment to any particular man. The implication is that such women will support themselves at least in part through their sexual relations with men and the gifts and money these men give them. In the village setting, these women receive male guests who generally arrive after dark and leave before light and who give the women gifts of either money or goods. While others in the village may happen to know the identity of these men, theirs is not a socially recognized relationship and it is not discussed openly. One reason for the secrecy is that it is sometimes prominent local married men who visit these women. If they begin seeing each other more regularly, the man may begin to compensate her with gifts as well as money. The woman may at some point decide to be exclusive with the man, even though their relationship is not socially recognized and they are not living together. It is generally treated as less of a secret at this point. If the couple decides to move in together, they will generally make their relationship socially known by formally introducing the partner to family members, especially parents. There is no exchange of bride price or expensive gifts. At this point, they are socially considered to be married.

As this account suggests, the exchange of sexual services for money has been common in the rural life in northern Madagascar. There is no moral condemnation. Rather, people see it as a legitimate way for a woman to supplement her living, given the relative difficulty for women in undertaking traditional farming activities (Gezon 2002). During a conversation with one woman in the Antankarana village who was describing her life as a *mangangy tovo* before she got married, she proclaimed: "I have to live, don't I?" As Feeley-Harnik suggests, this cultural model of sexuality derives from gendered ideas about making a living. Writing about the region of Majunga, a northern coastal city, she found that "both women and men saw men as living more from work, while women lived more from gifts, especially the gifts they received from men" (1991:280). This is the case for both single and married women.

Jennifer Cole (2009), writing about the central coastal city of Tamatave, identified these kinds of exchanges as taking place within a framework where, unlike the Western ideal of selfless love, love and affect are not abstracted from practical and material considerations. In her analysis, she counters common perceptions of these kinds of interactions as representing the heartless nature of African women who engage in purely instrumental relationships with men. Cole draws on Mauss's assessment of the social role of gifts to point out the reciprocal nature of these arrangements. She also cites literature that points out how economic relations shape the meaning and experiences of love, arguing that "emotions and materiality might, in fact, be deeply intertwined" (2009:111).

Meanings of love and practicality shift as conditions change. As Diego Suarez formed in the late 1880s, women moved there, bringing with them their attitudes toward sexuality. The city came into being when the French established it as a military base and administrative center. From the beginning, it was a multi-ethnic town, attracting Creoles (farmers of French descent) from Réunion Island and Ile Sainte Marie, escaped slaves (called Makoa) from elsewhere in Madagascar, those of Merina descent from the central plateau of Madagascar, those from the Comoros Islands, and even people from local rural areas looking for an opportunity to seek their fortune.

According to the lay scholar Cassam Aly (2004), while local men at first disdained the city, the women did not. He explains that because of local marriage customs that permit women to divorce after one year, there were numerous single women in Diego Suarez who were not tied down to the rural villages. Not only were the rural women single and free to travel, but single women were expected—even in the rural areas—to make a living, in part through their remunerated sexual relations with men (Gezon 2002). Aly explains that in the precolonial 1880s, these single women traveled to the new town in search of distraction and luxury items such as cloth and jewelry. They found employment as domestics and sexual partners, much as described by Luise White (1990) for colonial Nairobi. Because of the scarcity of European women, these women often lived with men in these domestic cum sexual partner relationships.

My interactions with older women revealed that these relationships were often highly enjoyable for Malagasy women, involving opportunities for entertainment that were not available to those who do not associate with the foreigners. I met several old women in Diego and in the rural areas who recounted with laughter their stories of riding in cars and juggling several men at a time, gleefully recalling this bygone era. In addition to providing immediate pleasure, these relationships allowed women to earn enough money to obtain land and build a house in their home village or in the nearest town to which they would return when they got older. Many did just that.

From a colonial economic and social perspective, these relationships facilitated the social reproduction of the men stationed there. From a French nationalistic perspective, involving identity, affect, and desire, these relationships raised fears of assimilation—that the men would become so ensconced in the native milieu as to lose the sensibilities of their supposedly superior civilization (Saada 2005; Stoler 2002). A postcard from Diego Suarez without a date, but seemingly from the early twentieth century at the latest, both denigrates these Malagasy women, or *ramatoas*, as Other, and extols their virtues as nursemaids and objects of desire. One postcard, written by a certain Habouzit, reads:

If you want good game,

True clothed monkeys,

That we call Ramatoa,

Dressed in frilly clothes;

In Tanambao [one of the *quartiers populaires*/working class neighborhoods of Diego Suarez] we find what we want

For poor and vain men

For tooth aches

It is surprising

There is no need for medicine,

These wise women

Like pictures

Are good for giving fillings.

Refrain:

Ramatoa, Ramatoa go

To give me pleasure

Save your memories

Ah! Ramatoa, Ramatoa go

Close your hut of bamboo

Of you I become drunk

Postcards such as these, whimsical as they may have seemed (and distasteful as this one appears today), reminded men of their primary connection to Europe by encouraging them to disparage their relationships with Malagasy women. Rather than becoming indigenous or remaining entirely European, however, the men and their Malagasy women often developed hybrid identities (Saada 2005). Ann Stoler (2002) has called attention to the sexual politics of colonial empire, where who has sex with whom is carefully socially engineered and monitored, as is the question of what to do with offspring of various kinds of couplings. In this context, race, intimacy, and state projects of economic imperialism and political citizenship are intricately linked.

The women purchased clothing and jewelry that allowed them to culti-vate a new urban style, enviable among their Malagasy neighbors—they were neither entirely rural Malagasy nor French. They developed tastes and domestic sensibilities grounded in their Malagasy upbringing but influenced by their colonial associations. Many older women tell stories of having enjoyed accompanying men in their youth. Razoky, for example, had two children, but had also had three abortions, claiming that she did not want children because she was enjoying life too much to want to raise them. With a mischievous smile, she explained: "*Tia la vie loatra*" ([I] like[d] life too much). "La vie" is taken from the French word for life, but in Malagasy it has vernacular connotations and might be likened to saying "I liked to party too much."

What this brief look at colonial history suggests is that Diego Suarez has provided economic and sexual opportunities for Malagasy women since its inception in the 1880s. Similar approaches to sexuality and livelihoods predate the development of colonial city and continue to exist in the cities and the rural areas in the north (Cole 2010). Being a single, sexually active woman is not only socially acceptable but also highly respected. In fact, I was often told that a woman who does not demand some kind of immediate material compensation for sexual relations with a man who is not her boyfriend or husband is shameless and has no self-respect. She is the one given a derogative moniker (*barbo*), with connotations of being a "slut." In response to the interview question: "How do you decide whom to marry?" one woman responded: "He gives you things, and then love comes. Money and love go together" (*tia miaraka vola*).

Women who regularly engage in transactional sex, seeking partners in bars and night clubs (often referred to as "prostitutes"), are called "*makorely*," from the French *la maquerelle* ("madame," female keeper of a prostitution house) and *mirondy* (to make the rounds) (Feeley-Harnik 1991:295 and n. 62, p. 560). Many of these seek sexual and affective relations with foreigners, especially European men. Being a *makorely* has somewhat more negative connotations than a *manangy taovo*, but tolerance is common in Diego Suarez and there is a high level of social acceptance. What they have in common, however, is that they both receive gifts (often money) in exchange for sexual relationships.

A source of income for many single women in Diego continues to be the money they get from the men with whom they have sexual relations—be they causal encounters or steadier, long-term liaisons. Whether women are seeking European or local men, one way to meet them is at one of Diego's many discos—some of which target the expatriate crowd, but many of which are frequented almost entirely by locals. These women at times develop long-term relationships with the men they find at discos, and some even get married and move to Europe with their husbands. Other women, not necessarily *makorely*, get to know foreign men through written correspondence and leave Madagascar to get married (Cole 2010).

Those who primarily seek local men may invite them into their own home instead of going to a hotel, and they often engage in this alongside other financial pursuits. They may be referred to as a *mangangy tovo*, often translated simply as *"célibataire,"* or unmarried woman. Their liaisons may also turn into longer term relationships, but even if so, they may have simultaneous relationships with more than one man, especially if the men are married. Razoky, an older woman still working as a domestic, explained how she once had one married (Malagasy) man who came to her house, and after that she would go to a hotel to meet the director of the bank. She proclaimed that *"Lehilahy iraiky tsy mamelon'tena!"* (One man isn't enough to make a living). As this anecdote suggests, the line between *makorely* and *mangangy tovo* is actually blurry in practice.

Some unmarried women remain with one man, even if they are his *deuxième bureau*. The practical advantage of this is that the man will generally pay for all or most of a woman's expenses, including rent, food, clothing, etc. This arrangement is more precarious interpersonally, however, since the wife may become jealous and resentful and try to harm her. On an emotional level, the *deuxième bureau* may become strongly attached to the man and become jealous of the wife. As reported above, many married women report being afraid that their husband's *deuxième bureau* will try to harm them.

Whether because of financial resentment or affective attachment, emotions run high among people involved in *deuxième bureaux*, and domestic violence is not unheard of. Razoky was keenly aware of the emotional pitfalls of relationships with married men. She told me that she had been in love with her first and only husband and had suffered greatly when he went off with other women. She finally tired of it and left him. Since then, she explained, she made sure that she did not fall in love again. Anytime she began to feel close to someone, she would leave him. She never wanted to feel longing (*ngoma*) for a man again. Her strategy of being with several men at a time and having few children was partly driven by financial practicality and partly by emotional pragmatism and lifestyle decisions. For many men and women alike, livelihood choices are not merely mechanical responses to economic cost-benefit calculations.

Stella, on the other hand, had been the *deuxième bureau* of a Malagasy ship captain for five years in 2004. They have two children together. She works at a local fish cannery. Stella told me that his wife knows about it and is angry. He left his wife once, but she came back to him, Stella imagined, because she still loved him and because they have children together. Stella explained that when he is in town he sleeps in her house and not with his wife, although he still gives his wife money. In telling me about this, Stella seemed physically tired and emotionally exhausted by this arrangement. She said that she does not love him anymore, and they fight often (apparently about the fact that he is still married). She does not want to leave him because she doesn't want him to take the children and she is still hoping that he will build her a house in her father's village. She used to go to the disco and have casual boyfriends when he was gone, but she is older now and tired of it.

With regard to making a living through other kinds of labor, it is generally acceptable and even expected that women—married or single—will work. The most common activities for Malagasy women living in the *quartiers populaires* are working for others doing domestic chores (e.g., cooking, house cleaning, washing clothes) and selling either from their home or at the market. Some of the older women discussed how it was easier to get domestic labor during the colonial era. One older single woman in Joffreville, recognized by others in town as being poor, noted that when the French left, she returned to Joffreville, where she worked as a day laborer on others' farms.

Some women choose to be single and feel quite strongly about it being a better choice than being with a man. One relatively successful single woman (by the standards of her peers in the *quartier populaire*) owned a neighborhood boutique and bar. She said in an interview that she did not want a husband or children. Men always have *deuxième bureaux*, she explained, and those women can bring a wife harm. Another woman, a relatively prosperous khat seller living in Joffreville, explained that many married men have approached her, wanting her for a *deuxième bureau*. She said that she had no interest in developing a relationship with a man because he would be likely to want to get some of her money. She would rather pursue her livelihood alone. Mary, the woman who has had nine husbands, acknowledged that even though it was considerably easier financially with an employed husband, she would not be worried about making a living if she were single again. She could always go back to her village home, if necessary. She talked about the importance of women being economically independent to free them from the constraints of having to have a husband. She praised local efforts at securing public works projects that would employ women in manual labor.

Many women considered being single to be preferable if it was possible to make a living without a man. Recall that this view of relationships exists side by side with the view that marriage is an ideal platform for a financially beneficial partnership and that marriage is the ideal context for raising children. Ideologies of marriage are fluid, and there is a range of views and practices that locals interpret as reasonable. Because of the demands of farming and the flexible opportunities in the city, it may be that more rural people embrace marriage as a livelihood strategy while women in the city embrace the benefits of being single. But in all locations, cognitive frameworks explicitly link financial practicalities with affairs of the heart. The following story of Francine's life illustrates how these ideas inform flexible livelihoods, interpersonal and affective strategies, and states of being.

Flexibility: A Life Story

The story of Francine illustrates how people adapt to difficult, changing, and unpredictable economic and relationship situations through *flexibility and diversification.* Worldviews come into being through a process that could perhaps be referred to as cultural modeling. The lives of individuals illustrate how cultural modeling takes place, as people engage with received and internalized cultural understandings in light of their own life circumstances. Through the examination of a single life, we see how cultural understandings become motivations, which, in turn, instigate action (Holland 2002 [1992]). More specifically, Francine's life story reveals her strategies for engaging with khat production and trade. What her story suggests more broadly is that these economic options—continuously filtered through the lens of interpersonal attachments—offer women relative independence.

Francine was a young woman in her late twenties when I got to know her in 2004. She was born and raised on Amber Mountain in the most rural and isolated part of Joffreville, near the official entrance to the park, amid khat fields. She was of Betsileo and Merina descent, and her ancestors have lived in the area for several generations and were buried there. Many members of her family had worked for the park or in tourism.

Francine lived in Diego Suarez when I met her and began to work with her. She was not highly educated and had worked at a variety of jobs both in Joffreville and in the city, including farmer, domestic, cook on forest-based research and tourist expeditions, ecological guide, and trader. She worked for me for several months in 2004 as a primary informant and research assistant. Besides being a lively and engaging person, her life captured the dynamics of flexible adaptation to changing interpersonal and economic situations. She had been married and widowed; she maintained ties to the khat-growing rural area; and she was continually seeking out new ways of finding personal satisfaction and making economic ends meet—and often the two were intricately linked.

Even though I lived with her and spoke with her nearly every day, I formally recorded an interview with her toward the end of my stay. In that format, I was able to ask about and capture her own words in describing so many aspects of her life that I had been getting to know slowly over several months in the course of everyday conversation.

Showing Love and Building Assets: Buying Land

Francine was married and lived with her husband, Charles, in Diego Suarez. He worked at the port authority and had a decent salary by local standards. They met in 1995, at which time she was his *deuxième bureau*. Charles was her only lover until 1999, when she sensed his affections had turned away from her and he began seeing other women. She began seeing a French man until he left for France one year later. During the time she was with the French man, she continued to see her future husband, but not regularly. After the French man left in 2000, she and Charles reconciled. He had divorced his wife, and he and Francine got married in Joffreville, at her parents' house. She moved moved into his house in Diego Suarez. About eighteen months after they married, he began seeing one of his old mistresses again. He died about a year before I met Francine. From her telling, he was brutally murdered out of jealousy by his long-time mistress.

His marriage with Francine had been wrought with tension. He had had many affairs, which he concealed with only the minimal formality. Francine talked of having suffered greatly because of this. She told stories of having gone to his mistress's house in the middle of the night demanding that her husband come home, screaming at the woman, and nearly getting herself arrested for the disturbance she caused. She reports having physically harmed him in anger, but he apparently never hurt her. In recalling this period of her life, the intensity of her feelings was apparent.

She explained that he after she caught him at his mistress's house one night, he was afraid to come back into their house. The reason was "because I had hit him with a piece of wood [on his leg] and it hurt him badly. Yeah, that is the way to quickly deal with men who fool around. I hit him hard" (*fòtony izy navy takako nivangoako vango kakazo etonazy nivonto karaha igny. Ia, zegny eky malaky aminakahy izy koa lehilahy maherihery andra eto fo ataoko mare hoe*).

What made the offenses of his affairs tolerable, she explained, was that each time she got upset, he would buy her something of value, even if she hit him. Each time, he would apologize and then go the bank to give her money to buy whatever she wanted. Francine described how her husband would take out one to two hundred dollars worth of local currency—a significant amount equaling at least two months' salary. She purchased items such as furniture and gold jewelry with the money he gave her in compensation. As explained above, these gifts let the community know that the man still loves (*tia*) his wife. The gift erases the social shame she feels, knowing others are gossiping about her and speculating about the nature of their relationship. For Francine, it restored her own feelings of love (*fitiavana*) for him. She also recounted that she believed that the mistress who had seduced and eventually killed him had sought the help of dark magic. Her husband agreed with this assessment, and they had even sought out counter-treatment from a diviner, but to no avail. He continued to see the mistress, and she eventually stabbed and maimed his body when he was too drunk to resist. He died of these wounds.

It seemed to me that Francine stayed in the relationship in part out of a deep sense of affection for him. She acknowledged that she had truly loved him and felt he had loved her (*misy fitiavagna; mifankatia*). I asked her during our recorded interview how she knew he loved her. First, she explained that it is a sign of love if you miss someone, or feel a longing for them (*ngoma*) when they are not present. No matter how long you have known each other—be it several years or a few months, "*Anao tsy maintsy* ngôma fo!" (You just miss them!), she exclaimed emphatically.

The interpretation of the reasons for their *fitiavana* is telling about local understandings of love and livelihood.

> *Ary fiheritreretako izy ndrêky, tegna nampangôma izy, nanambady izy voalohany, rô tsisy raha voafôrognondrô koa tsy rô niteraka fo; nisaraka rô. . . .* Nanambady izy faharoe, tsisy raha voaforognondrô fa rô niteraka araiky avy eo rô nisaraka. Zahay ndrêky zegny fivadiany zahay tsy niteraka fa zahay hitako mba nafôrofôrogno raha ely. Zahay nahazo aomby, zahay nivanga tany. . . . Nahavory vôla zahay nivanga tôles.

What I think really made him long for [*ngoma*] me was that in his first marriage, the only thing they accomplished was to have a child. They broke up. With his second wife, they also did not accomplish anything besides having one child, and they broke up. We, on the other hand, we had no children but accomplished something together. We bought cattle and land. . . . We put our money together to buy sheets of tin.

Francine has never had any children. This was a cause of great concern and some distress to her. Nevertheless, she was confident that her and her husband's industriousness not only made up for it, but was in the end a more positive indication of the strength of their love for each other:

> *ndrê izy vakivava nivolagna fa tegna anao hoy izy anjarako. Anao zaza marigny volagniny fa, naro vadiko volagniny fa tsy nahavita hevitry karaha hevitrinao'ty hoy izy.*

He even swore to me that "It's really you," he said, "who is my destiny/fate" (*anjara* means destiny/fate, and *–ko* indicates the personal possessive). "You are very young," he said, "but I have had many wives," he said, "and [I] have never been able to put my ideas together with someone as well as I can with you," he said.

The purchase of land was a marker of marital success, made particularly important by the extent of her husband's philandering. Part of Francine's objective in buying the land was to make a sound financial investment, and part of it was to make a public statement about the nature of her relationship with her husband. They used their joint resources to buy nonirrigated land for growing khat in Joffreville, near where she grew up. They planted the khat, and she was able to hire a family member to tend her khat field in her absence. Her khat was coming to maturity when I was there in 2004, and she was beginning to get some return on her investment in the form of khat receipts.

Francine's case diverts from the marital ideal explained above, especially as it ended in the tragedy of murder related to the jealousy of a *deuxième bureau*. It illustrates, however, how people negotiate and adapt to difficult, changing, and unpredictable economic situations and intimate relationships, showing how the two domains of livelihood and love overlap. Despite the tragedy of the *deuxième bureau*, or perhaps because of her decision to purchase land and materials with her compensation money, the relationship between Francine and her husband resulted in accumulated wealth and conformed to the ideal of a matched destiny.

Regarding khat specifically, Francine's story illustrates how khat provides opportunities for women not just as traders, but also as landowners, even in absentia. Whether women live on site or away, they can be entrepreneurs by hiring people to work their khat. The nature of khat production, which requires less day-to-day management and is arguably less labor intensive than farming, requires only some weeding, monitoring for theft, and harvesting. The more management- and labor-intensive activities of regular weeding, regulating irrigation, and applying pest control substances need not be undertaken for khat production to be successful.

Relationship Ideals: Building a Home

At the time of the interview, Francine was in a new but serious relationship with a young man named Richard. She discussed the pressures they were feeling to get married and form a household, expressing some ambivalence while stating her intention of moving in with him and eventually getting married according to local customs. Her deliberations and explanations reveal important aspects of local relationship ideals—specifically, the relationship between marriage and material goals. This case points out the ideals of joint strategies for building financial assets as a couple, while maintaining some independence for the woman. It provides an additional way of understanding how *fanaraka anjara* involves not only intimate relationship ideals but also economic ones.

Francine's first words in the interview were of caution—that forming a household is a serious commitment and both people needed to be ready to move beyond jealousy. She also was aware that the woman who raised her fiancé— Richard's paternal uncle's wife, whom he calls "*mamaely*,"[2] or "little mother," was skeptical of her because she'd been widowed. His father's sister (called *angovavy*), on the other hand, who also lived in the same compound, was encouraging the union. His *mamaely* was also her younger sister's mother-in-law: Her sister had married this woman's oldest son and lived in their compound on the outskirts of Diego Suarez. Francine's boyfriend also lived in the compound and would take Francine to live with him there when they married.

Despite Francine's misgivings, she talked of the certainty of their getting married and the details of which house they would live in at first on the compound. She also talked about her plans for their future together: She explained: "I look for money; he looks for money; and we will put this money together. When we have gathered money, we will think about buying sheets of corrugated tin (for constructing a house)" (*Zaho mitady vola, izy mitady vola, volanay aminjay zegny mivory. Amin'ny moment volanay mivory amin'izay mahita hevitry ely mivanga tôles*). She explained how she had already purchased a good number of sheets of tin (probably left from her first marriage) and would contribute them to the construction project. They would do as her sister had done: First, build a house on her husband's land and then plan to build one for the wife on her family land. Eventually, she hoped that they could purchase land of their own in the city and either move the house onto it or build another one. She concluded by pronouncing this as a general norm: "That's how marriage is. Just about only like that" (*Karaha zegny vadiagna. Presque fo eky*). Because of the fragility of relationships and the frequency of breakups, Francine was in a vulnerable position, even though it is culturally recognized that she should get a home on her own land (particularly when it is outside the city, in her ancestral village), which was a second priority.

Francine did end up moving in with Richard. When I returned four months later, I learned, however, that they were breaking up. She explained that his family had never accepted her and that he had become unbearably and unreasonably jealous. Francine's sister and other close family members confided to me that Francine seemed to be flagrantly having an affair with a neighborhood man— inviting him over and closing the door. Whatever the case, Francine would reassess her options and move on, in terms of both her intimate relationships and her livelihood strategy. Sometime after 2007, I learned that she had returned to her home in Joffreville and lived alone, though surrounded by extended family, working successfully in the tourism industry, guiding and cooking for tourists.

Gender and Agency in the Global System

Francine's case represents one person's active involvement in shaping the course of her life, taking advantage of opportunities and managing constraints. Although uneducated and living on one of the poorest margins of the global system, her life choices reveal her agency amid considerable limitations. In a similar observation of market women in Ghana, Gracia Clark confronts the stereotype that African women are passive victims of globalization. "These market women are shrewd, determined fighters" (Clark 2010:23), she writes. They "need not be passive to be victims of the tall odds stacked against them as Africans, as women, and as members of the world's poor majority" (p. 23).

Anthropologists have deconstructed the purported tendency of globalization to bring about homogeneous cultural and economic change (Appadurai 1990; Hannerz 1989). The widening gap between the rich and poor globally lays the framework for radically different experiences of and responses to new forms of global flows of information and capital. James Ferguson (2006) refers to the "global shadows" in identifying spaces on the margins of the system, where people can only dream about having gainful employment in a country with a developed transportation, communication, and social services infrastructure—and with it, access to modern technology and forms of transportation. The lack of these resources has led to countless localized economic, political, and cultural adaptations (Comaroff and Comaroff 1993).

Opportunities and constraints associated with change are not evenly distributed among local populations. Neither the "global" nor the "local" is a homogeneous category, and understanding how this works on the ground requires deconstructing "communities" to reveal social differentiation at many levels. Gender—along with age, ethnicity, and social class—is a common marker of difference in access to social resources. In the 1970s, feminist scholars emphasized studying women—a long-neglected segment of the population. In two seminal collected volumes, entitled *Toward an Anthropology of Women* (Reiter 1975) and *Women, Culture, and Society* (Rosaldo and Lamphere 1974), scholars introduced new ways of analyzing gender as a critical basis for stratification within communities. Scholars such as Karen Sacks (1974) identified ways of identifying relative status of women within their communities, pointing out that women often have less access to such social goods as personal autonomy, decision-making ability, and respect.

Later feminist studies moved away from a focus solely on women and emphasized the relationship between gendered individuals, considering gender as a relationship. Karen Brodkin, for example, recently identified "gender as a socially structured relationship of unequal power in a particular locale" (2007:xiii). This broad view of gender as structured inequality opens the frame for recognizing that gender is not just about women and is not necessarily binary (subdivided into two groups, namely men and women). It is also powerfully cross-cut by such dynamics as race, class, age, sexuality, and other factors of differentiation.

The focus on women has tended to remain in gender studies, despite criticisms that doing so merely replicates essentialist binary frames for understanding gender differentiation. Instead of positing any kind of universal womanhood or of focusing on women in an analytical vacuum, however, contemporary focus on women examines gendered systems with a focus on women. The emphasis on women remains because of their often-neglected, marked status. Recognizing the danger in essentializing "women" or "men" as a priori categories, a pattern nevertheless emerges whereby the gender category associated most commonly with female sexual anatomy nearly always holds a lower social status and remains systematically overlooked in studies that do not explicitly analyze gender (e.g., Banerjee and Bell 2007). Economic crises do not affect the poor equally, but tend to hit women the hardest when and if they are the ones feeding children, keeping fires stoked with diminishing stocks of combustibles, and are less well educated and therefore less able to participate in a literate, globally oriented economy. Such is the case in Madagascar.

Differentiation exists among women also in Madagascar, as traders and farmers have a different relationship with khat from consumers. While production and distribution activities provide many women with a considerable income by local standards, women in consuming households may experience interpersonal tension and economic hardship as their household budgets may be reduced by khat consumption. Others, however, enjoy chewing khat with their partner, and some even told me that they like it when he chews because it makes him more industrious and helpful around the house. The important point is that no gender category can be taken as homogeneous: Women, in this case, experience the khat economy differently and, as a result, have different khat-related health outcomes.

A recent edited volume by Gunewardena and Kingsolver (2007b), entitled *The Gender of Globalization: Women Navigating Cultural and Economic Marginalities*, takes on the question of how women negotiate the effects of globalization—often experiencing increased disempowerment, but sometimes taking advantage of new opportunities. The book makes two important points: First, women's experiences intersect with existing forms of social inequality, both among women and between women and men. In northern Madagascar, rural men have many advantages over women, with their greater access to the means of production, including land, beasts of burden, and any kind of machinery (including tractors or vehicles) or technology distributed in the formal economy (Gezon 2002). In the urban areas, women face the same constraints that women do in many parts of the world: having high numbers of female-headed households, less education, higher illiteracy rates, and less familiarity with formal institutional culture than men. Despite their lower access to resources, however, women are actively involved in the informal sector of production, trading, and other low-capital entrepreneurial activities. Because of the low level of labor input, single women, as absentee landowners, can hire a man to tend her khat for her and still earn a profit, particularly if the laborer is honest in giving her the khat that is her due. Recall that this is the case of Francine discussed above.

Existing gender relations—with culturally acceptable flexible marriage and partnership arrangements and acceptance of women's economic activity—allow and even encourage women to be entrepreneurs and to participate in the growing opportunities afforded by the khat economy. On the production and distribution end, many women in northern Madagascar enjoy opportunities that help them survive extreme poverty. Carla Freeman also argues that changing entrepreneurial activities in Barbados must be understood in the local context. She presents middle-class entrepreneurship as "a flourishing new expression of a long tradition of a Caribbean cultural model known as 'reputation' " (2007:3), which is rooted in African traditions and creole expressions of creativity, especially in the lower classes.

The second point that Gunewardena and Kingsolver make (2007a:3–11) is that women's (and, I might add, men's) agency is socially and culturally constrained—by factors such as the availability of economic opportunities and gender ideologies. It is important to note, for example, that although khat selling provides an indisputable opportunity for women in Madagascar, it also leaves them vulnerable because the quasi-legal status of khat makes it susceptible to being repressed at any time.

What we refer to as globalization is not a top-down project that is imposed without question on actual people in specific locales. Rather, local people interpret the dynamics with which they are faced, adapting them to local conditions. Global and local spheres co-produce each other, as each is influenced by the other. Anna Tsing's concept of "friction" captures this sense: "As a metaphorical image, friction reminds us that heterogeneous and unequal encounters can lead to new arrangements of culture and power" (2005:5). Global and national institutions, such as the World Bank or USAID, do not unilaterally shape local conditions. The growing khat economy, for example, represents what might be considered an unintended consequence of globalization: The poverty resulting from uneven global capital flows and structural adjustment programs has led to innovation in the informal economy rather than heightened participation in the formal global capitalist economy from which so many are excluded.

Khat may provide an opportunity for local people, ironically, *because* of and not *despite* the shadow that neoliberal restructuring casts on this part of the world. Women in particular find opportunities *because* khat, a sometimes-legal drug, is silenced on the national margins and out of a formal watchful eye, where literacy is not needed. Women's autonomy and entrepreneurial spirit have facilitated the establishment of the khat economy.

Models of Intimacy and Economy: Gender, Globalization, and Health

Stories such as those presented in this chapter reveal the processes through which women and men assess their opportunities and constraints to make decisions, taking many factors—affective as well as economic—into consideration. "Love" and relationships, motivated by complex—and often internally contradictory—desires for fulfillment, provide important lenses through which people engage in cost-benefit analyses about economic engagements. Scholars have argued about the relationship between Western romance and monogamous marriage and neoliberal capitalism. Anthony Giddens (1993) notes the nineteenth-century origin of the importance of romance as a basis for marriage partner selection in Europe. Through its emotionally intimate bonds, the emotionally privileged relationship between husband and wife established the primacy of the household as a site of emotional and physical reproduction, detached from other social obligations. Ilouz (2007) writes that what made intimacy both a psychological and a political affair was that "it stipulated that partners ought to relate to each other in an egalitarian fashion" (p. 28)—an autonomous, individualistic concept of personhood that is critical to the individualistic free enterprise, liberal democratic model.

Povinelli (2006) makes a connection between the rise of companionate marriage—the "intimate couple" (p. 16)—and a break from the broader social obligations of extended kin. She recognizes Habermas in noting that this coincided with political and economic individuality, where people act as pure human subjects, unfettered by social definitions or obligations. Povinelli writes: "Indeed, one of the key dimensions of the fantasy of intimate love is its stated opposition to all other forms of social determination even as it claims to produce a new form of social glue" (2006:190).

Among all but the poorest classes in North America and Europe, intimate monogamy has presented an ideal that has undergirded late modern capitalism: When most middle-class men have been assured of a stable job, women's income has been considered supplementary, and women's work has frequently been seen as a threat to the family (Margolis 2000). Although the nuclear household is actually in the minority in the United States, this ideal has structured, and has been structured by, political and economic practices of a seemingly contradictory companionate individuality.

In Madagascar, in contrast, both relationship ideals and economic dynamics are different. There are few formal sector jobs. Women are often the heads of household, and even when not, they are expected to contribute financially. Marriages do not tend to last. The discourses regarding marriage or romantic partnerships idealize economic partnership and children, but emotional intimacy is not the measure of a meaningful relationship as it is in the companionate model. These attitudes facilitate flexibility and make sense for people living in an economy on the global margins. They enable people to respond to rapidly changing conditions, characterized by uncertainty and the need to live day to day. Attention to the politics and economics of intimacy reveals that adaptation and accommodation to global and national economic and political shifts occur within the intimacy of the home as well as in more formal spaces (Padilla et al. 2007).

Women have a long history of making the margins work for them (Clark 2010; Freeman 2000), although they also suffer disproportionately with the radical economic and political transformations of globalism and neoliberal doctrines (Gunewardena and Kingsolver 2007b). As a legal but silenced drug, khat provides unique opportunities to women as a lucrative, virtually unregulated (informal, quasi-legal) substance. Opportunities for income mean opportunities to spend money on culturally valued items, including higher quality health care and nutritional foods. In a critical examination of health, evaluating a drug crop such as khat requires examination of the multiple ways in which khat affects the health of human populations. Direct effects of consumption constitute only one kind of effect.

I argue that indirect effects, such as income earning and its related impact on health, must also figure into a discussion of khat's overall social impact. Possibilities for interpersonal and economic flexibility, coupled with relationship autonomy, provide women traders and farmers with a framework from which they can negotiate when they do find themselves in a disadvantageous position. Outside of the khat economy, women continue to have lower status, especially in the formal economy where formal education and male status correspond with distinct advantages. Khat is not the final solution to women's lower status or to the marginal economic standing of northern Madagascar in general. It does provide a local means of adapting to poverty—a context in which many women can negotiate a relative advantage. This discussion of gender and economy grounds the next two chapters of the book, which examine khat on the margins of the global economy, considering the politics of consumption, discourses of drug effects and legalization, and khat's relationships to the state.

Notes

1. The USAID HIV/AIDS Country Profile for Madagascar, dated September 2010, estimates the percentage of adults living with HIV to be less than 0.1%, making it "one of the few low-prevalence countries in sub-Saharan Africa." http://www.usaid. gov/our_work/global_health/aids/Countries/africa/madagascar.html (accessed June 14, 2011).
2. "*Mamaely*" is the typical term of reference for one's father's brother's wife. It is also used for one's mother's younger sisters.

7

THE LOUD SILENCE OF GREEN GOLD: WAR ON DRUGS, STATE SILENCE, AND ALTERNATIVE DEVELOPMENT

In 2004, I was in my living room in the northern city of Diego Suarez, casually interviewing a well-connected man about the khat trade. I felt him hesitate about revealing too many details. I had been warned of this by the university professor who introduced me to this man, and who was also sitting in the room during the interview. Even though the university professor did not know much about khat himself, he surmised that there was a kind of khat "mafia" that was rather secretive. In my studies of the khat trade, I found no evidence of any actual organized control over it, as it seems to be dominated by small-scale farmers and traders alike (albeit with some controlling a far greater market share than others). But one of the man's statements made me consider that this air of secrecy may be less about how trade is organized and more about the cultural politics of khat. In discussing its legality, he got very serious, looked me in the eye, and stated that the authorities could never make it illegal because if they did there would be a revolt.

Khat is a hub in a nexus of struggles in Madagascar: about conservation and land use, about the social effects of drugs, about tensions within Madagascar between coastal peoples and those from the highlands, about symbolic affiliations with the West as opposed to some sort of Islamic or Arab other, and about competing visions of economic development. Khat's pharmacological effects, along with perceptions of its effects on society, influence its legal status globally as well as nationally. Whether or not a drug crop is legal, then, has implications for rural livelihoods, land use practices, and public health initiatives.

Evaluating the effects of khat as a drug must include a discussion of the larger political and economic framework that constrains it. This analysis follows a critical medical anthropology (CMA) approach by focusing on how our cultural constructions of a substance lie embedded within political and economic processes at multiple scales of analysis, including global ones. It also considers how attitudes toward substances contribute to the creation and perpetuation of social relationships, underscoring uneven access to power, prestige, and wealth (Baer et al. 2003:34; Singer and Baer 2007:33).

I begin by examining the international War on Drugs, considering its rhetoric and impact on the legal status of khat globally. I then continue with a discussion of its quasi-legal status in Madagascar, in particular, and the related state silence surrounding it. The chapter ties in with academic discussions of globalization in suggesting that khat's current local success may, paradoxically, be due to this very marginality—that is, the need to survive in the global shadows (Ferguson 2006). Its production and trade provide for the continued existence of those who fall into the cracks of the global capitalist economy that is characterized by massive flows of capital, large-scale projects, demands for relatively high levels of education, and wage labor. It also includes equally massive unemployment in the formal sector and poverty-level living conditions for many. This may also explain the state's silence, which allows for the undisputed vitality of the khat economy while enabling the Malagasy state to continue to court external aid. This discussion of the global margins engages reflections on gender and women's livelihood strategies for survival in particular.

I conclude the chapter by exploring some of the implications of this silence for northern Madagascar: It allows the economy to thrive despite the neoliberal reforms of globalization. Yet this freedom to pursue an alternative path to economic development has come at a cost, as it does not come with centralized agricultural extension supports nor does it lend itself easily to investigations of the potentially negative health effects of khat.

International Drug Control

Khat, a mild stimulant with amphetamine-like properties, has been illegal in the United States since the early 1990s and in Canada since the late 1990s. It is also illegal in much of Europe (with the United Kingdom and Holland as notable exceptions). In the United States, khat became illegal because it contains cathinone and cathine, both of which were added to the UN Convention on Psychotropic Substances in 1988: The United States, as a signatory to the convention, scheduled the substances. Cathinone has been designated as Schedule I, which is the most restrictive category. After having been picked, cathinone transforms gradually into cathine, a Schedule III drug, which is not illegal to possess. After about twenty-four to forty-eight hours, there is no cathinone left. In 1993, the U.S. Federal Register clarified that by scheduling khat's constituent alkaloids, the khat plant itself was being so scheduled. Armstrong (2008) points out that legal debates exist over khat's legal status in the United States, with defense attorneys arguing, in some cases successfully, that khat itself is not controlled because it does not always contain cathinone, the criminalized component. Furthermore, the U.S. Food and Drug Administration makes no reference to khat as a controlled substance, although it does specifically identify cathinone as such. Haggling over the legal status of the khat plant has not, however, prevented ongoing enforcement of a ban on the khat plant, as a quick Internet search for "khat bust" reveals. In August 2010, for example, 400 bundles, with an estimated street value of $250,000, were confiscated in the greater Atlanta region (http://www.foxnews.com/us/2010/08/17/ga-police-bust-man-rare-african-drug/; accessed September 23, 2011). In May 2011, more than 300 pounds of khat, with an estimated value of more than $95,000, were confiscated in Washington, D.C. (McCabe 2011 [http://washingtonexaminer.com/local/crime-punishment/2011/05/ethopian-cafe-owner-arrested-major-khat-bust; accessed September 23, 2011]).

Khat's principle active compound, cathinone, has been placed in a category that includes morphine and heroin. As explained in Chapter 3, many social and medical scholars question this placement of a relatively mild stimulant into such a harshly regulated drug category. Scholarship on khat's effects identifies it as incapable of the radically altered behavior, social disruption, and addictive dysfunctionality associated with narcotics. In most of the places it is consumed, khat is strongly associated with the forging of interpersonal bonds and affective ties. The cultural settings of its consumption contain boundaries that bracket its dosage and integrate it into functional social practice. Prescriptions exist for dosage, whom to chew with, foods and drinks to mix it with, and, importantly, for appropriate behavior to be exhibited during the time the high is felt most strongly. Overwhelming criticism still comes from certain quarters, however. Its condemnation is often based more on subjective judgments as to the drug's social effects than on medical considerations of its physical and mental health effects (Abebe et al. 2005).

Western opinion of khat has varied tremendously historically. Early travelers often found it quaint and amusing, while criticism increased in the early twentieth century, as Western control over the Middle East and Africa increased.

Perceptions of khat reveal clearly the CMA perspective that larger political and economic contexts shape cultural constructions. Khat, like many other drugs, has, effectively, been a canvas upon which people have painted their hopes and fears.

The War on Drugs

Concern over psychoactive substances in general coincided with the rise of organized biomedicine in the West and the increasing control of pharmacological substances toward the end of the nineteenth century. Before that, opium had been a common ingredient in medications as early as the colonial period in the United States. By the mid-1800s, opium-based medicinals were widely marketed to and heavily consumed by the white middle-class public—women in particular. Since the effects were little known, addiction was common.

Negative opinion of opium, of which there is evidence as early as the mid-nineteenth century, can be linked to several factors, including health concerns, discrimination against the immigrant Chinese population, and most importantly, because of a concern over England's rising economic status. Growing public concern with addiction focused on housewives and the working class. Baer et al. (2003:181) note, for example, that concerns about opium's impacts on health were raised by Engels, in 1845, who decried opium-based patent medicines that were rampant among Britain's working classes. Legal actions against opium were also a reaction against opium smoking among U.S. Chinese, originally imported as laborers. It is worth noting that the association between Chinese and opium is largely a result of British imperialism, when the British fought the Opium Wars of the mid-1800s for the right to sell opium to the general Chinese population. The result was, by one estimate, that one-tenth of all Chinese became addicted to smoking opium, and they took this addiction with them to the United States (Baer et al. 2003:181; Singer 2004). With the U.S. depression of the 1860s, the Chinese came to be viewed as undesirable and their opium smoking was condemned (Singer 2008b).

Even deeper concerns about opium emerged in the context of an international opium conference convened in the United States in the early 1900s, which resulted in the Harrison Act of 1914. These concerns focused not on health or even xenophobia, but on the concern that the British were gaining economically over the United States because of their opium sales to China (Baer et al. 2003:187). By restricting the distribution of over-the-counter opiates and empowering only physicians with the right to dispense the drug, the Harrison Act put pharmaceutical decision-making more squarely in the hands of the medical profession in the United States.

Singer (2008b) points out that a look across the spectrum of drug control reveals that racist and classist concerns have consistently been significant driving forces in condemning drug use. For example, concerns about marijuana in the 1930s (when it was originally controlled by imposing a high tax) were linked to U.S. Mexicans, who had originally arrived to meet labor needs during the Great Depression but had come to be seen as no longer necessary (Baer et al. 2003:176). Cocaine was similarly associated with African Americans as early as the turn of the twentieth century. Later debates over marijuana in the twentieth century place it squarely within the realm of fear of counterculture and rebellious youth. Scholars have likewise surmised a connection between khat and mistrust of immigrant Somali populations (Armstrong 2008).

Control of the use of psychoactive substances, beginning in the early twentieth century, not only shored up the hegemony of biomedical practices and the pharmacological industry, but also came to symbolize American middle-class values— and to point toward a way to ward off threats to the moral standing of the nation. This concern culminated in the War on Drugs, for which the first seeds were laid in the late 1960s. Richard Nixon, in seeking a way to gain the presidential office by playing on the fears of the middle-class white American public, found a way to conflate heroin, an inner-city and African American drug, with marijuana, which was associated with hippy counterculture (Baum 1996). Massing writes about Nixon that: "Marijuana, hashish, and LSD were, in his view, turning a generation of Americans into long-haired, love-beaded, guru-worshipping peaceniks" (2000:97). In a campaign speech in 1968, Nixon pronounced that drugs are "decimating a generation of Americans" (quoted in Massing 2000:97).

Under Nixon, the War on Drugs resulted, ironically, both in making drug use a criminal act and in making treatment widely available for heroin addicts. Although originally conflated for the purposes of the presidential campaign, marijuana was not treated as a serious drug through much of the 1970s. For all of Nixon's anti-drug assertions, his national Commission on Marihuana and Drug Abuse delivered a report in 1972 that essentially let marijuana off the hook as a dangerous drug. It explained that there is little danger of psychological or physical harm from intermittent use of cannabis. Popular concern over the drug was not due to its pharmacological properties, the report stated, but instead to its association with counterculture and its perceived threat to the moral order. Marijuana "becomes a symbol of the rejection of cherished values" surrounding family, duty, and country (quoted in Baum 1996:71). From the point of view of the users, the report stated, the disjuncture between marijuana's mild effects and the strong sanction against it breeds contempt for civil society. According to Baum, "The commission was telling Nixon, in effect, that the real marijuana problem wasn't the drug but the war on the drug" (1996:71).

Throughout the 1970s, marijuana paraphernalia was widely available, and President Jimmy Carter's speech writer even consulted with the head of NORML, an organization for the legalization of marijuana. He devised a strongly pro-legalization speech—which was intercepted by another staff member and never delivered to the public. While advocating for the retention of civil penalties for marijuana, President Carter did publically "support legislation amending Federal law to eliminate all Federal criminal penalties for the possession of up to one ounce of marihuana" (Baum 1996:95) in 1977. With the arrival of President Ronald Reagan in 1980, the tide turned strongly against legalization, led significantly by parent groups concerned about the effects of marijuana on youth. Many had been hopeful that Clinton would revive the legalization debate, but he did not. The War on Drugs escalated, affronting basic civil liberties and laying increasingly heavy emphasis on enforcement and criminalization, and unevenly targeted minority youth, especially African American males. In addition, Reagan drastically reduced the treatment infrastructure implemented by Nixon. The War on Drugs in the United States illustrates that perceptions of drugs are politically situated and shift depending on political interests. It also illustrates that these perceptions have consequences for real people in ways that perpetuate social inequalities.

War on Drugs' Effects

Critics of the War on Drugs point out that it has failed miserably. More and more potent drugs are available than ever before, and the justice system is clogged with drug-related cases, costing the American taxpayer unprecedented amounts of dollars and perpetuating racial oppression through profiling and uneven targeting (Baum 1996; Massing 2000; Singer 2004). A recent report from the Global Commission on Drug Policy (2011) states in the first sentence of its executive summary: "The global war on drugs has failed, with devastating consequences for individuals and societies around the world" (p. 2). It goes on to acknowledge that "vast expenditures on criminalization and repressive measures directed at producers, traffickers and consumers of illegal drugs have clearly failed to effectively curtail supply or consumption" (p. 2).

Even though the primary goals have met with failure, however, Singer points out the importance of identifying secondary goals, which have, in fact, been successful. Among these, he notes domestic aspects: middle-class individuals can blame drugs without looking at the deeper root causes of addiction, such as poverty related to a shifting global economy and the lack of an adequate publically funded social safety net. In addition, inmates and addicts provide cheap labor—as prisoners and as people on the streets who accept poorly paid jobs (Singer 2004:297).

On the global front, concerns about drugs domestically interrelate closely with foreign policy concerns. In addition to ending drug abuse within its borders, one of the stated goals of the War on Drugs is to stem the flow of illegal drugs into the United States. One effect of making drug use a legal rather than a public health issue is that the drug-producing nations are targeted. In its relations with drug suppliers, U.S. practice has been contradictory and inconsistent. Just as the original control of opiates under the Harrison Act was more about political economy than about health, so has been foreign policy under the War on Drugs. Issues of power and geopolitical interest have consistently shaped actions.

According to Singer (2004:290), the U.S. government has been involved in "a continued pattern of using drug money to finance covert (and often illegal) U.S. government-sponsored activities against disliked foreign regimes." Bullington (2004), for example, notes that U.S. support of Chaing Kai-Shek during the Red Scare days undermined the U.S. prohibition initiatives because of the Chinese leader's known involvement in the drug trade. Singer (2004:290) points out that in the early 1960s, members of the National Security Council were implicated in the smuggling of narcotics into the United States from Cuba. By the late 1960s, the CIA was assisting a Laotian warlord who was gaining control of the opium trade in that region of Southeast Asia and was a major supplier of heroin to the United States. The CIA, under Carter, also supplied opium-growing Afghani peoples with weapons and logistic support in the wake of the Soviet invasion in 1979. Scholars surmise that the support contributed not only to the anti-Soviet cause, but to the record crops of poppies produced during that time (Levins 1996, cited in Singer 2004), as markets for food commodities were disrupted by the war (Draper 2011). Heroin derived from those poppies flooded into the United States.

Heroin production in Afghanistan has continued to be politically charged. Draper (2011) explains that in 1991, Afghanistan surpassed Myanmar as the top illegal opium producer. When the Taliban took power in 1996, the Islamist government agreed not to crack down on producers and in exchange received heavy covert financing from trafficking groups. In July 2000, however, the Taliban leader declared that opium production was a violation of Islam. Enforced through violence and threats, poppy production declined by about 90% the following year. When the United States invaded Afghanistan in 2001 and toppled the Taliban, production of opium again spiked, encouraged by the Taliban who then used its profits to fund their insurgency. Bullington noted that as the result of the replacement of the Taliban by a U.S.-supported regime, "Afghanistan opium has once again flooded the market" (2004:30).

The United States has also opportunistically dealt out sanctions against producing or trafficking nations depending on their relationship to U.S. interests.

South American nations that received no sanctions in 2007, despite their status as contributing to drug proliferation, include Bolivia, Colombia, Venezuela, and Peru (Singer 2008b:81). In a similar critique, Chien et al. (2000:297–298) argue that the United States does not merely ignore drug trafficking, but appears to actually facilitate it in some cases through both its covert action (by the CIA) and obvious lack of oversight over those activities by governmental agencies. The case of U.S.-backed Nicaraguan Contras illustrates their point: The Contras were major traffickers of cocaine, with knowledge and even support of the CIA, shielded by less covert dimensions of policy. Chien et al. write: "Abetting the drug traffic has served not a rogue CIA, but rather longstanding U.S. foreign policy aims" (2000:298).

U.S.-dominated drug policy has had devastating consequences for countries and for producers involved in the drug trade. The case of coca in South America provides a particularly poignant example. Singer (2008b) points out that the stated focus of the "Andean program" has been on the eradication of coca bushes. Yet over 50% of the millions of dollars that have been given in aid by the United States has gone directly to the Colombian military operations to buy airplanes and helicopters and to train Colombian military personnel. With U.S. approval, they have used these resources to fight a fifty-year-long war against leftist insurgents and at the same time destroy coca fields. This has led to massive intimidation, torture, and death throughout the country. There have also been disproportionate eradication efforts in areas of oil exploration and extraction. Singer (2008b) concludes that, overall, the extent of the interruption of the cocaine commodity chain is small compared to the amount of money spent to stop it. The toll of the War on Drugs has undoubtedly been heavy on South American peasants and has ranged from loss of physical security to loss of livelihoods (Sanabria 1993). It is undeniable that international drug policy programs have effectively resulted in the control of marginalized people and places.

The rhetoric of the War on Drugs tends to lead to a uniform lumping of Schedule I substances as dangerous and in need of eradication. In so doing, it ignores traditional practices of socially integrated consumption (e.g., Conzelman 2006) and the role of these crops in rural economies as a safety net for farmers suffering the lowering of prices of other agricultural crops. Khat also exists in this global context of wars on drugs and strategic foreign policy. Malagasy government agents cannot ignore this in their relations with the West.

Khat in Global Context

Khat is not illegal in all Western nations. In the United Kingdom, the active compounds (cathinone and cathine) face similar restrictions, but the plant form remains legal. The history of prohibition of all forms of khat in the United States suggests that it was not due to its perceived potential for harm alone, but rather for distinctly political reasons. Recall that khat was officially named as a Schedule I drug in the United States and accordingly subject to full prohibition in the early 1990s at the time of the botched U.S. invasion of Somalia and the collapse of the Somali state. Several scholars assert that this is not a coincidence: Beckerleg writes: "The move to outlaw khat's main active ingredient appears to have been a response to the unhappy experience of the United States in Somalia when their troops were driven back from Somali soil by militiamen, allegedly high on khat" (2008:752; see also Anderson and Carrier 2009).

Even though discussions about khat had been taking place in the U.S. Department of Health and Human Services (DHHS) since 1988, it was four years later, in November of 1992, that the assistant secretary of the DHHS recommended that cathinone be placed in Schedule I. In January 1993, the rules and regulations of its legality were officially published (http://www.erowid.org/plants/khat/khat_law1.shtml; accessed January 30, 2011). At the time of the Somali invasion in late 1992 and 1993, reporters portrayed images of khat-crazed youth incited to violence by the substance (Klein 2007) and associated it with a long-standing history of Somali war lords battling for power (e.g., http://news.bbc.co.uk/2/hi/africa/6155796.stm; accessed September 23, 2011). The 2001 film, *Black Hawk Down* (Columbia, Sony Pictures), further entrenched these popular perceptions of khat. More recently, khat has been associated with gun-brandishing crazed Somali youth and pirates.

Lately, there have been suggestions both in the media and in academic scholarship associating khat revenues with terrorism. There are few facts that support this claim, however. Evidence presented in Harvey Kushner's book *Holy War on the Home Front* (2004) seems to merely be the following syllogism: Khat is mainly traded and used globally by Muslims from "failed states"; we don't know where the money from khat goes; therefore, khat is funding Islamic terrorist organizations. Discourse on the politics of khat in the United States illustrates how the fear of terrorism and rogue wars abroad reverberates within Western nations. A newspaper article reporting the need for tougher penalties for khat smuggling makes an implicit case for a link between khat and terrorism: Smugglers are using "informal systems to transfer money that have been tied to terrorists in the past" (http://www.washingtontimes.com/news/2008/oct/13/dc-seeks-tougher-penalties-for-khat/?page = all; accessed September 23, 2011). In addition to the concerns about drug effects, there were also stated concerns about the sheer volume of profit to be made from its sale: Wholesalers can pay $1 for a kilogram and can sell it for $700, according to a DEA agent. The agent expressed fears that the money may be being funneled into terrorist organizations in East Africa (http://www.anyuakmedia.com/ethionews72806. html; accessed September 23, 2011).

Even in the United Kingdom, where khat is legal, the threat of prohibition continuously looms. A number of campaigns to ban khat have been launched, and newspapers often conflate it with stronger substances: For example, *The Guardian* ran a piece on khat in 2004 with the headline "This has the same effect as ecstasy and cocaine.... And it's legal" above a photograph of a bundle of khat leaves. Such campaigns have resulted in the government conducting research into whether khat should be prohibited, and one such piece of research led the government in 2006 to conclude that a ban would not be appropriate.[1] However, more campaigning has led the government to ask for further research on the substance with a view to a ban, while a shadow minister from the opposition Conservative party has stated that her party would ban khat if they win the next election.[2]

Suspicion of khat within Somali immigrant communities does not just come from those of Anglo descent. What makes the campaign especially powerful is that many of those driving it forward are Somalis themselves: Effective lobbying by Somali groups who perceive khat as an impediment to Somali integration into life in the United Kingdom is the crucial aspect of the khat debate there. These groups make their case in meetings with local MPs, in media articles, through petitions, online blogs, and even on YouTube; their power should not be underestimated, as such groups played a role in bans on khat in Canada and Scandinavia.[3]

Colonial History of Legality

Over the last 100–200 years, khat chewing has spread beyond immediate areas of production within the Horn of Africa and Yemen, facilitated by advances in transportation. Ethiopia and Kenya are the two main producers in East Africa. Yemen is also a major producer, with production concentrated in what was formerly North Yemen. It is now consumed throughout East Africa and countries in the western Indian Ocean as well as throughout the world in diaspora nations.

While khat itself has never been under international control, individual governments since the colonial era have struggled—often in vain—to prohibit khat production and/or consumption. Such attempts have to be understood in the context of a growing international concern with psychoactive substances that began with opiates in the late nineteenth to early twentieth centuries and expanded to include more and more substances.[4] Prohibition became the default solution to problems associated with such substances, and, as a consequence, prohibition has been hailed as the answer to the problem of psychoactive drugs, including khat.

Carrier and Gezon (2009) explain that the earliest colonial attempt to control khat was effected by the British in the Protectorate of Somaliland in 1921. They banned cultivation of khat within the territory, and those wishing to consume it legally had to possess a license (BritishSomaliland 1923:291–292). Facing a vibrant black market economy, the British decided to drop the ban (Gebissa 2004:54–55). Again in 1939, the colonial government reinforced measures against people transporting or growing khat (Cassanelli 1986:252). These measures were quickly undermined by improved transportation infrastructure between Ethiopia and the protectorate.

By mid-century, further measures were instigated to combat a substance now seen by many as having serious negative health and social effects: Kervingant (1959), writing about French Somaliland (later Djibouti) for the UN Office on Drugs and Crime, claimed that khat use caused increased susceptibility to disease and numbed mental faculties and led to family breakdown as members may turn to begging, theft, or prostitution to satisfy cravings. The author concluded with the recommendation that it is "desirable that it should be abolished, and for this purpose measures for the gradual prohibition of the use of khat will shortly be adopted in the territory" (1959:unpaginated). Gebissa (2004) reports that the French government in Djibouti first implemented policies to curb khat imports and consumption in 1952 but that consumption actually tripled in three years.

In the British protectorate and colony of Aden, which later became South Yemen, people consumed imported khat in great quantities. A ban on khat imports to Aden Colony (but not the Aden Protectorate) in 1957 caused a flurry of reactions not only in Aden but also in Ethiopia, Aden's major supplier. A little over a year later, the ban was revoked because it had failed to prohibit consumption and caused the government to lose much revenue (Brooke 1960).

In Kenya, colonial authorities tried to control khat through a number of ordinances in the 1940s and 1950s. These initially introduced a permit system for trade and consumption within Kenya, but then later attempted to prohibit it completely in northern Kenya where it was seen as most problematic. While such measures proved ineffective, other colonial officials, notably in Meru, pushed for the colony to export khat to Aden as a source of revenue (Anderson and Carrier 2009). Khat was caught between the aim of suppressing consumption and promoting trade. From all this, it is clear that the khat's legality is shaped not only by social concerns but also by economic concerns that are quite independent of its drug effects. Gebissa writes: "Health reasons were cited to justify the [1957 ban in Aden] ban, but contemporary sources agree that the main reason was to prevent hard currency from draining into Ethiopia" (2004:90).

Wherever khat consumption was banned during the colonial era, the result was not reduced khat use but rather loss of government income from taxes and from increased anti-smuggling expenditures. A fascinating dynamic is that the major supplier of khat—Ethiopia—was not a colony, so its economy could not be controlled, nor could its economic gains help any Western empire grow. Ethiopia had only been under European rule for a brief period from 1936 to 1941, when it was controlled by the Italian fascists.

After independence, during the socialist era, in 1972, Mohsin al-Aini, the British-educated prime minister of Yemen, launched a campaign against khat that fell just short of banning it. Kennedy (1987:21) surmises that this probably contributed to his political downfall three months later. Nevertheless, the prime minister was not the only one who disliked khat and found it an impediment to development. Even today, despite khat's national popularity, some educated Yemenis still campaign against it (Cooper 2000). The president, Ali Abdulla Saleh, himself has an ambivalent position on khat (Kandela 2000). In 1999, he announced that he would reduce his own chewing habit to weekends only, and he encouraged others to do the same (http://news.bbc.co.uk/2/hi/middle_east/365221.stm; accessed September 23, 2011).

Postindependent Somalia also banned khat in 1983 under President Mohamed Said Barre. A government pamphlet cited damage to the national economy and the social fabric as the main reasons for the ban, but khat's association with government opposition, and "the sense that khat was contributing to the undermining of the economy and, by extension, of the regime, may have been a major factor in the decision to ban it" (Cassanelli 1986:251–252). This ban caused great resentment in northern Somalia toward the southern-based government (Dool 1998:46), while allies of President Barre were allegedly allowed to smuggle in khat that was then sold "by individuals from clans supporting the government" in Kismayu and Mogadishu (Goldsmith 1997:476). The collapse of the Somali state in 1989 put an end to the charade of a ban, and khat became a significant revenue generator for warlords there, prompting some to label it a "conflict good" (Cooper 2002:936). More recently, Islamists who took control temporarily of Mogadishu, Kismayu, and other towns in 2006 attempted to restrict khat: Their announcement that khat would be prohibited during Ramadan prompted demonstrations in Kismayu.[5] Today, khat continues to be sold openly with no sanction, taxation, or regulation since there is no stable government in place.

In Kenya and Ethiopia, the sources of khat chewed by U.K. Somalis, it remains legal and appears immune to prohibition, thanks to its economic importance. However, debate still rages over how it should be classified, couched in discussions about whether or not it is a drug (Carrier 2008). Such is the power of the transnational rhetoric of the War on Drugs that being labeled a drug leads to khat's conflation with illegal substances, prompting further questioning as to why it is still legal. In Kenya, this debate is decades old (since the 1930s), and while those attacking it use the language of the War on Drugs, the language of culture and tradition has often been invoked by those defending khat, especially by ethnic Meru. The British recognized this and were impressed by khat's ceremonial significance during colonial times. Although they made attempts to ban the substance in the rest of the country, they were happy to let ceremonial usage continue among the Meru. Both sides debate in detail the pros and cons of khat consumption for the individual's and society's well-being, while in effect the debate is rendered impotent by the crop's economic power. In the words of Gebissa (2008:798), "the real issue is not 'to ban or not to ban,' but how to use the present khat-generated prosperity in a way that will also benefit the next generation."

Quasi-legal Status in Madagascar

Khat is illegal in many European countries, including France, Germany, Italy, Scandinavia, and Ireland. It is legal in others, such the United Kingdom, The Netherlands, Greece, Portugal, and the Czech Republic (Armstrong 2008). It is legal, or what Cassanelli has referred to as "quasi-legal," throughout much of Africa—meaning that its status is ambiguous, poorly understood, or surrounded with discussions about possible prohibition. Khat, Cassanelli writes, is a political symbol and "is always susceptible to manipulation for political ends" (1986:254). As explained in Chapter 3, these discussions are often tied in with assessments of its health and social effects.

Khat is legal in Madagascar, but some citizens believe it is not. Many wonder if there will be moves to prohibit it, and occasionally rumors spread that it might become illegal, causing significant tension in Diego Suarez and its environs. One of the few mentions of khat in the searchable online news media reported that in 2008, authorities had to explicitly denounce rumors of prohibition as false to quell the discontent (http://www.madagascar-tribune.com/Victimes-d-une-campagne-de,5322.html; accessed March 11, 2008). Two related factors affect the status of khat within Madagascar: (1) the global political climate of the U.S.-led War on Drugs, which focuses on prohibition at home and eradication abroad; and (2) the link between drug control and all forms of international aid. This international political climate puts pressure on Westward-leaning heads of state to comply with U.S. and other Western priorities.

Former president Marc Ravalomanana (2002–2009), who was in control during much of the span of this research, is reputed to have commented (though it has never been substantiated) that Madagascar will never see significant economic development as long as the youth are strung out, spending their afternoons chewing khat. The president's opinion was shaped in part by his strong Westward-leaning stance, embracing not only structural adjustment reforms but also more cultural aspects of the political hegemony of conservative American politics—in particular, the Christian right—for example, by having the country foot the bill to have several dozen students educated at the conservative Christian university, Abilene Christian University (ACU) in Texas. Of the campus, Ravalomanana remarked that "the thing that most impresses me about ACU is the heart and soul of its people. You are committed to doing your best and at the same time, you are faithful to God. That is very important to me" (http://www.acu.edu/events/news/archives2005/050207_madagascar_follow_up.html; accessed September 23, 2011).

Ravalomanana has been a practicing Christian and active as a lay vice-president of his denomination (FJKM—the Reformed Protestant Church in Madagascar). People in Madagascar associate khat with Islam, since the places where khat is most heavily consumed are Yemen, Ethiopia, and Somalia, where most of the chewers are Muslim. The president's—as well as many politicians' and common peoples'—opposition to khat is multifaceted, revealing a suspicion of stimulants that are not accepted in the West and indicating skepticism of non-Western forms of expression.

The international drug scene also takes shape locally through the framework of existing internal state politics. At this level, international issues combine with national ones, playing themselves out in the context of longstanding tensions. These issues often have little to do with drugs or international pressure, and they may be expressed through discourses of ethnicity, religion, and with reference to a history of national governance. These tensions have been particularly strongly revealed in presidential politics in recent decades. Ravalomanana's affiliation with Christianity does not merely signal an alliance with the West, but also with people who have traditionally practiced that particular form of Christianity—the Merina of the central highlands.

The division between the highlands and the coast has roots in a precolonial era, when the imperialist Merina state polity subjected many coastal kingdoms to its control. The division was further reinforced during the colonial conquest, as it was reified to some degree by the opposing British and French forces (Raison-Jourde and Randrianja 2002; Vérin 1990). The coastal Antankarana people of the far north, for example, sided with the French against their Merina enemies in the mid-1800s (Gezon 2006). The Merina, located in and around what is today the capital city of Antananarivo, were being supported by the British at the time. It wasn't until later in the century that the French directly fought the British for control over Madagascar and won. During the colonial period, fiscal, educational, and hiring policies tended to favor the central highlands and its people (the capital, Antananarivo, is located near the center of this area). Independence struggles often made reference to this division if only to decry it, calling for a single united Madagascar.

The influential postindependence president Didier Ratsiraka (1975–1993, 1997–2002), who led the socialist revolution in the mid-1970s, is from the coastal region, and in the later years of his presidency, he supported federalist administrative policies favoring the relative independence of the coastal provinces. Nevertheless, for much of his period in office, his government perpetuated the same bias toward investing in the central highlands in terms of such factors as infrastructure and education. In the early 1990s, civil unrest forced Ratsiraka from office for several years, but in 1997 he was reelected and served until 2002. Through the 1990s, Ratsiraka continued to support federalism and succeeded in granting the coastal provinces more administrative autonomy in all areas. He also actively supported Islam, which has a stronger presence on the coasts than in the predominantly Christian high plateau. Former president Marc Ravalomanana came to power in a heavily contested election in 2002 against President Didier Ratsiraka (see Marcus and Razafindrakoto 2003). This election effectively pitted the coastal areas against the central highlands of the country, and the province of Antsiranana in the north (Diego Suarez is the capital) was one of the last to hold out against Ravalomanana's forces.

The discourse surrounding khat sometimes engages these traditional geographic and ethnic divisions. Since Malagasy newspapers rarely mention khat, it is difficult to trace this discourse systematically. In one particularly salient reference to it, a young Malagasy scholar I met at a conference in the mid-2000s told me that contributors to certain Malagasy blogs were stating that, nationally, opinions of khat were another iteration of the coast-highlands divide—with those originating from coastal areas supporting khat and others condemning it. It is clear, however, that throughout Madagascar, khat is associated with the northern coastal region where it is grown and with its people.

State Silence

Despite the centrality of khat to the economy of the north, and despite the raging criticism of khat heard informally, the media in Madagascar is curiously silent on the topic. In a search of Malagasy newspapers online, I only found a few references to khat. One in 2005 was a human interest editorial in the *Madagascar Tribune* educating readers—most likely targeted to an audience in the capital city—who may not know much about khat. It referred to khat as the "green gold" of the northern coastal region (Narcisse 2005 [http://www.madagascar-tribune. com/admin/voir_article.php?id = 9629; accessed November 2, 2006. No longer online; in author's files]), commenting on its stimulant effects and its role in bringing wealth to the region. Despite local rumors about the national president's disapproval of khat, I was not able to find references to any official position in the print media while I was there or in online news media since then. Moreover, reports of khat-crazed or lazy delinquent youth on khat were nowhere to be found in the media, despite khat's detractors' frequent laments about it in casual conversation. If the state has a position on khat—either positive or negative—it has not made it known.

The newspapers' quiet stance on khat echoes a general national silence that goes beyond media to include an absence of any kind of targeted regulatory policies (including taxation) or agricultural extension initiatives. As for taxation, the municipality that is the central point for the major production area, Antsalaka, has implemented a tax on all khat that is sold. People pay by the basket. Revenue from khat has funded municipal projects, including a municipal building, and infrastructure improvement, including water and electricity. In Joffreville, taxes are not collected regularly or consistently, and records of tax revenues are incomplete.

In terms of agricultural extension activities, khat is not officially targeted by economic development projects as the recipient of aid or expert knowledge. Joffreville has been the focus of many economic development and conservation projects funded by NGOs, foreign governments, and the Malagasy government. Here, there have been projects for bee keeping, potato growing, poultry raising, introduction of fruit trees, water systems, tourism, national park maintenance, and so on, but khat has received no expert attention, despite fears that it may have an impact on forests and food systems (see Chapter 4).

Why the ambivalence toward khat?

I argue that an important reason for this silence is connected to the state's dependence on foreign aid and on its commitment to development as defined by the agents and institutions of the global capitalist economy. Two issues are salient: (1) khat is illegal in much of the West; and (2) Madagascar has committed to neoliberal economic reforms in exchange for aid. Understanding the current situation requires a brief history lesson: President Ratsiraka first came to the presidency in a rejection of the West as a socialist gaining inspiration from Mao and assistance from Libya and the USSR. Nevertheless, he cooperated closely with the international lending institutions, borrowing heavily in an approach referred to as "*investir à outrance*," meaning to invest to the utmost. The debt burden increased and revenues fell as projects for industrialization were never realized or met with failure. By the early 1980s, the Malagasy government was no longer able to pay down its loans (Barrett 1994; Gezon 2006; Mukonoweshuro 1994). It sought relief from the International Monetary Fund (IMF) and accepted the conditions of structural adjustment. It received a total of fourteen adjustment credits during the 1980s, making Madagascar one of Africa's most comprehensive structural adjustment projects (Hewitt 1992).

The kinds of conditions imposed by structural adjustment were the devaluation of currency, which lowered the cost of exports from Madagascar but caused prices to soar for Malagasy consumers, privatization of nationalized enterprises, lowering of trade barriers for those wanting to import goods into Madagascar, and the removal of subsidies for farmers (Rajcoomar 1991). Toward the end of the 1980s, structural adjustment carried with it commitments toward conservation—hence the burgeoning of conservation activity in Madagascar in the early 1990s (Gezon 1997b; Kull 1996).

It is worth noting that despite these draconian measures to bolster the economy, the country remained impoverished. The country's gross domestic product (GDP) declined by 26% between 1979 and 1991, and the Malagasy spent 85% of their export earnings servicing their debts by the late 1980s (Gezon 2006; Mukonoweshuro 1994). Even though these measures did not result in financial well-being for the country, the government's compliance with the demands of structural adjustment ironically earned the World Bank's acknowledgment as one of the "star pupils" in the structural adjustment experiment (Rajaonarivony 1996:96). The World Bank went so far as to deem it one of the "economic miracles" of Africa (Hewitt 1992).

The status of khat in Madagascar is currently negotiated in this political and economic framework of impoverishment and economic dependence on the West. As a recipient of considerable Western aid, the status of khat in the United States and other powerful Western nations is of potential concern to the Malagasy state. Rosaleen Duffy has noted a transition from the politics of conditionality, where international loans and aid depended on formal conditions of structural adjustment in the 1980s and 1990s, to what she identifies as post-conditionality, characterized by "participation, stakeholders and partnership" (2006:734). The U.S.-led politics of drugs can affect other nations, either directly through force and conditionality (such as the drug wars in South America) or indirectly through persuasion and the will to participate in "good governance," as defined by international institutions. While he was president, Marc Ravalomanana's alignment with the Christianity and the English-speaking political, economic, and educational world sent a clear message of participation and partnership to Western nations. Under these conditions, he was not likely to embrace khat, which is not only illegal but also associated with Islam and terrorism.

An additional factor in considering the reasons for state silence is that khat's production and distribution are local, with few opportunities for expansion to export markets. Because it is not exported, khat is not a potential or actual source of hard currency for the state. One reason it is restricted to the domestic economy is because production volume is low. This means it would not be profitable to invest in a dedicated airline infrastructure to send it quickly to places where it is legal, such as the United Kingdom and other western Indian Ocean destinations. Another reason for state silence is that khat is illegal in the place with which northern Madagascar has the most active airline ties—Réunion Island, a French overseas department that lies less than 1,000 miles to the southeast of Diego Suarez. The large Malagasy population there would happily purchase khat if it were available. From stories I heard, small amounts are smuggled in through personal networks, but nothing on a commercial scale. As it is, khat circulates primarily in the northern region of Madagascar, and secondarily throughout other urban areas within Madagascar, where it is increasingly shipped by air. In the end, while it fuels the domestic economy, it does not raise the GDP of the country or bring in hard currency from abroad.

It is uncertain how strongly the United States and other Western nations will pursue khat's illegality in the future, but its legal status, combined with its impracticality as a vehicle for global capitalist development, makes it risky for the Malagasy government to endorse.

Effects of State Silence

Silence on khat facilitates continued smooth social relations between the Malagasy state and its donors. Recent theories of the state explore secondary effects of silence—specifically, how it opens up space for certain kinds of political practices, identities, and knowledges. An important distinction exists between *the state as an ideological construct*—an ideal symbolized by flags, for example, and *the state as a set of practices*, both symbolic and bureaucratic (Hansen and Stepputat 2001; Mitchell 2006). It is a common error to conceptualize the state as a homogeneous entity with a uniform will of its own and the capacity to act in a consistent manner, where all employees agree with each other and act together to enforce the same principles. Studies of colonialism were some of the first to demonstrate the significance of internal disagreements and even contradictions in state governments. They pointed to a state apparatus that lacked the unified will and capacity to act decisively with which it is often credited (Cooper and Stoler 1997). This perspective on the state—as fragmented and even disorganized—also helps us understand the Malagasy state's lack of a unified voice on khat, considering the range of opinions and uneven stake in this cultural and economic commodity across the nation. An important effect of state silence, then, is the possibility of coexisting contradictory discourses about the place of khat within the Malagasy nation, which, in the end, allows the informal khat economy to thrive.

What is "the state?" Who are the "authorities" that people fear might make khat illegal? The state is a social construct that cannot be analyzed without considering the actual people who represent it. Monique Nuijten (2004) argues that even though the state cannot be identified as an a priori actor, it has salience as a cultural set of practices. She usefully identifies three aspects of state practices: "the idea of the state"; "the state machine," or sets of bureaucratic practices; and "the culture of the state." This latter phrase she defines as "the practices of representation and interpretation which characterize the relation between people and the state bureaucracy and through which the idea of the state is constructed" (2004:211). This involves imagining community (Anderson 2006) through cultural practices of "narrative, medial ritual, pageantry, and public works that link the public sphere to the domestic and local scenes" (Aretxaga 2003:396).

With this deconstructed definition of the state, it becomes possible to identify the situated and performed nature of state actions and ideologies. The seemingly unified state needs as much explaining—if not more—as the fractured, seemingly dysfunctional one. Gupta and Sharma (2006) have argued that "to the degree that 'the state' is represented *as if* it had coherence and unity, an enormous amount of cultural work has to go into securing that coherence" (p. 291; emphasis in original). Despite the apparent consistency of the state, as evidenced in repetitive bureaucratic procedures, people nevertheless often subvert or appropriate policy agendas that are, then, never implemented as officially intended. This disconnect is often evaluated from the outside as failure, or in the worst cases, as corruption (Mathews 2008; Shore and Haller 2005). But as Gupta and Sharma point out, this very "failure" of policy may, in fact, "lie at the very heart of the institutional organization and reproduction of states" (2006:292).

In writing about adherence to internationally imposed development agendas, David Mosse notes that although bureaucrats may consent to dominant, formal models, they may also "make of them something quite different" (2004:645), hence subverting formal agendas in practice. States are shifting entities, dependent on everyday bureaucratic actions and their appropriations and (re)interpretations by participants. James Scott, in *Seeing Like a State* (1998), argues that inherent in the ability of a state to survive, in fact, is its flexibility to modify practices given the exigencies of specific locales and situations. This perspective challenges notions of strict legality and bureaucratic procedure as the norm or even as a realistic or desirable state of affairs. It opens up the possibility of seeing noncompliance with formal procedures and policies, and even what is thought of as corruption, as ubiquitous and even, perhaps, necessary.

Not only are states internally differentiated, but state relations with global institutions are never as straightforwardly compliant as they might appear. Rosaleen Duffy (2006) writes specifically about environmental agendas of conservation, where millions of dollars of aid have been linked conditionally to Madagascar's commitment to conservation, obligating the government to establish national policies and a bureaucratic system of enforcement. Duffy argues that Madagascar is not merely the pawn of global finance and political institutions, however, despite appearances to the contrary. Imposed agendas are implemented in a fragmented way, not always in compliance with original intent. She writes that state and global "boundaries are turbulent, and they are neither wholly national nor completely global, but are instead a complex mix" (2006:734). Arguing for the negotiated aspect of states, Duffy says that "global environmental governance might be thought of more fruitfully as a system of practices and regulations that are still emergent and incomplete" (p. 745). One might suggest that they will, by their very nature, remain emergent and incomplete. In a similar way, the status of khat in Madagascar is constantly negotiated, and despite, its legal status, there is no unity of attitude toward it, despite state commitments to Western agendas. That Madagascar skirts international disdain for khat could be considered another silence—another case of "don't ask, don't tell."

Studying silences reveals that within stability lie the seeds of change, since bureaucratic silence does not make a phenomenon disappear. The relative local autonomy of the khat economy is a potentially fragile state of affairs, as state and global power ebbs and flows in the context of shifting daily practices. Increased attention to the international drug war or internal tensions, for example, could draw attention to the khat situation in Madagascar, evoking a more specific and perhaps punitive state response to khat growing, like that in centers of coca and opium production (Singer 2004). This would not only affect local livelihoods, but it could threaten the fragility of civil order. Khat repression is not as likely as it has been for coca production in South America or poppies in Southeast Asia, in part because the War on Drugs has focused on criminalizing commodity chains that end with a U.S. drug user, and there are few khat chewers in the United States aside from relatively small Somali diaspora communities. Nevertheless, a change in international focus—such as a strategic interest in the western Indian Ocean and Horn of Africa—could have an effect on attitudes toward khat production. For now, as long as it is listed as a Schedule I drug, and as long as Madagascar turns to the West for aid and as a role model, khat will probably never be the recipient of state or internationally sponsored agricultural extension activities, nor will its role in the prosperity of the north officially be recognized.

Alternative Development?

This perspective on the state allows for an examination of silence as negative space that opens up possibilities. Most analyses of states consider the consequences of what actions are taken, not the opportunities that are opened up by the silences. In the case of khat, of interest is what the state, as a governing bureaucratic body, does *not* attempt to do and even avoids doing—namely articulating and enforcing a consistent, formal stance on khat. The focus of analysis can then shift to the cultural knowledge and practices that are made possible by the silences. *This perspective of the state—as diverse and emerging—ultimately sheds light on the failure of both state and global governance institutions (such as NGOs, donors and lenders) to define local practices and landscapes.* Even though the state may choose to appear to support the U.S. ban on khat, and even though many state representatives (including, perhaps, the former president) would personally prefer to see it prohibited, a practice of silence allows the state to avoid taking an official stand. Doing so would obligate them to act, and that would cause considerable political and economic instability throughout the nation. Khat's quasi-legal status—officially legal but always with a barely visible question mark floating above it—allows for a wide range of attitudes and responses toward it. *Ignoring the informal khat economy enables the state to court external aid while not disrupting the life's blood of the economy of the north.*

This official state silence on khat both constrains and opens up possibilities for action. Not only does it reinforce solidarity between the Malagasy state and global governance institutions, it also, unwittingly, reinforces a divide between Western-based models of economic development and locally based alternatives—in this case, khat. The human interest newspaper article from the *Madagascar Tribune* in 2005 (http://www.madagascar-tribune.com/admin/voir_article.php?id = 9629; accessed November 2, 2006) referred to khat as a "development bank" for the north. The author reported an interview with a khat farmer who proudly stated that, "now, our township has solar panels, four wheel drive vehicles, and satellite television." The economic opportunities that khat provides come, ironically, because of and not despite the shadow that neoliberal restructuring casts on this country. They come to fill in the gaps of poverty that neoliberal reforms entail (see Figure 7.1).

In his analysis of "global shadows," James Ferguson notes that places on the political and economic margins throughout Africa and much of the global south are not just waiting to catch up. They are, instead, parallel economies without which the formal economy could not exist (Ferguson 2006:16). The khat economy, for example, has come into being *because* it allows survival for those who fall between the cracks of the formal economy. This case is similar for many drug economies around the world, including the United States and

Figure 7.1   Satellite dishes in Antsalaka provide evidence of the prosperity of some khat farmers

other industrialized nations, where drug dealing and drug production provide an income to large numbers of the population. Marijuana cultivation, for example, is common in several economically depressed areas of the United States and Canada (Katz and Whitaker 2001; Nguyen and Bouchard 2010).

The idea of alternative modernities acknowledges cultural differences in the ways in which people experience recent technological innovations and geopolitical and economic hegemonies. People interpret change through the lens of existing cultural practices and forge syncretic practices that do not merely mimic the West (e.g., Comaroff and Comaroff 1993; Knauft 2002). This perspective is important because it counters the misconception that globalization is leading toward, or reflects, a single world culture patterned on Euro-American development. Arturo Escobar (2008), in discussing localized economic development in

Columbia, identifies *alternatives to modernity* as an important concept, referring to "the emergence of subaltern knowledges and identities in the cracks of the modern colonial world system. These knowledges point at both a reappropriation of global designs by subaltern local histories and the possible reconstruction of local and regional worlds on different logics" (p. 162).

In proposing this viewpoint, Escobar is careful not to suggest that what we see on the ground is wholly outside the global capitalist economy; rather, he seeks to de-center the financial powerhouses as the unmarked category of analysis. His view privileges multiple centers, focusing on what he calls "a network of glocal histories constructed from the perspective of a politically enriched alterity" (2008:167).

Ferguson argues that focusing merely on global diversity, "a happy story about plurality and non-ranked cultural difference" (2006:192), risks becoming "a way of avoiding talking about the . . . political economic statuses of our time, and thus, evading the question of a rapidly worsening global inequality and its consequences" (p. 192). In other words, certain modernities have greater power, prestige, and wealth than others. The khat economy represents a locally oriented informal economy, true to the capitalist ideal of price being a function of supply and demand, but outside the bounds of the global capitalist political economy led by international capital and finance institutions, and, despite its creativity, it remains embedded in poverty and lack of access to quality education, health care, and other social goods that are part of the official economy.

Gender and the Margins

Women are key players in the global margins in Madagascar, as they are around the world, and as they have been historically. The women I met in Madagascar, whose lives were presented more fully in Chapter 6, navigate economic opportunities and limitations to ensure their own survival and often that of their families. The silence of khat at the national level keeps open a space for women's informal activities as they struggle to adapt to harsh economic conditions. Many studies by anthropologists and others have demonstrated that people—especially the poor—suffer from structural adjustment and neoliberal economic reforms that devalue currency, raise consumer prices, and encourage production for export. Men and women alike suffer greatly: Neither have adequate access to literacy and stable employment. Women's frequent obligation to dependent care, along with their relatively lower access to formal education and income, often puts them at a disadvantage vis-à-vis men, however. Gunewardena and Kingsolver (2007b) point out, in negotiating the effects of globalization, that women often experience increased disempowerment. In some contexts, however, they are able to take advantage of new opportunities.

Recent studies in gender and sustainability suggest that paying attention to women's strategies is important not only because they are frequently overlooked, but more importantly because they often have a high stake in ensuring subsistence survival and are at the forefront of adaptation to livelihood-threatening change (Gezon n.d.). Women are not inherently more capable than men at adapting to economic hardship. They certainly do not always follow paths that lead to the betterment of their households. It would be a mistake to ascribe women with essentialist qualities and assume that, by virtue of being a woman, an individual has certain proclivities or sensibilities. Nevertheless, certain patterns in women's behavior can be ascertained. To the extent that women do find themselves responsible for household reproduction, including the long-term care of individuals, they tend to be acutely aware of opportunities for making this happen. Without romanticizing women, we can still acknowledge the value of noticing what women, in conjunction with others, are doing to adapt for survival, taking care to acknowledge that not all women are alike.

Informal economies have been an important domain for women throughout the world, especially where they have fewer opportunities than men in the formal economy. Motivated and entrepreneurial, women have long been skillful at making ends meet (Clark 2010; Freeman 2000; Weismantel 2008). In the context of globalization, they face not only gender discrimination but also an increasingly entrenched social stratification that makes it hard for men and women alike to survive at the bottom. In Madagascar, women's exceptional skills at making ends meet fuel the khat economy and provide an impetus for general survival. Khat—and other informal entrepreneurial activities globally—may provide an opportunity for women, ironically, *because* it is silenced, on the national margins, out of a formal watchful eye, where literacy and formal education are not needed; and because of the depth of local poverty that valorizes women's long-standing practice of making ends meet.

Khat has provided an opportunity for income and flexibility for many women. As third-wave feminism (Anzaldúa 1990; Lorde 1984) has emphasized, however, women are differentiated by such factors as ethnicity and race, class, age, and other factors. In the Madagascar context, it must be recognized that while khat provides a living for some women, it increases the stress on other women whose husbands use scarce household resources to purchase it. It is indeed very expensive compared with other daily consumables, with one small-to-medium-sized pack of khat costing the same as a meal for five people. Women traders and farmers dealing in khat, on the other hand, have experienced tremendous gains relative to other commodities or services they could produce and offer instead.

Khat clearly presents an alternative to Western-led global capitalism as a form of survival in northern Madagascar. The fact that it is an internationally regulated psychoactive substance gives it a unique opportunity as well as a constraint: Its controlled status globally makes it risky for the state government to explicitly regulate this highly lucrative, locally legal commodity. Growers and traders continue to enjoy a high profit margin relative to other agricultural commodities with little government oversight. Silences allow for the expression of the otherwise forbidden, but they also suppress discussion. In the case of khat, the positive effects of a vibrant semiautonomous economy are offset by a lack of centralized attention to issues of agricultural productivity and sustainability, on the one hand, and issues of public health related to khat, on the other (see also Odenwald 2007:17).

Conclusion

Khat is a site of struggle over vision, combining material survival with ideological orientation and affective affiliation. It is a relatively mild psychoactive substance whose route of administration as a chewed leaf places inherent limitations on the quantity of its active properties that can be consumed in any given sitting. Khat is therefore instructive because it provides a broad canvas onto which it is possible to project worries or express commitments. Impressions of it as a hard or light drug develop in a cultural context and are not based directly on the unstable pharmacological properties of the stimulant itself (with cathinone, a Schedule I drug, changing into cathine, a Schedule III drug after twenty-four–forty-eight hours). The struggle over vision includes a moral imaginary that touches on issues of identity and global attachment to the West versus the Middle East and the Indian Ocean as well as issues of health, mental well-being, class anxieties, and work ethic that tend to accompany discussions of recreational drugs.

Evaluating the effects of a drug entails examining the broad political economic contexts in which it is produced, traded, and consumed. Ethnographic understandings of local experiences, perceptions, and cultural contexts of drug use stand alongside nonlocal dynamics that affect the structural conditions of availability and attractiveness of involvement in drugs. In this manner, a study of drugs entails multi-sited analysis, paying attention to anthropological concerns with how world system and local conditions mutually affect each other (Marcus 1995). This chapter has examined the effects of global perceptions of drugs, in general, and khat, in particular, in historical and contemporary perspective. In recent times, the War on Drugs has significantly shaped global and national understandings of khat, which have generally condemned the substance as dangerous to physical, mental, and social health. This negative view has intersected locally with cultural politics of ethnic and regional identity. It has also shaped the ways that national leaders have accommodated and appropriated norms, expectations, and conditions related to visions and practices of international development. For those who look to Western development models, khat is often seen as an impediment to economic development. Despite the negative evaluation of khat, the Malagasy state has not openly condemned its use or attempted to suppress its production. This silence has had the effect of opening up an informal economic space for the people, women in particular, of this northern region, providing income opportunities to farmers and traders.

When considering khat's drug effects, it is imperative to consider these larger, often seemingly unrelated political, economic, and cultural apprehensions and hopes. Evaluations of the health effects of psychoactive substances cannot be disentangled from cultural, political, and economic considerations. Reasons for negative evaluations of many psychoactive substances are couched in international foreign policy interests, as well as national political economic interests, and are not necessarily closely linked to the way they actually affect the lives of individuals. In the end, khat in Madagascar provides multiple economic opportunities and benefits and relatively few costs to society or the environment. Its ambiguous status, however, creates an underlying anxiety over its future.

Notes

1. The recommendations of the U.K.'s Advisory Council on the Misuse of Drugs, which the government accepted in 2006, are available online at: http://www.homeoffice.gov.uk/publications/alcohol-drugs/drugs/acmd1/khat-report-2005/Khat_Report_.pdf?view = Binary/ (accessed September 23, 2011).

2. See: http://www.guardian.co.uk/commentisfree/2008/jun/15/drugspolicy.somalia (accessed September 23, 2011).

3. In Australia, where khat can be imported by permit holders, there are similar campaigns. See, for example: http://www.theaustralian.news.com.au/story/0,25197,24063019-5006785,00.html (accessed September 23, 2011).

4. United Nations Office on Drugs and Crime, *A Century of International Drug Control* (Vienna, 2009) (http://www.unodc.org/documents/data-and-analysis/Studies/100_Years_of_Drug_Control.pdf; accessed September 23, 2011), offers an historical survey of international regulation that began with the 1909 Shanghai Opium Commission.

5. See the report of September 22, 2006, on the BBC website: http://news.bbc.co.uk/1/hi/world/africa/5369958.stm, and http://news.bbc.co.uk/2/hi/africa/6157216.stm (accessed June 15, 2011).

8

DRUG EFFECTS:
A HOLISTIC PERSPECTIVE

"Mom, not to be disrespectful or anything, but why would anyone care about khat in Madagascar?" This is the question my son, Adam, who was ten years old at the time, posed when I explained I was writing a book about it. What he meant to ask was why I would take the time to write about such an obscure topic that had, he imagined, so little interest to anyone outside of Madagascar. In this closing chapter, I make the case that khat in Madagascar provides an opportunity to reassess critically the meaning and structural effects of drugs in society and to recognize the complexities of their embeddedness in the social, cultural, economic, political, and environmental aspects of social life from local to global contexts. The case of khat gives us a way to break out of the now hardened polar perspectives of drugs as good or evil.

Thus far, the chapters in this book have analyzed khat from multiple angles, considering it from the perspectives of: (1) the physical and mental effects on individuals of psychotropic substances; (2) the social effects of its production, trade, and consumption; (3) the effects on both those who gain financially from it (farmers and traders) and those whose households budgets may be strained by money spent on consumption; (4) whether or not khat production displaces subsistence food production; and (5) the effects of global discourse against drugs (for example, the War on Drugs) on khat's local viability as a commodity and recreational activity. The emphasis of this analysis is that understanding any drug's effects requires examining multiple fronts, including individual, social, political, and economic aspects. Every substance that affects the central nervous system to influence perceptions, emotions, and behaviors is likely to have both costs and benefits. It is the task of concerned citizens, health specialists, and scholars to tease these out in a nonmoralistic, nonjudgmental way to best address problems while acknowledging advantages.

Drugs and Health: Definitions and Perspectives

The World Health Organization (WHO), in the preamble to its constitution in 1946, defined health as "a complete state of physical, mental and social well-being, and not merely the absence of disease or infirmity." In a similar way, Baer et al. (2003) propose a critical medical anthropology (CMA) definition of health "as access to and control over the basic material and nonmaterial resources that sustain and promote life at a high level of satisfaction" (p. 5). Baer et al.'s definition addresses critiques of the WHO definition—that it is out of touch with practical issues of human rights and the unevenness of access to health care globally (Saracci 1997), and therefore needs to reconsider its definition of health (Awofeso 2005). Nevertheless, it shares an emphasis on health as subjectively experienced as a state of well-being, marked by an individually perceived sense of satisfaction.

The role of recreational drugs in these definitions of health is tricky to define: As Saracci (1997) points out, physical health and a mental sense of well-being may be at odds with each other for a cigarette smoker. This brings up ethical issues pitting personal freedom against public health, which prioritizes the health of the group over individual interests (Charlton 2001). In arguing for personal freedom in access to psychiatric drugs such as Prozac, Charlton points out that making substances illegal means that the potential harm to society (of addiction, or of acts committed while under the influence) outweighs the potential benefit to the individual (e.g., of producing an enjoyable effect, counteracting anxiety, or reducing pain). A public health perspective, however, tends to neglect subjective aspects of drug use in favor of statistical measures of mortality and disease states. Charlton argues that for many psychiatric substances, individuals ought to have the right to make decisions about which ones they feel will benefit them. Adults already have this right with regard to alcohol, an addictive substance that is subject to much abuse. He concludes by stating that given "the essentially political nature of Public Health, and the way in which it can so easily be made to serve the interests of government against both individuals and populations— then individual freedom seems the best starting point for rational policy. . . . The *primary* safeguard against the abuse of Public Health is personal freedom"

(2001:68). From this perspective, a subjective experience of pleasure and social ease is a valuable outcome of a drug experience, and it connects with the definitions of health above, which emphasize well-being and personal satisfaction.

Substances that make people feel good can provide benefits to the consumers themselves, to people in their social networks, and to the physical environments in which they live, or they can be a source of harm. Recognizing and addressing benefits as well as harms becomes the legitimate domain of a civically minded and ethical public health approach. In the end, public health and personal freedom approaches must each have a place.

Studying Drug Effects

The first step toward this kind of holistic approach is good clinical observations and scholarship about drug effects. This includes pharmacological analysis, as well as knowledge about the drug context, or "setting" (Zinberg 1984), including the global political economy, the physical environment, gendered social relationships, and cultural and discursive conceptualizations. It also includes reported individual expectations, perceptions, and experiences of the substance, referred to by psychologists as "set" (Zinberg 1984). Scholars such as medical doctor Andrew Weil and Winifred Rosen (2004) have done much to popularize the need for education regarding drug effects. They insist that their readers distinguish drug use from drug abuse, understanding abuse not to be inherent in the substance itself, but rather in having "bad relationships with drugs" (Weil and Rosen 2004:2). They define a good relationship as one where people remain physically "healthy and fulfill their social and economic obligations" (Weil and Rosen 2004:24). Use of illegal drugs does not necessarily mean that the user is engaging in drug abuse: some users have healthy relationships with a given substances, while others do not. Weil and Rosen acknowledge, along with many other scholars (Zinberg 1984, for example), that expectations about drug effects and the social, physical, and cultural setting of consumption "can modify pharmacology drastically" (Weil and Rosen 2004:27). Therefore, understanding broad contexts of drug use is critical. Faulty assumptions about drugs can lead to easy but misguided conclusions about them, which, in turn, can influence the actions people take to mitigate or encourage their use.

Khat provides a relevant example of this: An amphetamine is a psychologically dependence-producing, or addictive, stimulant. Stimulants, sometimes referred to as "uppers," temporarily increase mental and physical function, making people feel awake. People often take these to remain alert for work or study, or to stay up for late-night recreation, such as at rave parties. The "high" is often followed by a significant lowering of functionality and mood. Examples of stimulants are methamphetamine, cocaine, Adderall, caffeine, and khat, whose active psychotropic properties have been identified as amphetamine-like (Kalix 1992). Narcotic drugs, on the other hand, are depressants that slow down brain function. They are derived from opium or a synthetic derivative of it and produce a stupor, relieve pain, and induce sleep. Narcotics include heroin, opium, many prescription pain killers (including codeine, Oxycontin, and Vicodin), and Valium. Narcotics produce physical dependence that results in physical withdrawal symptoms when an individual attempts to lessen or eliminate use. While both are potentially debilitating and dependence producing, amphetamines and narcotics are very different drugs, pharmacologically speaking.

Despite these differences, "narcotic" is a heavily charged, overused word that is commonly associated with any drug considered dangerous. The popular press often falsely refers to khat, a stimulant, as a narcotic. One report in the *Washington Post* describes a former school teacher in Somalia: "Now she earns a living dealing khat, a narcotic plant that when chewed yields a jittery high and feelings of invincibility that later melt and leave the user in a lethargic stupor" (Wax 2006). Even the *New Scientist* referred to khat as a narcotic in its report entitled "Narcotic Khat Gets Sperm Going" (Ainsworth 2004). The two drug categories have significantly different medical effects, and narcotics are, from a pharmacological point of view, much more likely to be debilitating to social functioning than unrefined, nonsynthesized, and therefore mild, stimulants, such as caffeine, coca leaves, and khat.

The Case of Khat: A Holistic Perspective

Khat provides an instructive case study for examining the broader context of a particular drug. This analysis has linked social, cultural, ecological, political economic, experiential, and medical perspectives, resulting in a holistic biocultural account. In addition to being a drug, khat is a vital part of the economy of northern Madagascar. That it is a drug shapes its viability as an economic resource. Conversely, that it is economically lucrative influences its availability as a consumable substance.

Political Ecology and CMA

Khat is one of the most significant factors in the environmental and economic transformation in the Mount Amber region of northern Madagascar, which lies on the edge of a protected forest. The growth of the khat economy since the 1980s has had implications for how land is used (khat as opposed to other crops;

khat perhaps at the expense of forest), how inhabited spaces transform in rural areas as khat money fuels the expansion of villages into towns with expanding infrastructural needs, and the possible spread of risks associated with pesticides used in khat production. Based on observation and interviews with farmers on location, my recent visits to the region suggested that forests are coming increasingly under pressure because of khat production. Nevertheless, none of the political officials or conservation agents I spoke with mentioned this as a serious concern—in fact, some feel khat is beneficial as a deterrent to erosion. With regard to the fear that khat is replacing food crops, many farmers said that in addition to growing khat, they would like to plant more food crops, such as beans, tomatoes, and carrots. Problems such as lack of markets, poor water management, and deteriorated roads make that difficult. With careful attention to agricultural, forestry, and social factors, both khat and food production could be treated as complementary parts of a system.

Political ecology is a theoretical approach that many environmental anthropologists have engaged to understand how powerful contests over access to resources shape and are shaped by local human-environmental interactions. Scholars examine local power struggles (Bassett 1988; Gezon 1999b) as well as the ways in which political economic dynamics at national and global levels (Hecht and Cockburn 1990) affect how local people negotiate the ways in which they use—or don't use—resources of the physical environment. Both political ecology (PE) and CMA examine the actual conditions of health (CMA) and environment (PE), politically negotiated *access* to them, and the *discourses* that shape them. This analysis of khat in Madagascar links PE and CMA concerns. In this case, the conditions of concern are the *forest*—related to the production of khat, *livelihoods*—related to the production and distribution of khat, and the *health* of the local people—related to the consumption of khat and access to high-quality nutrition. National and international discourses about khat—regarding it as a dangerous drug, as associated with terrorism and Islam, and as an anathema to economic development—are linked to powerful outside economic and political interests that shape both land use and physical health locally.

Other CMA studies have engaged a PE approach in an integrated analysis of environmental, physical, and mental health. This has occurred in response to a strong call by CMA theorists to link health analyses with external factors (Singer 1989, 1990). Many of these studies have focused on ways that environmental injustice affects, if not determines (often negatively), quality of health care and environmental health effects. In one landmark study, Janice Harper (2002) teased out the health effects of unequal access to environmental resources as a conservation project was established in Madagascar. She found that as a result of the conservation efforts of the Ranomafana National Park, the local people were prohibited from access to medicinal plants and other forest resources—such as land for farming, tree ferns for selling, and materials for local construction. The result was lowered nutrition due to loss of potentially available land, decreased access to direct health care from the medicinal plants, and diminished indirect access to health care for which payment is required because of their loss of income. In the midst of severe poverty and a high mortality rate, she identified any loss of access to resources as life threatening. Other studies have focused on unequal exposure to risks associated with environmental change—for example, related to global warming (Baer and Singer 2009) and control over fisheries resources (Richmond et al. 2005).

My analysis of khat production shares this growing interest in integrating health issues into broader political economic and ecological contexts, but it diverges from former studies that have focused on the negative impacts of environmental change on health, emphasizing how the poor are victims of globalization. Instead, the impact on health of this environmental transformation (increased khat production) is not necessarily negative, since it increases incomes and purchasing power of farmers and traders, thereby increasing access to health care and nutritious foods. It is potentially negative, however, in how it affects consumers and their households because the relatively high cost of khat prevents some from purchasing household needs, including food. This study evaluates how a lucrative drug plant affects the ways that people choose to modify the physical environment: in this case, by cutting down some forests, by planting khat bushes that stabilize soil, and through the transformation of rice and vegetable fields into khat fields. Khat has allowed many people to adapt to the devastation of globalization by providing a living for many in one of the poorest nations in the world.

Social Differentiation: Commodity Chains and Gender

The khat economy takes place through social networks of relationships. The commodity chain approach I have taken permits a nuanced examination of the processes through which khat becomes available and widely used, highlighting the different kinds of relationships that people have with khat. This approach traces production (farming), through distribution (trade), to consumption. A feminist perspective, with a focus on women's livelihood strategies, reveals the ways that access to khat as a resource has unevenly touched people's lives. In northern Madagascar, the effects of khat on women have been uneven: Some benefit from increased opportunities for income generation as farmers and traders, and others suffer the effects of lowered household budgets as household members (often husbands and sons) use scarce resources to purchase khat.

In a review of the medical anthropology literature on women, Marcia Inhorn (2006) points out that medical anthropology has much to contribute to traditional medical approaches to gender, and to women's health in particular. One of the themes she found in the medical anthropology literature is that race, class, and other forms of differentiation intersect gender, and that these factors have a significant effect on health experiences. In several studies, for example, scholars pointed out "the role of poverty as the major risk factor for women's contraction of the HIV virus" (Inhorn 2006:361).

Another theme Inhorn highlighted was the effect of patriarchy on women's health, considering such issues as loss of autonomy, nutritional deprivation, and son preference and their effects on health. In her own work, for example, she studied the cultural politics of infertility, which gives men in a patriarchal society considerable control over women (Inhorn 2006). The study of khat contributes to an understanding of how gender stratification affects women's health opportunities. While Inhorn (2006) calls for "more ethnographic texts that also successfully theorize the health-demoting effects of patriarchy in women's lives" (p. 361), the case of khat reveals a different but related dynamic, which is the empowerment women experience in a higher status setting. Freedom to divorce and engage in economic activities autonomously provides women with greater access to income and greater freedom to make their own health care and nutritional decisions.

A feminist CMA perspective grounds any analysis in an awareness of both the ability for individuals to make decisions about their lives and the structural factors of unequal power relations that constrain and frame the decisions they can make (Gunewardena and Kingsolver 2007a). Chapter 6 explored the realm of decision-making about involvement in the khat economy—as farmers, sellers, consumers, or spouses of consumers—considering the range of factors that people take into consideration, including the ideals and realities of intimate relationships as well as straight economic rationality. Women flexibly manage their options within the context of general poverty, high rates of illiteracy, limited income-earning possibilities, relative social autonomy, and desires for relationship fulfillment. They do this within a gendered space of highly masculine khat consumption and associated cultural identities, as described in Chapter 2.

Identity and Meaning in the Drug Experience: Opiate of the Masses or Emancipation?

In addition to being an economic means of survival, the consumption of khat contributes to establishing new cultural modes of expression locally. Khat is widely chewed by people in northern Madagascar, cutting across generations, national origins, and ethnic identity. A significant exception is that it does not tend to be chewed by people who strongly identify culturally with the high plateau region of the country, especially those who claim Merina ethnic identity (from the region in and around the national capital) who have recently immigrated to the region. Some of the most prominent of chewers are young men, who publically chew khat in groups in the afternoons or chew as they work, for example, as taxi drivers. Khat serves as an identity marker on several different levels—for masculinity, youth, and as a Malagasy person of northern coastal descent. It is strongly associated with a particular kind of masculinity—one associated with hip youth culture. As Mbima (2011) argues for Madagascar, and Mains (2010) and Ahmed (2010) argue for Ethiopia, in many places where it has recently been taken up as a practice, khat serves as a central symbolic focus for new forms of identity that replace narrow ethnic and religious affiliations, especially among young men. This is positive to the extent that it permits new forms of civic engagement and mutual understanding.

The recreational aspect of khat chewing raises larger questions about the social and individual significance of drug experiences. Drug consumption is a powerful experience that takes people out of their ordinary everyday lives and opens their minds to alternative ways of understanding and experiencing the world. In many cultural contexts, drug-induced states are socially structured and highly valued (Coomber and South 2004b). Evidence suggests that the desire to alter one's consciousness is deeply ingrained in the human experience. One study suggests that attraction to the taste and smell of ethanol in rotting fruit may have been selected for in many nonhuman fruit-eating species, including primates. Dudley (2004) suggests that the adaptive value of ethanol attraction was because of its association with the higher sugar content and nutritional reward of ripe fruit and for the inebriating effects of alcohol at very low doses, which may encourage consumption of food.

Psychotropic substances also facilitate and deepen social connections, which is key to our basic survival as a species. They do this by distancing people from interpersonal competitiveness and the demands of everyday responsibilities and by binding them in the affective and cognitive affirmation of commonly held worldview and values. Brian Hayden (2003) has written about the prehistory of religion and the cognitive origin of the capacity for religious experience. He has pointed out that an important effect of religious experience is social bonding through ritual, through what Emile Durkheim referred to as "collective effervescence." Hayden (2003) suggests that significant bonding occurs in the context of ecstatic experiences, induced through drumming, chanting, and psychotropic drugs. In commenting on Hayden's work, psychologist Matthew J. Rossano writes that euphoric states induced through ritual do not only enlighten individuals involved in the ritual, they also contribute to the formation of strong social alliances within and between groups (Rossano 2005).

The social and individual effects of ritual and nonordinary experiences have been debated. Analyzed as a kind of ritual inversion, where the mundane is subverted and replaced with an alternative way of being, drug-induced altered states of consciousness can provide a way of "letting off steam." Seen as an "opiate of the masses," drugs can also be seen as blinding people to the harsh realities of class oppression. From the emic perspective of khat chewers in Madagascar, there is no consensus on its effects, and opinions continuously shift. Nevertheless, many laud the feeling of the high that khat provides and find it a pleasurable way of spending time with friends, opening the door to lively and engaging conversation. They also derive satisfaction from participating in new cultural forms and in-style ways of being Malagasy (see also Carrier 2005a). In the quieter, more introspective moments of the khat experience, many claim that it opens their mind to new ideas and helps them plan for their future. It is also valued as an aphrodisiac. Some chewers—and critics of those who chew—point out that even though people get big ideas while they are chewing khat, the plans are rarely if ever realized and only distract them from their harsh economic situations.

These disparate perceptions raise the question of what the overall result of recreational drug use is for individuals in society: Do their benefits (self-actualization, pleasure, and social bonding) necessarily come with the price of alienation from nonconsuming members of their primary social networks? Do they necessarily accompany lower social status (status as power, prestige, and wealth) and become a blind escape from class oppression? Or do drugs, on the other hand, lead to self-improvement and increased social opportunities? These are questions in the minds of many Malagasy as they themselves struggle to understand this new phenomenon of khat. As Bennett and Cook (1996) point out, anthropological studies of drugs have often focused on drug use from the consumer's points of view, developing accounts that seem to condone their consumption. These studies often reveal and reject common assumptions that illegal substances are necessarily harmful to individuals and communities.

In his analysis of drugs and poverty, however, Singer (2008a:41) condemns use of certain drugs (tobacco, for example), arguing that they are barriers to the well-being of consuming populations. He invokes Sidney Mintz's analysis of sugar as a cheap appetite suppressant, and he cites British promotion of opium in China in the 1800s to suggest that drug addictions among working people often serve the interests of the powerful. Singer convincingly argues that an important aspect of their use is in "self-medicating the hidden injuries of oppression" (Baer et al. 2003:169). Singer's analysis reveals the importance of evaluating drugs from both emic and etic perspectives, considering both local perceptions and experiences, and evaluations based on analysis of a broader cultural political economy. He valuably reminds anthropologists of the shortsightedness of binary thinking about drugs as either good or bad. In terms of practical action, Singer's analysis points to the need for interventions that not only target users but also the larger political and economic phenomena of poverty and social stratification that frame the contexts in which people consume drugs.

To return to the above set of questions, khat's effects cannot be pigeon-holed in the abstract. Even within northern Madagascar, experiences vary based on the amount chewed, the set and setting of chewing, and the actual social relationships surrounding consumption. Considering a cross-cultural perspective, Coomber and South (2004b) make the argument that drug use is not necessarily damaging, rather there are many cases that reveal "positive, integrative and functional contributions of drug use to the social-health of particular communities of people" (p. 16). Characteristics of these positive drugs are that they are "integrated into many facets of everyday life" (p. 16) and often have ceremonial or ritual meaning. Andrew Weil and Winifred Rosen (2004) argue that instead of thinking of substances as being "good" or "bad" in and of themselves, it makes more sense to evaluate individuals' relationships with them. They present characteristics of a good relationship that include being knowledgeable about the nature and effects of the substance as a chemical, experiencing a sustained beneficial effect of the drug, ability to stop using it at will, and lack of adverse side effects of drugs on health or behavior, recognizing that this will vary among individuals. Although addressing a primarily U.S. audience, their criteria are useful in thinking about differences among individuals within any given study group, where some have healthier relationships with drugs than others. A public health intervention focusing on addressing drug abuse would do well to analyze the specific indicators of khat consumption that point to well-being or lack thereof, paying attention, for example, to defining what "adverse" means in the Malagasy context.

Khat: "Good" or "Bad"?

So what's the overall verdict for khat? Can any generalizations be made? Based on almost a decade of research, I argue that in terms of both health (physical and mental) and economic development, the overall effect of khat has been benign, tending to have a neutral to beneficial influence. Economically, it has clearly been beneficial to farmers and traders. Emerging local markets for khat in Madagascar, combined with ideal ecological conditions for growing it, vitalize the local economy. Its relatively mild psychotropic effects reduce its threat to consumers and their communities, and the physical health effects do not appear significant (as opposed to tobacco and alcohol), based on existing studies.

These factors add up to making khat a viable economic alternative for many people in northern Madagascar. The informal khat economy has permitted these people, on the margins of the global economy, to survive in conditions where they have little chance for upward mobility—or even basic survival (see also Ferguson 2006). As a country, Madagascar's gross domestic product (GDP) per person was about $1,000 per year in 2010, which puts it 217th in the world—nearly at the bottom. To put this into perspective, it contrasts with the United States, where the GDP per person was $47,400 in 2010 and ranked 10th highest in the world.

This thriving local informal economy may become increasingly important to local well-being in the wake of the global financial crisis. Consumer households may not gain directly from khat's economic strength, but they may indirectly feel the ripple effects of cash flowing in the local economy. This is important to health, as studies show that reduction of real poverty leads overall to better nutrition and greater access to health care. Therefore, khat may be an instigator rather than a barrier to local development, albeit a kind of development that is alternative to the vision of global financial institutions based on hard currency and commodity export.

In terms of social relationships, there are two tendencies: On the one hand, khat chewing contributes favorably to social relations between same sex peers among youth and men and to the making of postethnic cultural identities. On the other hand, frequent chewing can also lead to strain within families as chewers divert valuable resources to pleasure consumption instead of meeting the needs of dependents. Frequent peer-group chewing sessions within the home can also usurp the domestic space available to children and other family members, leading to early alienation of children from the home (Mbima, personal communication). Despite the social problems, it is important to note, based on my interviews and surveys, that khat's negative effects on family systems have been exaggerated (see also Beckerleg 2006). In addition, problems associated with khat seem to be as much related to the lure of leisure in the context of poverty as to the effects of the psychotropic substance itself. This suggests, in affirmation of Singer's stance, that efforts to address problems of khat need also to deal with the lack of jobs, inaccessibility of high-quality education, and other aspects of entrenched poverty.

Globalization and Discourse

Answering the question of whether or not khat is "good" for people in northern Madagascar is not sufficient for understanding it as a CMA phenomenon since local conditions of use are also affected by the global context. As a quasi-legal drug, khat provides a unique set of political and economic constraints and opportunities. Because of how emotionally charged reactions are to them, perceptions of psychotropic substances have dramatic effects in terms of global policy and local interventions. These are not always positive for growers, as in the case of the extensive destruction to opium and coca fields in Southeast Asia and South America in the wake of the War on Drugs. Because of its relatively inconspicuous status on the global stage compared with opium and coca, however, khat has slipped under the radar in Madagascar. Although it is illegal in the United States and much of Europe, no government has made it the target of an eradication campaign. There is currently no serious talk of making khat illegal in Madagascar, but its increasing negative perception in the West, coupled with national-level anxieties surrounding it within Madagascar, could prompt a reevaluation of its legal status.

This study points to the unique ways in which discourses on psychotropic substances engage states and global institutions, producing effects at local levels. In Madagascar, there is a silence around khat: Although rumored to be reviled by government officials, there is little to nothing in the popular media in Madagascar about khat and even less that condemns it. In addition to the media silence, khat is not directly taxed beyond the most local level, nor is it the target of agricultural extension projects—despite its lucrative nature. An important reason for this silence is connected to the state's dependence on foreign aid—coming from nations such as the United States that do not condone the use of khat—and its commitment to neoliberal economic reforms. Since khat is only consumed within Madagascar, it is not a source of hard currency from export sales, and therefore does not contribute to the raising of the country's GDP. These two factors make khat an unlikely target of positive governmental attention. However, by not repressing or publically condemning the informal khat economy, the state does not risk disrupting the life's blood of the economy of the north and creating a hotbed of political instability.

The loud silence toward khat affects people's livelihood and health, however, by shaping their access to, experience of, and information about this substance. On the negative side, it discourages analysis of and intervention into the public health effects of khat and keeps khat out of formal discussions of agricultural, environmental, and economic development interventions. On the positive side, the silence and marginality allow for the building of community and the flourishing of an informal economy where women and the poor tend to thrive, thereby increasing their access to quality nutrition and health care.

Khat and Coca

Many people point out the similarity between khat and coca: Both are stimulants whose leaves are chewed by local people with neutral to positive effects. Both are labeled as "drugs" with "high abuse potential" by WHO and many governments. They are different in that coca is refined into cocaine through chemical processing, increasing its potency dramatically. The khat plant, in contrast, has been known to be dried for preservation but not processed into a more concentrated form. A more potent form can be synthesized in a laboratory into methcathinone, used for both medical and recreational purposes, but the khat plant is not needed for this, while for cocaine, the plant is needed. Unlike khat, coca production has been the target of a heavily funded U.S.-backed War on Drugs since the early 1970s, when President Nixon declared drugs "public enemy number one" (Singer 2008b:75).

Khat is not chewed widely outside of Yemen and the Horn of Africa and their diaspora communities (especially Somalis), whereas cocaine in its different forms has been a drug of choice various for segments of the U.S. population, with the wealthy preferring its powder form and the poor tending toward the less expensive rock crystal form, called crack, that produces a high when heated. Unfortunately for producers, the War on Drugs has focused more heavily on eradicating drug production in supplying countries than on reducing dependence and abuse within its own borders (although it has spent considerable amounts on incarceration of users and distributers). What may have begun as a genuine interest in addressing social problems related to addiction in the United States soon began to answer to the interest of U.S. foreign policy interests in fighting communism and protecting sources of oil. As Singer has stated, the War on Drugs "has been driven at least in part, or at times primarily, by the global geopolitical designs of U.S. foreign policy, rather than by a concern for the harmful effects of drug use" (2008b:76).

Khat and coca have some apparent similarities, including route of administration (being chewed by local people as a stimulant) and common labeling as harmful drugs, which makes both of them prohibited substances. Their differences are significant, however: History and status of use in the global north, chemical effects of its various forms, domestic political agendas in the United States, strategic position of producing and trafficking nations, civil wars in producing countries, the environmental conditions of production, and the acquiescence or resistance of each individual involved in these economies all contextualize the differences between khat and coca.

Drug Use and Abuse: Public Health Concern or Criminal Activity?

Accounts of drugs tend to lean toward totalizing assessments of their use: Across the board, they are either portrayed as harmful, benign, or perhaps even manifestly socially beneficial in establishing bonds between people and reinforcing integrative culturally held values. Dichotomous assessments of drugs as good or bad mask complexities on two levels: First, *drugs, such as khat, can have both positive and negative effects within a given community.* On the positive side, khat is an important source of income for many; it is a satisfying form of leisure; and it is closely linked with new forms of urban multicultural/multiethnic identity and sociability. On the negative side, drawbacks include some deforestation (though most fields are not carved from the forest, as discussed in Chapter 5) and the diminishing of subsistence food production due to the conversion to khat fields (though reduction of food crop production cannot easily be linked to the rise of khat). Khat can also have some adverse health effects—though these are not well understood and appear to be mild when compared with the often devastating effects of heavy use of other drugs, such as alcohol, heroin, cocaine, and methamphetamine. Finally, it can strain the social relationships of consumers because of the high purchase price of khat and the time it takes away from other primary relationships. Problems at the household level, though real, are not ubiquitous, and they tend to be exaggerated by those who disapprove of khat.

A second level of complexity stems from this last qualified negative aspect of khat: *Within any community, some people have healthier relationships with drugs than others.* This presents two interrelated challenges: One question is how to address individual cases of abuse—where consumption takes away from a person's health, defined as their physical, mental, and social well-being. This is in keeping with a public health approach that seeks to modify individual risk behaviors in consumption practices. This supports interventions such as detoxification and rehabilitation programs. Nutbeam (2000) points out that historically, public health approaches have not only focused on individual behaviors but on the social conditions that negatively affect health. During the Industrial Revolution, for example, public health initiatives addressed the living and working conditions of the laboring classes. What is needed today, argues Nutbeam, is an approach that combines macro analysis of structural conditions with sensitivity to differences in individual responses to these conditions. He writes: "Health status is influenced by individual characteristics and behavioral patterns (lifestyles) but continues to be significantly determined by the different social, environmental, and economic circumstances of individuals and populations" (p. 260).

With increasing sensitivity to broader socioeconomic impacts on health, many public health initiatives have been designed to address underlying influences on poor health choices. An example would be smoking: In addition to education campaigns addressed at smokers, there is support for policy that would restrict promotion and access to tobacco (Nutbeam 2000). It also involves holistic drug treatment programs. In one such program that Merrill Singer (1993) helped design, culturally sensitive interventions addressed not only the direct condition of addiction, but also interrelated needs of addicted pregnant women, including childcare, medical care, and transportation to services. The goal of the program was not only to halt damaging addictions but also to break a cycle of poverty that goes hand-in-hand with the addictions. A critical approach to drug treatment, argue Baer et al. (2003), involves recognizing the larger political and economic underpinnings of destructive individual behavior.

Despite the logic of a public health approach to drugs, however, many governments, including that of the United States, have opted instead to place a stronger emphasis on criminalizing illegal drug use, no matter what the relationship between the user and the substance. One fear is that drug use leads to criminal behavior and therefore must be repressed. This has meant, as Baer et al. (2003) lament, that "American society is ambivalent about investing resources in drug treatment. Such existing programs are often underfunded and inadequate for the scale of the problem at hand" (p. 224). Indiscriminately making drug users criminals deprives individuals of potentially empowering treatments to address debilitating dependencies and ignores underlying structural roots of dependency. In the case of illegal drugs, it also takes away the opportunity for healthy relationships with drugs.

From a policy perspective, approaches to drug use have been characterized as aiming either toward completely ridding a nation of drugs, on the one hand, or on reducing harm to individuals and society, on the other (Mares 2006). The drug-free-nation option has characterized the United States and has fueled both the War on Drugs and anti-drug campaigns at home. The stated goal of the War on Drugs has been to eliminate the supply of drugs from the market (see Chapter 7 for a more extensive critique of the War on Drugs). Educational campaigns occur according to the precepts of the U.S. D.A.R.E. (Drug Abuse Resistance Education) program. It has been widely disseminated to children in grades K–12, and aims, according to its website, to give "kids the skills they need to avoid involvement in drugs, gangs, and violence" and to teach them "how to resist peer pressure and live productive drug and violence-free lives" (http://www.dare.com/home/about_dare.asp; accessed May 18, 2011). These statements equate drugs with violence and do not acknowledge an option for healthy relationships with drugs. A critical irony is that this program ignores blatant and culturally acceptable violations of their stated goal, sending children home to scold their parents for enjoying even an occasional drink of alcohol.

The drug-free approach that criminalizes users also ignores the enormous social costs of enforcing such laws. MacCoun and Reuter (2001) outline a taxonomy of drug-related harms according to the categories of health, social functioning, public order, and criminal justice. Many of the costs are directly related to the fact of its illegal status and the consequences of enforcement. The authors write, for example, that "direct criminal justice costs in the current regime are on the order of tens of billions of dollars" (p. 108).

The "harm-reduction" approach, in contrast, seeks to mitigate the effects of harmful chemical dependency on individuals by providing such services as needle exchange and treatment programs. It rests on the fundamental assumption that drug use and abuse will continue to exist at some level—that zero tolerance is not a realistic option. The harm-reduction approach is a response to the zero tolerance approach and rests on two main critiques: First, zero-tolerance strategies have failed to eliminate drug use, leaving harms to individuals and society intact. Second, many of the harms associated with drug use stem from the enforcement policies themselves (MacCoun and Reuter 2001:386).

Richard Nixon is often credited with both introducing the War on Drugs and championing the harm-reduction approach. He spoke like a hard-line law-and-order advocate, associating drugs with violent crime and rebellious youth, and of "decimating a generation of Americans" (quoted in Baum 1996:12). He committed the nation to fighting illegal drugs both at home and abroad. As part of his fight against drugs, he recognized that the problem stemmed from hard-core users, and he embraced the harm-reduction approach by implementing extensive methadone treatment programs for heroin addicts. According to Massing, "When Richard Nixon became president in 1969, the nation was in the grip of a serious heroin epidemic. In a few short years, his administration managed to bring it under control" (1998:271). As chronicled by Baum (1996), the harm-reduction approach turned into a full-scale War on Drugs by the 1980s, criminalizing drug use and eliminating most funding for harm-reduction initiatives.

Drug policy experts overwhelmingly call for reform in how our nation understands and addresses the problem of drugs. The recent report of the Global Commission on Drug Policy (GCDP) (2011) condemns the War on Drugs as a failure. It is worth noting that members of this commission are high profile international figures, including Kofi Anan, former secretary general of the United Nations; George Schultz, secretary of the treasury under President Nixon and secretary of state under President Reagan; Paul Volker, former chairman of the U.S. Federal Reserve; and former heads of state of Mexico, Colombia, Brazil, Greece, and Switzerland.

Together, these commissioners came to a consensus that comprehensive reforms are needed in global and national drug policies. In the introduction, they write of the "the global drug problem as a set of interlinked health and social challenges to be managed, rather than a war to be won" (GCDP 2011:4). They make many recommendations, one of which is to "replace the criminalization and punishment of people who use drugs with the offer of health and treatment services to those who need them" (p. 10). They encourage a strong public health approach that resists stigmatization of drug users. On the criminal side, the report encourages lighter sentences or even decriminalization of small-scale users and dealers. Law enforcement emphasis should instead be placed on addressing violent drug-related crime and organized drug trafficking. They end the report by entreating policy makers around the world to act urgently, because "the war on drugs has failed, and policies need to change now" (p. 17).

Scholars have long pointed out the need for drug policy reform. Massing (1998), in making a claim for increased attention to treatment initiatives, calls for a recognition that "the main threat to young people is not the occasional, experimental use of drugs but their regular use" (p. 175). MacCoun and Reuter (2001) acknowledge that treatment alone will not solve the drug problem and that other social policies targeting issues of poverty (housing, health care, education) are needed to address drug problems. They do not call for an end to all criminalization of the drug trade. They look to European examples of prohibition that is selective and targeted, including shorter terms for offenders, attention to racial profiling, and less intrusion on civil liberties. Their recommendations suggest focusing enforcement on use that is demonstrably associated with social problems like health and crime—a change that would severely reduce the scope of current drug enforcement initiatives.

Critical medical anthropologist Merrill Singer points out that distress about illegal drug use is not merely top-down—it is not just confined to law enforcement agents. Those concerned with the disparities of class and the plight of the poor are also alarmed at current patterns of drug use. Singer points out that the harmful effects of drug use tend to fall on the poor. He writes: "Drugs, including both legal and illegal varieties . . . contribute to maintaining an unjust structure of social and economic relations" (Singer 2008a:230). Furthermore, "feelings of hopelessness and powerlessness in a community have been found to be good predictors of health risk and health, and, as well, the appeal of psychotropic drugs" (p. 234). In response, many people within poor communities have launched what Singer has called "an alternative war on drugs" (p. 239), where community members engage in grassroots campaigns to reduce the presence of both legal (e.g., by limiting advertising) and illegal drugs their neighborhoods.

Model for Assessing Drugs

Harmful individual relationships with drugs, as well as broad-based political economic concerns about the presence of drugs within given communities, drive initiatives to combat their negative effects. With regard to khat, the ideal would be to launch a public health initiative that is well intentioned, nonmoralistic, and sensitive to individual experiences with drugs—acknowledging that the problem is not the plant itself but rather with individual relationships with it. Efforts to reduce its direct harmful effects on users would be combined in a multi-agency effort to address poverty by encouraging an increase in available social services (such as health and education) and economic opportunities. In the case of khat in Madagascar, an integrated approach would include taking a close look at agricultural issues of productivity and the balance of khat and food production. Forest issues need to be examined to analyze the extent of deforestation due to khat and the issues of land tenure that frame it. Culturally sensitive medical studies of the health effects of khat would frame direct public health interventions. Such a holistic approach would be robust enough to acknowledge the positive aspects of khat while addressing problems in a culturally sensitive way.

A model for assessing a drug within a community will take an expanded health system approach. It considers multiple factors, including the *pharmacological assessment* of the drug; the behavior and perceptions of *users* (perceptions are sometimes referred to as "set"); and the *social and cultural context* of use, including legal status, other substances that may be taken in tandem with the drug in question, and the way in which the substances fits into other cultural practices (sometimes referred to as "setting"). It also evaluates the broader social context of use, examining *perceptions and behavior of nonusers*. These nonusers include people within the social networks of users as well as those in official positions at the local, national, or global level who address public concerns regarding use, including health care workers, enforcement agents, policy makers, religious leaders. Finally, it considers the *broader socioeconomic and political framework within which the drug commodity chain exists* and within which use takes place, attuned to a broad range of issues, such as the availability of social services, opportunities for productive income-earning, and ecological and agricultural contexts of production. The first three concerns: drug action, set, and setting (Zinberg 1984) have been the traditional focus of drug studies. CMA broadens this traditional concern with setting to include a focus on the wider social networks and political economic dynamics that frame drug use.

The outcome is an assessment of what constitutes use and abuse—of the nature of both positive and dysfunctional relationships with the substance, which can then guide culturally appropriate interventions that protect the rights of some while addressing the needs of others.

Conclusion

Why would anyone outside of Madagascar care about khat? This is the question posed by my son that opened the chapter. First, khat provides a significant scholarly case study of cultural and economic survival on the global margins.

Second, in a more applied sense, it has relevance for analyzing the effects of drugs in general, and for conceptualizing interventions that can account for the complexities of their effects. As this analysis has revealed, uniform judgment of the health effects of any given psychotropic substance is not as useful as analyzing broad-based costs and benefits. Practical interventions targeting any drug will account for both the advantages it affords people—subjective as well as clinically measurable—as well as the costs it imposes.

Taking a stand on khat or any drug requires complex evaluation of their multiple effects, which may include both negative and positive aspects: It can be beneficial to some and harmful to others, for example. Understanding these complex dynamics requires a holistic understanding grounded not only in individualistic mental and physical health perspectives, but also in political economic, social, and cultural contexts. As stated previously, *the danger in analyzing any drug lies in black and white, often moralistic thinking that fails to see the complexity of the issues at stake.* Interdisciplinary education for health care workers, with a strong grounding in social as well as natural sciences, is an important step toward effective interventions. Health care professionals may not be able to directly impact policies of the War on Drugs, which are deeply rooted in foreign policy objectives, or influence policies regarding the criminalization of drugs, which are tightly embedded within larger social anxieties about race and poverty. They can, however, through each individual served, each program implemented, and each medical study designed, help shift the balance toward a context-sensitive approach to drugs, well-being, and overall sense of satisfaction with life.

In Madagascar, khat has multiple meanings—a lucrative local crop for farmers and trade for sellers, a pleasurable diversion for many, a marker of modernity for some, and a problem for some, but local perceptions are generally favorable. More negatively nuanced meanings are evoked as one moves from local to regional to national to global levels of analysis and are intimately related to policy rather than the medical and social consequences of its consumption.

Perhaps what saves khat from being targeted by the U.S. War on Drugs, like coca and poppies, are its natural properties of being a mild stimulant in leaf form with a short lifespan of potency that cannot be easily converted into an (illegal) export crop. In its natural form, the drug seems not to be particularly problematic in terms of health issues, violence, or criminal activity, and the plant itself is not needed to produce the synthetically much stronger form. Under these circumstances, the state allows khat to fulfill a local need and make contributions to the local economy in a marginalized area of Madagascar, thereby promoting political stability. However, khat does have the potential to become a larger national issue because of global policies tied to aid that affect not just drugs but also agriculture, conservation, and food security. Thus, at this time, there is an uneasy truce between the producers and the state, and the ensuing silence serves all parties well except, perhaps, those who "abuse" khat who, like addicts to other drugs, are blamed for their own problems.

This analysis of khat in Madagascar surely points to the importance of paying attention to the entire social, economic, and environmental context of khat, from local to global, and highlights the increasing relevance of using critical approaches to understanding intertwined health and environmental issues that emerge in the context of drugs.

REFERENCES

Abebe, Almaz, Kelbessa Urga, and Lemma Ketema
  2005 Khat chewing habit as a possible risk behaviour for HIV infection: A case-control study. Ethiopian Journal of Health Development 19(3): 174–181.

Abebe, Dawit, Asfaw Debella, Amare Dejene, Ambaye Degefa, Almaz Abebe, Kelbessa Urga, and Lemma Ketema
  2005 Khat chewing habit as a possible risk behaviour for HIV infection: A case-control study. Ethiopian Journal of Health Development 19(3):174–181.

ACU News
  2005 President of Madagascar praises ACU during visit to campus: ACU News. http://www.acu.edu/events/news/archives2005/050207_madagascar_follow_up.html (accessed September 20, 2011).

Advisory Council on the Misuse of Drugs (ACMD)
  2005 Khat (Qat): Assessment of Risk to the Individual and Communities in the UK. London: Advisory Council on the Misuse of Drugs, Home Office. http://www.homeoffice.gov.uk/publications/alcohol-drugs/drugs/acmd1/khat-report-2005/Khat_Report_.pdf?view=Binary (accessed September 29, 2011).

Ahmed, Hussein
  2010 Khat Consumption in Wallo, Northern Ethiopia. In Taking the Place of Food: Khat in Ethiopia. E. Gebissa, ed. Pp. 13–28. Trenton, New Jersey: Red Sea Press, Inc.

Ainsworth, Claire
  2004 Narcotic khat gets sperm going. New Scientist 183(2454):15.

Al-Hebshi, Nezar, and Nils Skaug
  2005 Khat (Catha edulis)—An updated review. Addiction Biology 10(4): 299–307.

225

Al-Motarreb, Ahmed, Al-Habori, and Kenneth J. Broadley

2010 Khat chewing, cardiovascular diseases and other internal medical problems: The current situations and directions for future research. Journal of Ethnopharmacology 132:540–548.

Aly, Cassam

2004 Ambalavelona, ou, L'insurrection anticoloniale dans le nord-ouest de Madagascar en 1898. Antananarivo: Éditions "Faire connaître le nord de Madagascar."

Anderson, Benedict

2006 Imagined Communities: Reflections on the Origin and Spread of Nationalism, Revised Edition. London and New York: Verso.

Anderson, David, Susan Beckerleg, Degol Hailu, and Axel Klein

2007 The Khat Controversy: Stimulating the Debate on Drugs. New York: Berg.

Anderson, David, and Neil Carrier

2009 Khat in colonial Kenya: A history of prohibition and control. Journal of African History 50(3):377–397.

Annals of the Association of American Geographers

1993 Special issue. Volume 8, Issue 2.

Anzaldúa, Gloria

1990 Making Face, Making Soul/Haciendo Caras: Creative and Critical Perspectives by Women of Color. San Francisco: Aunt Lute Foundation Books.

Appadurai, Arjun, ed.

1986 The Social Life of Things: Commodities in Cultural Perspective. New York: Cambridge Press.

1990 Disjuncture and difference in the global cultural economy. Public Culture 2(2):1–24.

1996 Modernity at Large: cultural dimensions of globalization. Minneapolis: University of Minnesota Press.

Aretxaga, Begoña

2003 Maddening states. Annual Review of Anthropology 32:393–410.

Armstrong, Edward G.

2008 Research note: Crime, chemicals, and culture: On the complexity of khat. Journal of Drug Issues 38(2):631–648.

Arnett, Jeffrey Jensen

2006 Emerging Adulthood: The Winding Road from the Late Teens through the Twenties. Oxford: Oxford University Press.

Awofeso, Niyi
    2005 Re-defining "health." Bulletin of the World Health Organization 83:802.

Baer, Hans and Merrill Singer
    2009 Global Warming and the Political Ecology of Health: Emerging Crises and Systematic Solutions. Walnut Creek, California: Left Coast Press.

Baer, Hans, Merrill Singer, and Ida Susser
    1997 Medical Anthropology and the World System: A Critical Perspective. Westport, Connecticut: Bergin and Garvey.

    2003 Medical Anthropology and the World System. Westport, Connecticut: Praeger.

Banerjee, Damayanti, and Michael Mayerfeld Bell
    2007 Ecogender: Locating gender in environmental social science. Society and Natural Resources: An International Journal 20(1):3–19.

Baré, Jean-François
    1980 Sable Rouge. Une monarchie du nord-ouest malgache dans l'histoire. Paris: Editions L'Harmattan.

Baron, Denis Neville
    1999 A memorable experience: The qat party. British Medical Journal 319(7208):500.

Barrett, Christopher B.
    1994 Understanding uneven agricultural liberalisation in Madagascar. Journal of Modern African Studies 32:449–476.

BasicNeeds
    2008 Mental Health and Development: A Model in Practice. Warwickshire, U.K.: BasicNeeds.

Bassett, Thomas J.
    1988 The political ecology of peasant-herder conflicts in the northern Ivory Coast. Annals of the Association of American Geographers 78(3):453–472.

Baum, Dan
    1996 Smoke and Mirrors: The War on Drugs and the Politics of Failure. Boston: Little, Brown.

BBC News
    2006a Somali khat protester shot dead. http://news.bbc.co.uk/2/hi/africa/6155796.stm (accessed September 20, 2011).

BBC News

    2006b Somali Islamists stage execution. http://news.bbc.co.uk/1/hi/world/africa/5369958.stm (accessed September 29, 2011).

Beckerleg, Susan

    2004 Living with Heroin at the Kenya Coast. *In* Drug Use and Cultural Contexts "Beyond the West": Tradition, Change and Post-Colonialism. R. Coomber and N. South, eds. Pp. 192–208. London: Free Association Books.

    2006 What harm? Kenyan and Ugandan perspectives on khat. African Affairs 105(419):219–241.

    2008 Khat special edition introduction. Substance Use and Misuse 43(6):749–761.

    2009 Khat chewing as a new Ugandan leisure activity. Journal of Eastern African Studies 3(1):42–54.

Bennett, Linda, and Paul W. Cook, Jr.

    1996 Alcohol and Drug Studies. *In* Handbook of Medical Anthropology: Contemporary Theory and Method, Revised Edition. C. F. Sargent and T. M. Johnson, eds. Pp. 235–251. Westport, Connecticut: Greenwood Press.

Bernstein, Henry

    1996 The Political Economy of the Maize Filière. *In* The Agrarian Question in South Africa. H. Bernstein, ed. Pp. 120–145. Portland: Frank Cass.

Biersack, Aletta, and James B. Greenberg, eds.

    2006 Reimagining Political Ecology. Durham, North Carolina: Duke University Press.

Blaikie, Piers M., and Harold Brookfield, eds.

    1987 Land Degradation and Society. New York: Routledge.

BritishSomaliland

    1923 The Laws of the Somaliland Protectorate. London: Stevens.

Brodkin, Karen

    2007 Foreword. *In* The Gender of Globalization: Women Navigating Cultural and Economic Marginalitites. N. Gunewardena and A. Kingslover, eds. Pp. xii–xv. Sante Fe: School for Advanced Research Press and James Currey.

Brooke, Clarke

    1960 Khat (Catha edulis): Its production and trade in the Middle East. The Geographical Journal 126(1):52–59.

Bullington, Bruce

    2004 Drug policy reform and its detractors: The United States as the elephant in the closet. Journal of Drug Issues 34(3):687–721.

Burawoy, Michael

1991 The Extended Case Method. *In* Ethnography Unbound: Power and Resistance in the Modern Metropolis. M. Burawoy et al., eds. Pp. 271–287. Berkeley: University of California Press.

Bures, Frank

2001 From civil war to the drug war: Immigrants are risking prison for a taste of home. Mother Jones 26:23–25.

Butler, Judith

1999 Gender Trouble: Feminism and the Subversion of Identity. New York: Routledge.

Carapico, Sheila, and Cynthia Myntti

1991 Change in north Yemen 1977–1989: A tale of two families. Middle East Report 170:24–29.

Carrier, Neil

2005a "Miraa is cool": The cultural importance of miraa (khat) for Tigania and Igembe youth in Kenya. Journal of African Cultural Studies 17(2):201–218.

2005b The need for speed: Contrasting timeframes in the social life of Kenyan miraa. Africa 75(4):539–558.

2007 Kenyan Khat: The Social Life of a Stimulant. Leiden: Brill.

2008 Is miraa a drug? Categorizing Kenyan khat. Substance Use and Misuse 43(6):803–818.

Carrier, Neil, and Lisa Gezon

2009 Khat in the western Indian Ocean: Regional linkages and disjunctures. Études Océan Indien 42–43:271–297.

Cassanelli, Lee V.

1986 Qat: Changes in the Production and Consumption of a Quasilegal Commodity in Northeast Africa. *In* The Social Life of Things: Commodities in Cultural Perspective. A. Appadurai, ed. Pp. 236–257. Cambridge: Cambridge University Press.

Castells, Manuel

1996 The Rise of the Network Society. Cambridge, Massachusetts: Blackwell Publishers.

Castro-Gómez, Santiago

2005 La hybris del punto cero. Bogatá: Universidad Javeriana.

Caton, Steven C.

1993 Peaks of Yemen I Summon: Poetry as Cultural Practice in a North Yemeni Tribe. Berkeley: University of California Press.

Chanler, William A.

1896 Through Jungle and Desert: Travels in Eastern Africa. London: MacMillan.

Charlton, Bruce G.

2001 Personal Freedom or Public Health? *In* Medicine and Humanity. M. Marinker, ed. Pp. 55–69. London: King's Fund.

Chevannes, Barry

2004 Ganja and the Road to Decriminalisation in Jamaica. *In* Drug Use and Cultural Contexts "Beyond the West": Tradition, Change and Post-Colonialism. R. Coomber and N. South, eds. Pp. 177–191. London: Free Association Books.

Chien, Arnold, Margaret Conners, and Kenneth Fox

2000 The Drug War in Perspective. *In* Dying for Growth: Global Inequality and the Health of the Poor. J. Y. Kim, J. V. Millen, A. Irwin, and J. Greshman, eds. Pp. 293–327. Monroe, Maine: Common Courage Press.

Chouvy, Pierre-Arnaud

2009 Opium and alternative development in Asia: What results? Revue Tiers Monde 3(199):611–625.

Clark, Gracia

2010 African Market Women: Seven Life Stories from Ghana. Bloomington: Indiana University Press.

Cole, Jennifer

2001 Forget Colonialism?: Sacrifice and the Art of Memory in Madagascar. Berkeley: University of California Press.

2005 The Jaombilo of Tamatave (Madagascar), 1992–2004: Reflections on youth and globalization. Journal of Social History 38(4):891–914.

2009 Love, Money, and Economics of Intimacy in Tamatave, Madagascar. *In* Love in Africa. J. Cole and L. M. Thomas, eds. Pp. 109–134. Chicago: University of Chicago Press.

2010 Sex and Salvation: Imagining the Future in Madagascar. Chicago: University of Chicago Press.

Comaroff, Jean, and John Comaroff

1993 Modernity and Its Malcontents: Ritual and Power in Postcolonial Africa. Chicago: University of Chicago Press.

Conzelman, Caroline S.

2006 Fieldwork in Coca County: Investigating Democracy and Development in the Bolivian Andes. *In* Dispatches from the Field: Neophyte Ethnographers in a Changing World. Andrew Gardner and David M. Hoffman, eds. Pp. 119–135. Long Grove, Illinois: Waveland Press.

Coomber, Ross, and Nigel South, eds.

    2004a Drug Use and Cultural Contexts "Beyond the West": Tradition, Change and Post-Colonialism. London: Free Association Books.

    2004b Drugs, Cultures and Controls in Comparative Perspective. *In* Drug Use and Cultures Contexts "Beyond the West": Tradition, Change and Post-Colonialism. R. Coomber and N. South, eds. Pp. 13–26. London: Free Association Books.

Cooper, Frederick, and Laura Ann Stoler, eds.

    1997 Tensions of Empire: Colonial Culture in a Bourgeois World. Berkeley: University of California Press.

Cooper, Neil

    2002 State collapse as business: The role of conflict trade and the emerging control agenda. Development and Change 33(5):935–955.

Cox, Glenice, and Hagen Rampes

    2003 Adverse effects of khat: A review. Advances in Psychiatric Treatment 9:456–463.

D.A.R.E.

    1996 About D.A.R.E. Los Angeles (http://www.dare.com/home/about_dare.asp, accessed May 18, 2011).

Date, Junko, Noritoshi Tanida, and Tatsuya Hobara

    2004 Qat chewing and pesticides: A study of adverse health effects in people of the mountainous areas of Yemen. International Journal of Environmental Health Research 14(6):405–414.

Diaz-Laplante, Jeannette, and Renate Schneider

    2011 Globalization as re-traumatization: Rebuilding Haiti from the spirit up. In review for Journal of Social Issues.

Dool, Abdullahi

    1998 Failed States: When Governance Goes Wrong! London: Horn Heritage.

Draper, Robert

    2011 Opium Wars. National Geographic 219(2):58–83.

Drug Enforcement Administration

    1993 Khat law: Federal legal status. http://www.erowid.org/plants/khat/khat_law1.shtml (accessed January 12, 2011).

    n.d. Drug scheduling: Drug Enforcement Administration. http://www.usdoj.gov/dea/pubs/scheduling.html (accessed September 20, 2011).

Dudley, Robert

    2004 Ethanol, fruit ripening, and the historical origins of human alcoholism in primate frugivory. Integrative and Comparative Biology 44(4):315–323.

Duffy, Rosaleen

2006 Non-governmental organisations and governance states: The impact of transnational environmental management networks in Madagascar. Environmental Politics 15(5):731–749.

Dupont, Hans, J.B.H.M., Charles D. Kaplan, Hans T. Verbraeck, Richard V. Braam, and Govert F. van de Wijngaart

2005 Killing time: Frug and alcohol problems among asylum seekers in the Netherlands. International Journal of Drug Policy 16(1):27–36.

Duranti, Alessandro

1997 Linguistic Anthropology. Cambridge: Cambridge University Press.

Durrenberger, E. Paul, and Nicola Tannenbaum

2002 Chayanov and Theory in Economic Anthropology. In Theory in Economic Anthropology. J. Ensminger, ed. Pp. 137–154. Walnut Creek, California: AltaMira Press.

Epstein, Arnold L.

1978 [1967] The Case Study Method in the Field of Law. In The Craft of Social Anthropology. A. L. Epstein, ed. Pp. 205–230. Delhi, India: Hindustan Publishing Corporation.

Escobar, Arturo

1995 Encountering Development: The Making and Unmaking of the Third World. Princeton, New Jersey: Princeton University Press.

2008 Territories of Difference: Place, Movements, Life, Redes. Durham, North Carolina: Duke University Press.

Fahim, Kareem

2006 30 Held on Charges of Smuggling East African Stimulant to U.S. In The New York Times, July 27. http://www.nytimes.com/2006/07/27/nyregion/27khat.html?scp=1&sq=30%20Held%20on%20Charges%20of%20Smuggling%20East%20African%20Stimulant%20to%20U.S&st=cse (accessed September 30, 2011).

Farmer, Paul

2000 Foreword to Dying for Growth: Global Inequality and the Health of the Poor. J. Y. Kim, J. V. Millen, A. Irwin, and J. Greshman, eds. Pp. i–xix. Monroe, Maine: Common Courage Press.

Feeley-Harnik, Gillian

1991 A Green State: Restoring Independence in Madagascar. Washington, D.C.: Smithsonian Institution Press.

Ferguson, James

1990 The Anti-Politics Machine: "Development," Depoliticization, and Bureaucratic Power in Lesotho. New York: Cambridge University Press.

2006 Global Shadows: Africa in the Neoliberal World Order. Durham, North Carolina: Duke University Press.

Fox News

2010 Ga. Police Bust Man with Rare African Drug. http://www.foxnews.com/ us/2010/08/17/ga-police-bust-man-rare-african-drug/ (accessed September 22, 2011).

Freed, Benjamin Z.

1996 Co-Occurrence among Crowned Lemurs (Lemur Coronatus) and Sanford's Lemurs (Lemur Fulvus Sanfordi) of Madagascar. Ph.D. dissertation, Washington University.

Freeman, Carla

2000 High Tech and High Heels in the Global Economy: Women, Work, and Pink-Collar Identities in the Caribbean. Durham, North Carolina: Duke University Press.

2007 Neoliberalism and the Marriage of Reputation and Respectability: Entrepreneurship and the Barbadian Middle Class. *In* Love and Globalization: Transformation of Intimacy in the Contemporary World. M. Padilla et al., eds. Pp. 3–37. Nashville: Vanderbilt University Press.

Friedberg, Susan

2001 To garden, to market: Gendered meanings of work on an African urban periphery. Gender Place and Culture: A Journal of Feminist Geography 8(1):5–24.

Friedman, Thomas L.

2000 The Lexus and the Olive Tree. New York: Farrar, Straus, Giroux.

2007 The World Is Flat: A Brief History of the Twenty-First Century. New York: Picador.

2010 It's about Schools. *In* The New York Times, February 9, p. A25.

Gamburd, Michele Ruth

2008 Breaking the Ashes: The Culture of Illicit Liquor in Sri Lanka. Ithaca, New York: Cornell University Press.

Ganguly, Kalyan

2004 Opium Use in Rajasthan, India: A Socio-Cultural Perception. *In* Drug Use and Cultural Contexts "Beyond the West": Tradition, Change and Post-Colonialism. R. Coomber and N. South, eds. Pp. 83–100. London: Free Association Press.

Gebissa, Ezekiel

2004 Leaf of Allah: Khat & Agricultural Transformation in Harerge, Ethiopia 1875–1991. Oxford: James Currey.

Gebissa, Ezekiel

2008 Scourge of life or an economic lifeline? Public discourses on khat (Catha edulis) in Ethiopia. Substance Use and Misuse 43(6):784–802.

2010a Khat in the Horn of Africa: Historical perspectives and current trends. Journal of Ethnopharmacology 132(3):607–614.

2010b Taking the Place of Food: Khat in Ethiopia. Trenton, New Jersey: Red Sea Press, Inc.

2010c Crop and Commodity: Economic Aspects of Khat Production and Trade. *In* Taking the Place of Food: Khat in Ethiopia. E. Gebissa, ed. Pp. 89–126. Trenton, New Jersey: Red Sea Press, Inc.

2010d Keeping Tradition and Killing Time: The Use and Misuse of Khat of Ethiopia. *In* Taking the Place of Food: Khat in Ethiopia. E. Gebissa, ed. Pp. 57–88. Trenton, New Jersey: Red Sea Press, Inc.

Gereffi, Gary, and Miguel Korzeniewicz, eds.

1994 Commodity Chains and Global Capitalism. Westport, Connecticut: Greenwood Press.

Gezon, Lisa L.

1995 The Political Ecology of Conflict and Control in Ankarana, Madagascar. Ph.D. dissertation, University of Michigan.

1997a Political ecology and conflict in Ankarana, Madagascar. Ethnology 36(2):85–100.

1997b Institutional structure and the effectiveness of integrated conservation and development projects: Case study from Madagascar. Human Organization 56(4):462–470.

1999a Of shrimps and spirit possession: Toward a political ecology of resource management in northern Madagascar. American Anthropologist 101(1):58–67.

1999b From adversary to son: Political and ecological process in northern Madagascar. Journal of Anthropological Research 55(1):71–97.

2000a The changing face of NGOs: Structure and communitas in conservation and development in Madagascar. Urban Anthropology 29(2):181–215.

2000b Women, politics and economics: Case studies from the Ankarana region. Taloha 13:239–260.

2002 Marriage, kin, and compensation: A socio-political ecology of gender in Ankarana, Madagascar. Anthropological Quarterly 75(4):675–706.

2003 The Regional Approach in Northern Madagascar: Conservation after the Integrated Conservation and Development Project. *In* Contested

Nature: Power, Protected Areas and the Dispossessed—Promoting International Conservation with Justice in the 21st Century. S. R. Brechin, P. R. Wilshusen, C. Fortwangler, and P. C. West, eds. Pp. 183–194. Albany: State University of New York Press.

2006 Global Visions, Local Landscapes: A Political Ecology of Conservation, Conflict, and Control in Northern Madagascar. Lanham, Maryland: AltaMira Press.

2010 Multi-sited Ethnography: Combining Analysis at Different Scales. *In* Society and Environment: Methods and Research Design. Ismael Vaccaro, Eric Alden Smith, and Shankar Aswani, eds. Pp. 238–265. Cambridge: Cambridge University Press.

n.d. Why gender matters, why women matter. Unpublished manuscript.

Gezon, Lisa L., and Benjamin Z. Freed
1999 Agroforestry and conservation in northern Madagascar: Hopes and hindrances. African Studies Quarterly 3(2):9–37.

Gezon, Lisa L., and Alex Totomarovario
2008 Encountering the unexpected: Appropriating the roles of researcher, teacher, and advocate in a drug study in Madagascar. Practicing Anthropology 30(3):42–45.

Gezon, Lisa L., Sean P. Sweeney, Benjamin Z. Freed, and Glen M. Green
2005 Forest Loss and Commodity Chains in Northern Madagascar. Report submitted to the National Geographic Society, Washington, D.C.

Gezon, Lisa L., Sean Sweeney, Glen Green, and Benjamin Z. Freed
2007 Forest Loss and Commodity Chains in Northern Madagascar: National Geographic Society. Grant No. 7413.03.

Giddens, Anthony
1990 The Consequences of Modernity. Stanford, California: Stanford University Press.

1993 The Transformation of Intimacy: Sexuality, Love, and Eroticism in Modern Societies. Stanford, California: Stanford University Press.

Global Commission on Drug Policy (GCDP)
2011 War on Drugs: Report of the Global Commission Drug Policy. http://www.globalcommissionondrugs.org/Report (accessed September 30, 2011).

Gluckman, Max
1958 Analysis of a Social Situation in Modern Zululand. Manchester, U.K.: Manchester University Press.

Goldman, Michael
2005 Imperial Nature: The World Bank and Struggles for Social Justice in the Age of Globalization. New Haven, Connecticut: Yale University Press.

Goldsmith, Paul

1997 The Somali Impact on Kenya, 1990–1993: The View from Outside the Camps. *In* Mending Rips in the Sky: Options for Somali Communities in the 21st Century. H. M. Adam and R. Fords, eds. Pp. 461–483. Lawrenceville, New Jersey: Red Sea Press.

1999 The political economy of mirra. East African Alternatives (March/April):15–19.

Good, Byron

1994 Medicine, Rationality, and Experience: An Anthropological Perspective. London: Cambridge University Press.

Goode, Erich

2007 Drugs in American Society, 7th Edition. Boston: McGraw-Hill.

Graziani, Manuela, Michelle S. Milella, and Paolo Nencini

2008 Khat chewing from a pharmacological point of view: An update. Substance Use and Misuse 43(6):762–783.

Green, Reginald Herbold

1999 Khat and the realities of Somalis. Review of African Political Economy 79:33–49.

Griffiths, Paul

1998 Qat Use in London: A Study of Qat Use among a Sample of Somalis Living in London. H.O.D.P. Initiative, ed. London: Home Office.

Griffiths, Paul, Michael Gossop, Simon Wickenden, John Dunworth, K. Harris, and C. Lloyd

1997 A transcultural pattern of drug use: Qat (khat) in the U.K. British Journal of Psychiatry 170:281–284.

Gross, Daniel R.

1971 The great sisal scheme. Natural History 80(3):48–55.

Gunewardena, Nandini, and Ann Kingsolver

2007a Introduction. *In* The Gender of Globalization: Women Navigating Cultural and Economic Marginalities. N. Gunewardena and A. Kingsolver, eds. Pp. 3–23. Santa Fe: School for Advanced Research Press.

2007b The Gender of Globalization: Women Navigating Cultural and Economic Marginalities. Santa Fe: School for Advanced Research Press.

Gupta, Akhil, and Aradhana Sharma

2006 Globalization and postcolonial states. Current Anthropology 47(2):277–307.

Habermas, Jurgen
    1987 The Theory of Communicative Action. Life World and System: A Critique of Functionalist Reason. Boston: Beacon Press.

Hailu, Degol
    2010 Agrarian Debacle and the Spread of the Dollar Leaf in Northern and Southern Ethiopia. *In* Taking the Place of Food: Khat in Ethiopia. E. Gebissa, ed. Pp. 127–148. Trenton, New Jersey: Red Sea Press, Inc.

Halbach, H.
    1972 Medical aspects of chewing of khat leaves. Bulletin, World Health Organization 47:21–29.

Hannerz, Ulf
    1989 Notes on global ecumene. Public Culture 1(2):66–75.

Hansen, Karen Tranberg
    2000 Salaula: The World of Secondhand Clothing and Zambia. Chicago: University of Chicago Press.

Hansen, Thomas Blom, and Finn Stepputat
    2001 Introduction. *In* States of Imagination: Ethnographic Explorations of the Postcolonial State. T. B. Hansen and F. Stepputat, eds. Pp. 1–38. Durham, North Carolina: Duke University Press.

Harper, Janice
    2002 Endangered Species: Health, Illness and Death among Madagascar's People of the Forest. Durham, North Carolina: Carolina Academic Press.

Hartley, Aidan
    2004 The Zanzibar Chest: A Memoir of Love and War. London: Harper Perennial.

Harvey, David
    1989 The Condition of Postmodernity: An Enquiry into the Origins of Cultural Change. Cambridge, Massachusetts: Blackwell.

Hayden, Brian
    2003 Shamans, Sorcerers and Saints: A Prehistory of Religion. Washington, D.C.: Smithsonian Books.

Heath, Dwight B.
    2004 Camba (Bolivia) Drinking Patterns: Changes in Alcohol Use, Anthropology and Research Perspectives. *In* Drug Use and Cultural Contexts "Beyond the West": Tradition, Change and Post-Colonialism. R. Coomber and N. South, eds. Pp. 119–136. London: Free Association Books.

Hecht, Susanna, and Alexander Cockburn

1990 The Fate of the Forest: Developers, Destroyers and Defenders of the Amazon. New York: Harper Perennial.

Heseltine, Nigel

1971 Madagascar. New York: Praeger.

Hewitt, Adrian

1992 Madagascar. *In* Structural Adjustment and the African Farmer. A. Duncan and J. Howell, eds. Pp. 86–112. London: Overseas Development Institute.

Hirsch, Jennifer S., and Holly Wardlow

2006 Modern Loves. Ann Arbor: University of Michigan Press.

Hjort, Anders

1974 Trading mirra: From school-leaver to shop-owner in Kenya. Ethnos 39:27–43.

Holland, Dorothy

2002 [1992] How Cultural Systems Become Desire: A Case Study of American Romance. *In* Readings in Gender and Culture in America. N. P. McGee and L. Stone, eds. Pp. 346–370. Upper Saddle River, New Jersey: Prentice Hall.

Hopkins, Terence K., and Immanuel Wallerstein

1986 Commodity chains in the world economy prior to 1800. Review 10(1):157–170.

llouz, Eva

1997 Consuming the Romantic Utopia: Love and the Cultural Contradictions of Capitalism. Berkeley: University of California Press.

2007 Cold Intimacies: The Making of Emotional Capitalism. Cambridge: Polity Press.

Inhorn, Marcia C.

2006 Defining women's health. Medical Anthropology Quarterly 20(3):345–378.

Jarosz, Lucy

1993 Defying and explaining tropical deforestation: Shifting cultivation and population growth in colonial Madagascar (1896–1940). Economic Geography 69(4):366–379.

Kalix, Peter

1990 Pharmacological properties of the stimulant khat. Pharmacology & Therapeutics 48(3):397–416.

1992 Cathinone, a natural amphetamine. Pharmacology & Toxicology 70(2):77–86.

Kalix, Peter, and Olav Braenden
    1985 Pharmacological aspects of the chewing of khat leaves. Pharmacology Reviews 37:149–164.

Kandela, Peter
    2000 Nargile smoking keeps Arabs in Wonderland. Lancet 356(9236):1175.

Kassa, Habtemariam
    2010 Khat and Livelihood Dynamics in the Harer Highlands of Ethiopia: Significance and Challenges. In Taking the Place Food: Khat in Ethiopia. E. Gebissa, ed. Pp. 149–166. Trenton, New Jersey: Red Sea Press, Inc.

Katz, Rebecca S., and Stephen Whitaker
    2001 Explaining accommodation and resistance in Kentucky. Crime, Law & Social Change 35:295–318.

Kennedy, John G.
    1987 The Flower of Paradise: The Institutionalized Use of the Drug Qat in North Yemen. Dordrecht, Holland: D. Reidel Publishing Company.

Kennedy, John G., James Teague, and Lynn Fairbanks
    1980 Qat use in North Yemen and the problem of addiction: A study in medical anthropology. Culture, Medicine and Psychiatry 4(4):311–344.

Kennedy, John G., James Teague, William Rokaw, and Elizabeth Rooney
    1983 A medical evaluation of the use of qat in North Yemen. Social Science Medicine 17(12):783–793.

Kenney, Martin, and Richard Florida
    1994 Japanese maquiladoras: Production organization and global commodity chains. World Development 22(1):27–44.

Kervingant, D.
    1959 The consumption of khat in French Somaliland. Bulletin on Narcotics 11(2):42.

Kingsolver, Ann E.
    2011 Tobacco Town Futures: Global Encounters in Rural Kentucky. Prospect Heights, Illinois: Waveland Press.

Kingstone, Heidi
    2009 Khat-crazed Kids: First Ever Interview with a Shipper Trading Cash for Crew. In The Washington Times. http://www.washingtontimes.com/news/2009/apr/29/khat-crazed-kids/print (accessed September 27, 2011).

Klein, Axel
    2007 Khat and the Creation of Tradition in Somali Diaspora. *In* Drugs in Society: European Perspectives. J. Fountain and D. J. Korf, eds. Pp. 51–61. Oxford, U.K.: Radcliffe Publishing Ltd.
    2008 Drugs and the World. London: Reaktion Books.
Knauft, Bruce M., ed.
    2002 Critically Modern: Alternatives, Alterities, Anthropologies. Bloomington: Indiana University Press.
Kottak, Conrad P.
    1980 The Past in the Present: History, Ecology, and Cultural Variation in Highland Madagascar. Ann Arbor: University of Michigan.
Kottak, Conrad P., and Elizabeth Colson
    1994 Multilevel Linkages: Longitudinal and Comparative Studies. *In* Assessing Cultural Anthropology. R. Borofsky, ed. Pp. 396–412. New York: McGraw-Hill, Inc.
Kottak, Conrad P. (with John Colwell, Lisa Gezon, Glen Green, Jean Aimé Rakotoarisoa, Robert Sussman, and Pierre Vérin)
    1994 Final Report of the CIESIN Pilot Project: An Integrated Approach to Deforestation, Conservation, and Development in Madagascar Using Satellite Images.2. http://www.westga.edu/assetsDept/anth/Final_Report_of_the_Ciesin_Pilot_Project.pdf (accessed September 30, 2011).
Kull, Christian A.
    1996 The evolution of conservation efforts in Madagascar. International Environmental Affairs 8(1):50–86.
    2004 Isle of Fire: The Political Ecology of Landscape Burning in Madagascar. Chicago: University of Chicago Press.
Kushner, Harvey (with Bart Davis)
    2004 Holy War on the Home Front: The Secret Islamic Terror Network in the United States. New York: Penguin.
Laillet, E.
    1884 La France orientale. Paris: Challamel.
Lambek, Michael, and Andrew Walsh
    1997 The imagined community of the Antankaraña: Identity, history, and ritual in northern Madagascar. Journal of Religion in Africa 27(2):25.
Lappé, Frances Moore, and Joseph Collins
    1977 Food First: Beyond the Myth of Scarcity. Boston: Houghton-Mifflin.

Larson, Pier M.
2000 History and Memory in the Age of Enslavement: Becoming Merina in Highland Madagascar, 1770–1822. Portsmouth, New Hampshire: Heinemann.

Leary, Timothy, Ralph Metzner, Richard Alpert, and Karma-Glin-Pa Bar Do Thos Grol
1964 The Psychedelic Experience: A Manual Based on the Tibetan Book of the Dead. New York: University Books.

Lorde, Audre
1984 Sister Outsider: Essays and Speeches. Trumansburg, New York: Crossing Press.

Lowry, Porter P., II, George E. Schatz, and Peter B. Phillipson
1997 The Classification of Natural and Anthropogenic Vegetation in Madagascar. *In* Natural Change and Human Impact in Madagascar. S. M. Goodman and B. D. Patterson, eds. Pp. 93–123. Washington, D.C.: Smithsonian Institution Press.

MacAndrew, Craig, and Robert B. Edgerton
2003 [1969] Drunken Comportment: A Social Explanation. Clinton Corners, New York: Percheron Press.

MacCoun, Robert J., and Peter Reuter
2001 Drug War Heresies: Learning from Other Vices, Times, and Places. Cambridge and New York: Cambridge University Press.

MacRae, Edward
2004 The Ritual Use of Ayahuasca by Three Brazilian Religions. *In* Drug Use and Cultural Contexts "Beyond the West": Tradition, Change and Post-Colonialism. R. Coomber and N. South, eds. Pp. 27–45. London: Free Association Press.

Mains, Daniel
2010 Chewing and Dreaming: Youth, Imagination, and the Consumption of Khat in Jimma, Southwestern Ethiopia. *In* Taking the Place of Food: Khat in Ethiopia. E. Gebissa, ed. Pp. 29–56. Trenton, New Jersey: Red Sea Press, Inc.

Marcus, George E.
1995 Ethnography in/of the world system: The emergence of multi-sited ethnography. Annual Review of Anthropology 24:95–117.

Marcus, Richard R.
2004 Political Change in Madagascar: Populist Democracy or Neopatrimonalism by Another Name? Johannesburg: Institute for Security Studies.

Marcus, Richard R., and Christian A. Kull
1999 Setting the stage: The politics of Madagascar's environmental efforts. African Studies Quarterly 3(2):1–7.

Marcus, Richard R., and Paul Razafindrakoto
2003 Participation and the poverty of electoral democracy in Madagascar. afrika spectrum 38(1):27–48.

Mares, David
2006 Drug Wars and Coffeehouses: The Political Economy of the International Drug Trade. Washington, D.C.: CQ Press.

Margolis, Maxine L.
2000 True to Her Nature: Changing Advice to American Women. Prospect Heights, Illinois: Waveland Press, Inc.

Martinez-Alier, Juan
2002 The Environmentalism of the Poor: A Study of Ecological Conflicts and Valuation. Northhampton, Massachusetts: Edward Elgar Publishing.

Massing, Michael
2000 The Fix. New York: Simon & Schuster.

Mathews, Andrew
2008 State making, knowledge, and ignorance: Translation and concealment in Mexican forestry institutions. American Anthropologist 110(4):484–494.

Mbima, Pierre
2006 Place du Français et Pratiques Linguistiques Non Conventionnelles Chez les Jeunes à Madagascar, Tome I. Thèse de Doctorat Nouveau Régime, Université de la Réunion.

2011 Le français "branché" des jeunes urbains de Diégo-Suarez à Madagascar: Le koroko ou la construction d'une identité mouvante. Paper presented at Anthropologie Comparative des Sociétés Insulaires de L'Ocean Indien Occidental Terrains et Theories, Paris, April 27–29.

McCabe, Scott
2011 Ethiopian Cafe Owner Arrested in Major Khat Bust. In Washington Examiner, May 3. http://washingtonexaminer.com/local/crime-punishment/2011/05/ethopian-cafe-owner-arrested-major-khat-bust (accessed September 27, 2011).

McElroy, Ann, and Patricia K. Townsend
2009 Medical Anthropology in Ecological Perspective. Boulder, Colorado: Westview Press.

Migdalovitz, Carol, coord.

1993 Somalia: A Report on Khat. Washington, D. C.: Congressional Research Service, Library of Congress.

Milich, Lenard, and Mohammed Al-Sabbry

1995 The "Rational Peasant" vs. Sustainable Livelihoods: The Case of Qat in Yemen. http://ag.arizona.edu/~lmilich/yemen.html (accessed September 27, 2011).

Miller, Franklin G., and Ted J. Kaptchuk

2008 The power of context: Reconceptualizing the placebo effect. Journal of the Royal Society of Medicine 101:222–225.

Minquoy, Vincent

2006 Quand la logique dépasse l'éthique: Le khat à Madagascar. Les Cahiers d'Outre-Mer 233:133–136.

Mintz, Sidney

1974 Worker in the Cane: A Puerto Rican Life History. New York: W. W. Norton & Co, Inc.

1985 Sweetness and Power: The Place of Sugar in Modern History. New York: Viking.

Mitchell, Timothy

2006 Society, Economy, and the State Effect. In The Anthropology of the State: A Reader. A. Sharma and A. Gupta, eds. Pp. 169–186. Malden, Massachusetts; Oxford: Blackwell Publishing.

Moerman, Daniel E., and Wayne B. Jonas

2002 Deconstructing the placebo effect and finding the meaning response. Annals of Internal Medicine 136(6):471–476.

Moore, Donald S.

2005 Suffering for Territory: Race, Place, and Power in Zimbabwe. Durham, North Carolina: Duke University Press.

Moore, Henrietta

1994 A Passion for Difference. Bloomington: Indiana University Press.

1999 Anthropology Theory Today. Malden, Massachusetts: Polity Press.

Mosse, David

2004 Is good policy unimplementable? Reflections on the ethnography of aid policy and practice. Development and Change 35(4): 639–671.

Mouawad, Jad

2009 Total, the French Oil Company Places Its Bets Globally. In The New York Times, February 22, page BU1.

Mukonoweshuro, Eliphas, G.
    1994 Madagascar: The collapse of an experiment. Journal of Third World Studies 11(1):336–368.

Nader, Laura
    1972 Up the Anthropologist-Perspectives Gained from Studying-Up. *In* Reinventing Anthropology. D. Hymes, ed. Pp. 284–311. New York: Random House.

Narcisse, R.
    2005 Le khat, l'or vert du nord. Madagascar Tribune. http://www.madagascar-tribune.com/admin/voir_article.php?id=9629 (accessed November 2, 2006). No longer online; in author's files.

Nencini, Paolo, and Abdullahi Mohamed Ahmed
    1989 Khat consumption: A pharmacological review. Drug and Alcohol Dependence 23(1):19–29.

Neumann, Arthur H.
    1982 [1898] Elephant-hunting in East Equatorial Africa. Durban, South Africa: Books of Zimbabwe Publishing.

Nguyen, Holly, and Martin Bouchard
    2010 Patterns of youth participation in cannibis cultivation. Journal of Drug Issues 40(2):263–294.

Nichter, Mark
    2008 Global Health: Why Cultural Perceptions, Social Representations, and Biopolitics Matter. Tucson: University of Arizona Press.

Nuijten, Monique
    2004 Between fear and fantasy: Governmentality and the working of power in Mexico. Critique of Anthropology 24(2):209–230.

Nutbeam, Don
    2000 Health literacy as a public health goal: A challenge for contemporary health education and communication strategies into the 21st century. Health Promotional International 15(3):259–267.

Nutt, David, Leslie A. King, William Saulsbury, and Colin Blakemore
    2007 Development of a rational scale to assess the harm of drugs of potential misuse. The Lancet (March 24–30):1047–1053.

Odenwald, Michael
    2007 Chronic khat use and psychotic disorders: A review of the literature and future prospects. Journal of Addiction Research and Practice 53(1):9–22.

Ong, Aihwa
2006 Neoliberalism as Exception: Mutations in Citizenship and Sovereignty. Durham, North Carolina: Duke University Press.

Padilla, Mark, Jennifer S. Hirsch, Miguel Munoz-Laboy, Robert E. Sember, and Richard G. Parker, eds.
2007 Love and Globalization: Transformations of Intimacy in the Contemporary World. Nashville: Vanderbilt University Press.

Page, J. Bryan, and Merrill Singer
2010 Comprehending Drug Use: Ethnographic Research at the Social Margins. New Brunswick, New Jersey: Rutgers University Press.

Pascal, Blaise
2000 Pensées. Paris: Livre de Poche.

Paulson, Susan, and Lisa L. Gezon, eds.
2005 Political Ecology, Across Spaces, Scales and Social Groups. New Brunswick, New Jersey: Rutgers University Press.

PCD (Plan Communal de Development) d'Antsalaka
nd Unpublished report (in French) by SAGE/UTR; in author's files.

Peet, Richard, Paul Robbins, and Michael Watts, eds.
2011 Global Political Ecology. Oxford: Routledge.

Peet, Richard, and Michael Watts
1993 Introduction: Development theory and environment in an age of market triumphalism. Economic Geography 69(3):227–253.
2004 Liberation Ecologies: Environment, Development, Social Movements. New York: Routledge.

Pine, Adrienne
2008 Working Hard, Drinking Hard: On Violence and Survival in Honduras. Berkeley: University of California Press.

Pollini, Jacques
2011 The difficult reconciliation of conservation and development objectives: The case of the malagasy environmental action plan. Human Organization 70(1):74–87.

Povinelli, Elizabeth A.
2006 The Empire of Love: Toward a Theory of Intimacy, Genealogy and Carnality. Durham, North Carolina: Duke University Press.

Quijano, Anibal
2000 Coloniality of power and eurocentrism in Latin America. International Sociology 15(2):215–232.

Quinn, Naomi, and Dorothy Holland
    1987 Culture and Cognition. *In* Cultural Models in Language and Thought. D. Holland and N. Quinn, eds. Pp. 3–40. New York: Cambridge University Press.

Raison-Jourde, F., and S. Randrianja, eds.
    2002 La nation malgache au défi de l'ethnicité: [table ronde tenue à l'Université de Paris VII]. Paris: Editions Karthala.

Rajaonarivony, Narisoa
    1996 The examination of the impact of IMF-supported program on the economic performance of low-income countries: The case of Madagascar, Ph.D. dissertation, Auburn University.

Rajcoomar, S.
    1991 Madagascar: Crafting comprehensive reforms. Finance and Development 28(3):46–48.

Raxworthy, Christopher J., and Ronald A. Nussbaum
    1997 Biogeographic Patterns of Reptiles in Eastern Madagascar. *In* Natural Change and Human Impact in Madagascar. S. M. Goodman and B. D. Patterson, eds. Pp. 124–141. Washington, D.C.: Smithsonian Institution Press.

Reiter, Rayna R., ed.
    1975 Toward an Anthropology of Women. New York: Monthly Review Press.

Ribot, Jesse C.
    1998 Theorizing access: Forest profits along Senegal's charcoal commodity chain. Development and Change 29(2):307–341.

    2005 Institutional Choice and Recognition: Effects on the Formation and Consolidation of Local Democracy. Report submitted to the World Resource Institute, Washington, D.C.

Richmond, C., S. J. Elliot, R. Matthews, and B. Elliot
    2005 The political ecology of health: Perceptions of environment, economy, health and well-being among 'Namgis First Nation. Health & Place 11(4):349–365.

Robbins, Paul
    2004 Political Ecology: A Critical Introduction. Malden, Massachusetts: Blackwell Publishing.

Rosaldo, Michelle Zimbalist, and Louise Lamphere, eds.
    1974 Women, Culture, and Society. Stanford, California: Stanford University Press.

Rossano, Matthew J.
    2005 The Religious Mind and the Evolution of Religious Forms. Paper presented at the Science and Religion: Global Perspectives, an International, Interfaith, and Interdisciplinary Conference, Philadelphia, June 4–8.

Rubin, Vera D., and Lambros Comitas
    1975 Ganja in Jamaica: A Medical Anthropological Study of Chronic Marihuana Use. The Hague: Mouton.

Rushby, Kevin
    1999 Eating the Flowers of Paradise: A Journey Through the Drug Fields of Ethiopia and Yemen. New York: St. Martin's Press.

Saada, Emmanualle
    2005 Entre "assimilation" et "decivilisation": L'imitation el le projet colonial republican. Terrain 44:19–38.

Sacks, Karen
    1974 Engels Revisited: Women, the Organization of Production, and Private Property. In Women, Culture, and Society. M. Z. Rosaldo and L. Lamphere, eds. Pp. 207–222. Stanford, California: Stanford University Press.

Sahlins, Marshall
    1972 Stone Age Economics. New York: Aldine Publishing Company.

Samson, Colin
    2004 The Disease over Native North American Drinking: Experiences on the Innu of Northern Labrador. In Drug Use and Cultural Contexts "Beyond the West": Tradition, Change and Post-Colonialism. R. Coomber and N. South, eds. Pp. 137–157. London: Free Association Books.

Sanabria, Harry
    1993 The Coca Boom and Rural Social Change in Bolivia. Ann Arbor: University of Michigan Press.

Saracci, Rodolfo
    1997 The World Health Organization needs to reconsider its definition of health. British Medical Journal 314:1409–1410.

Schaefer, Stacy B.
    2004 In Search of the Divine: Wixarilca (Huichol) Peyote Traditions in Mexico. In Drug Use and Cultural Contexts "Beyond the West": Tradition, Change and Post-Colonialism. R. Coomber and N. South, eds. Pp. 158–176. London: Free Association Books.

Schmink, Marianne, and Charles H. Wood

1987 The Political Ecology of Amazonia. *In* Lands at Risk in the Third World: Local-Level Perspectives. P. D. Little, M. M. Horowitz, and E. A. Nyerges, eds. Pp. 38–57. Boulder, Colorado: Westview Press.

Schopen, Armin

1978 Das Qat: Gerschichte und Gerbrauch des Genbmittles Catha edulis Forsk, in der Arabischen Republik Jemen. Wiesbaden, Germany: Franz Steiner.

Schuyler, Philip D.

1997 Qat, conversation, and song: A musical view of Yemeni social life. Yearbook for Traditional Music 29:57–73.

Scott, James C.

1998 Seeing Like a State. New Haven, Connecticut: Yale University Press.

Shore, Cris, and Dieter Haller

2005 Introduction—Sharp Practice: Anthropology and the Study of Corruption. *In* Corruption: Anthropological Perspectives. D. Haller and C. Shore, eds. Pp. 1–28. London and Ann Harbor, Michigan: Pluto Press.

Singer, Merrill

1989 The coming age of critical medical anthropology. Social Science and Medicine 28:1193–1203.

1990 Another perspective on advocacy. Current Anthropology 31(5):548–550.

1993 Project Recovery: A Substance Abuse Treatment Program for Hartford Women. Report submitted to the Hartford Foundation for Public Giving, Hartford, Connecticut.

2004 Why Is It Easier to Get Drugs than Drug Treatment in the United States? *In* Unhealthy Health Policy: A Critical Anthropological Examination. A. Castro and M. Singer, eds. Pp. 287–302. Walnut Creek, California: AltaMira Press.

2006 The Face of Social Suffering: The Life of a Street Drug Addict. Long Grove, Illinois: Waveland Press.

2008a Drugging the Poor: Legal and Illegal Drugs and Social Inequality. Long Grove, Illinois: Waveland Press, Inc.

2008b Drugs and Development: The Global Impact on Sustainable Growth and Human Rights. Long Grove, Illinois: Waveland Press.

Singer, Merrill, and Hans A. Baer

2007 Introducing Medical Anthropology: A Discipline in Action. Lanham, Maryland: AltaMira Press.

Smith, Neil
    1984 Uneven Development: Nature, Capital and the Production of Space. Oxford: Blackwell.

Spedding, Alison
    2004 Coca Use in Bolivia: A Tradition of Thousands of Years. *In* Drug Use and Cultural Contexts "Beyond the West": Tradition, Change and Post-Colonialism. R. Coomber and N. South, eds. Pp. 46–64. London: Free Association Books.

Spiro, Melford E.
    1982 Collective Representations and Mental Representations in Religious Symbol Systems. *In* On Symbols in Anthropology: Essays in Honor of Harry Hoijer. J. Maquet, ed. Pp. 45–72. Malibu, California: Udena Publications.

Stevenson, Jonathan
    1992 Krazy Khat: Somalia's Deadly Drug War. The New Republic 207(22):17–19.

Stevenson, Mark, John Fitzgerld, and Cathy Banwell
    1996 Chewing as a social act: Cultural displacement and *khat* consumption in the East African communities of Melbourne. Drug and Alcohol Review 15(1):73–82.

Steward, Julien Haynes
    1955 Theory of Culture Change: The Methodology of Multilinear Evolution. Urbana: University of Illinois Press.

Stewart, Kathleen
    2007 Ordinary Affects. Durham, North Carolina: Duke University Press.

Stoler, Ann Laura
    2002 Carnal Knowledge and Imperial Power: Race and the Intimate in Colonial Rule. Berkeley: University of California Press.

Strathern, Andrew, and Pamela J. Stewart
    2010 Curing and Healing: Medical Anthropology in Global Perspective. Durham, North Carolina: Carolina Academic Press.

Sussman, Robert W., and Glen M. Green
    1990 Deforestation history of the eastern rain forests of Madagascar from satellite images. Science 248:212–215.

Tefera, Hailu, Kebebew Assefa, Fufa Hundera, Tiruneh Kefyalew, and Tesfaye Teferra
    2003 Heritability and genetic advance in recombinant inbred lines of tef (Egragrotis tef). Euphytica 131(1):91–96.

Tefera, Tesfaye Lemma, and Daniel Start

2010 Market Incentives, Rural Livelihoods, and a Policy Dilemma: Expansion of Khat Production in Eastern Ethiopia beyond the Tesfaye. *In* Taking the Place of Food: Khat in Ethiopia. E. Gebissa, ed. Pp. 167–187. Trenton, New Jersey: Red Sea Press, Inc.

Tsing, Anna Lowenhaupt

1993 In the Realm of the Diamond Queen. Princeton, New Jersey: Princeton University Press.

2000 Inside the economy of appearances. Public Culture 12(1):115–144.

2005 Friction: An Ethnography of Global Connection. Princeton, New Jersey: Princeton University Press.

United Nations

1971 Convention on Psychotropic Drugs. New York: United Nations. http://www.incb.org/incb/convention_1971.html (accessed September 30, 2011).

1975 United Nations Narcotics Laboratory. Studies on the chemical composition of Khat III: Investigations on the phenylalkylamine fraction. UN document MNAR, 11.

Van Velsen, Jaap

1979 The Extended-case Method and Situational Analysis. *In* The Craft of Social Anthropology. A. L. Epstein, ed. Pp. 129–149. London: Pergamon Press.

Varisco, Daniel Martin

1986 On the meaning of chewing: The significance of qat (Catha edulis) in The Yemen Arab Republic. International Journal of Middle East Studies 18:1–13.

1997 The twin twigs: Coffee and qat in Yemen. World & I 12(7):216–228.

2004 The Elixir of Life or the Devil's Cud: The Debate over Qat (Catha edulis). *In* Drug Use and Cultural Contexts "Beyond the West": Tradition, Change and Post-Colonialism. R. Coomber and N. South, eds. Pp. 101–118. London: Free Association Books.

Vérin, Philippe

1990 Madagascar. Paris: Éditions Karthala.

Wagner, Mark

2005 The debate between coffee and qat in Yemeni literature. Middle Eastern Literatures 8(2):121–149.

Wallerstein, Immanuel

1974 The Modern World-System. Vol. I: Capitalist Agriculture and the Origins of the European World-Economy in the Sixteenth Century. New York/London: Academic Press.

Walsh, Andrew

1998 Constructing Antankarana: History, Ritual and Identity in Northern Madagascar. Ph.D. thesis, University of Toronto.

2001 When origins matter: The politics of commemoration in northern Madagascar. Ethnohistory 48(1–2):237–256.

Ward, Christopher

n.d. Yemen: CDR Building Block. Undated report Washington, D.C.: The World Bank. http://siteresources.worldbank.org/INTYEMEN/Overview/20150264/YEQat.pdf (accessed September 30, 2011).

Wax, Emily

2006 Khat Trade Rules Somalia. *In* Washington Post, April 16, http://www.washingtonpost.com/wp-dyn/content/article/2006/04/15/AR2006041500666.html (accessed September 30, 2011).

Wedeen, Lisa

2008 Peripheral Visions: Publics, Power, and Performance in Yemen. Chicago: University of Chicago Press.

Weil, Andrew, and Winifred Rosen

1983 From Chocolate to Morphine: Understanding Mind-Active Drugs. Boston: Houghton Mifflin.

2004 From Chocolate to Morphine: Everything You Need to Know about Mind-altering Drugs. Revised Edition. Boston: Houghton Mifflin.

Weir, Shelagh

1985 Qat in Yemen: Consumption and Social Change. London: British Museum Publications Limited.

Weismantel, Mary

2008 Foreword to At the Kitchen Table. *In* Kitchenspace: Women, Fiestas, and Everyday Life in Central Mexico. M. E. Christie, ed. Pp. ix–xvi. Austin: University of Texas Press.

White, Luise

1990 The Comforts of Home: Prostitution in Colonial Nairobi. Chicago: University of Chicago Press.

WHO

2003 WHO Expert Committee on Drug Dependence. WHO Technical Report Series. Geneva: WHO.

Wilson, Suzanne, and Marta Zambrano

1994 Cocaine, Commodity Chains, and Drug Politics: A Transnational Approach. *In* Commodity Chains and Global Capitalism. G. Gereffi and

M. Korzeniewicz, eds. Pp. 297–317. Westport, Connecticut: Greenwood Publishing Group, Inc.

Wolf, Eric

1966 Peasants. Englewood Cliffs, New Jersey: Prentice-Hall.

1972 Ownership and political ecology. Anthropology Quarterly 45(3):201–205.

1982 Europe and the People without History. Berkeley: University of California Press.

Zinberg, Norman E.

1984 Drug, Set, and Setting: The Basis for Controlled Intoxicant Use. New Haven, Connecticut: Yale University Press.

INDEX

ABOUT THE AUTHOR

Lisa L. Gezon is a cultural anthropologist who graduated from the University of Michigan in 1995. She has been at the University of West Georgia since 1996 and is currently a professor in the Department of Anthropology. Her primary research area has been in Madagascar, but she has also conducted research in Georgia and in Senegal, West Africa. She is interested in many facets of humans and their relationship to the material environment, including conservation and protected area management (Madagascar), health and wellness (Madagascar and the United States), and tourism (Madagascar). Her research on khat in Madagascar has been funded by the National Geographic Society, the National Science Foundation, and a U.S. Department of Education Fulbright-Hays Faculty Research Abroad Fellowship. Significant publications include *Global Visions, Local Landscapes: A Political Ecology of Conservation, Conflict, and Control in Northern Madagascar* (AltaMira, 2006) and *Political Ecology, Across Spaces, Scales and Social Groups* (co-authored with Susan Paulson), (Rutgers University Press, 2006).